INDIA BOOKVARSITY

**LOTUS CHOICES**

Editor: Mahendra Kulasrestha

# Hindu Social System

## First Famous Study

*By*

**The Celebrated French Missionary**

**ABBE J.A. Dubois**

'I believe the caste division to be in many respects the **chef-d' aevure,** the happiest effort, of Hindu legislation. It is simply and solely due to it that India did not lapse into a state of barbarism and reserved and perfected the arts and sciences of civilisation, whilst most of the other nations of the earth remained in a state of barbarism.

**—Abbe Dubois**

Translated from the French
and Edited by
HENRY K. BEAUCHAMP
Member of the Royal Historical Society
and Royal Asiatic Society

4735/22, Prakash Deep Building,
Ansari Road, Daryaganj,
New Delhi - 110002.

# Hindu Social System

## First Famous Study

*By*

**The Celebrated French Missionary**

**ABBE J.A. Dubois**

**Source:** ***Hindu Manners, Customs and Ceremonies***
**by Abbe J.A. Dubois**
**published in 1816.**



**Hindu Social System**

New First Edition—2013
ISBN: 978-81-8382-307-4 (PB)

*Published by:*
**LOTUS PRESS PUBLISHERS & DISTRIBUTORS**
Unit No. 220, Second Floor, 4735/22, Prakash Deep Building,
Ansari Road, Darya Ganj, New Delhi-10002
Ph.: 011-23280047, 32903912 • Mob.: 098118-38000
E-mail: lotus_press@sify.com

*Printed at:* Afcon Printer, Delhi

Editorspeak

# A Major Social Experiment

From the day one of human history, there have been societies and societies in various parts of our beloved planet earth, in different skin colours, from white to black, through yellow, brown and their various shades. In many lands just one particular shade prevailed, while in others more than one, belonging to independent racial communities, intermingled, clashing in most cases against each other to acquire supremacy—in which generally the fairer ones won the game, crushing the darker ones with extreme cruelty. It may be noted that the situation has continued till the last century, courtesy chiefly the European nations, the smallest one of whom, the English, has recently been counted as having attacked almost 90 percent of the whole world—of which we Indians have also been the victims.

The present writer is reminded of the Slavery Museum he had the occasion to visit in Liverpool a few years ago—while in that country known as 'Great' Britain—an eye-opener to the gory killings and atrocities of those (in)human beings. The American conquest of the tribes living there and the treatment given to the Negros by the Europeans in the past few centuries is another very dark chapter of white history.

India in this context has presented a totally different picture. The Hindus from the start made a well considered and equally well planned effort to organise society chiefly on an economic basis—a fact not underlined so far—and secondarily, on a religious basis, which formed the life-values and behaviour patterns of various communities living in the vast lands boundaried by the Himalayas from the west to east, and oceans all around in the south. There were four kinds of people all over: the Aryans in the north, Dravidians in the south, Kiratas in the east, and Nishadas all over—the skin colour varying from very fair to very dark, which situation still holds. There would have been clashes among them—as is the general characteristic of human beings—but the wiser among them did not let them attack any other and gave them a social structure to bring them together and to live cohesively, utilise their capabilities for everyone's growth and development. It was a substantial experiment in life and human resource management.

Thus the Varnashrama system came into existence. It is notable that the original divisions were four in both its parts, Varna and Ashrama which together formed a complete whole. They came to be subdivided into castes, representing the kind of work they did to earn their livelihood, which the author of this work regards as a 'civilising factor.' He emphatically states that 'the caste division in many respects...is the happiest effort of Hindu legislation.' Wow! surprised? He further states: **'I am persuaded that it is simpley and solely due to the distribution of the people into castes that India did not lapse into barbarism, and that she reserved and perfected the arts and sciences of civilisation,** whilst most other nations of the earth remained in a state of barbarism.'

He presents the case in some detail: 'Caste assigns to each individual his own profession or calling,...from father to son,...from generation to generation, makes it impossible for any person or his descendents to change the condition of life which the law assigns to him for any other.'

He further comments: 'Such an institution was probably the only means that the most clearsighted prudence could devise for maintaining a state of civilisation...' etc.

It's an entirely new point of view which not only Sister Nivedita but our own poet-philosopher Rabindranath Tagore alse endorse. The latter has also made a suggestion—which we have so far totally ignored—perhaps not even taken note of, unfortunately—that **the system was not 'mutated'—which we should now undertake in right earnest.** (I've presented this in required detail in my book **Tagore Select** published earlier in the present series.)

• • •

This is the first ever work on the subject of Hindu Society, which is most comprehensive, and is based on the author's first-hand studies in a very detailed manner, which includes the only descriptions of Suttee-burnings in the country. A French Christian missionary, he stayed in our country for a quite long time, learnt Sanskrit and Tamil, read classics, and tried to mix with people as one of them, changing his dress etc. to win their favour—in which he succeeded to a great extent. It is interesting that though his mission was to spread Christianity in the country, he came to the conclusion that it was an impossible pursuit—which he openly announced in no uncertain terms to his fellowmen. He wrote exhaustively, checked and rechecked it, adding further information as and when he collected it. He wrote in French and sold the MS to East India Company, who had it translated into English and published in England.

The work deals with society as well language and literature, military and justice systems—these are aspects on which almost nothing else is available, and the details are presented in a most interesting manner, reading like fiction, which greatly enhances its value.

Abbe Dubois was a remarkable person, even Maxmuller regretted having not heard about him and met him; his contribution to Indian studies is unusually significant, for which reason his work continues to be published and read till date. I've tried to make it more useful and systematically approachable by dividing it into more than one book and rechapterising it in view of the present day requirements. This is the second book, the first being limited to religion and mythology, and perhaps a third one, centred around the Ashramas, which will be called Life-time Planning and Management, will be published in due course. I sincerely hope that the reader will like and love it like I do. Amen!

# A Valuable Work

## F. Max Muller

It is difficult to believe that Abbe Dubois, the author of *Moeurs, Institutions et Ceremonies des Peuples de l'Inde*, died only in 1848. By his position as a scholar and as a student of Indian subjects, he really belongs to a period previous to the revival of Sanskrit studies in India, as inaugurated by Wilkins, Sir William Jones, and Colebrooke. I had no idea, when in 1846 I was attending in Paris the lectures of Eugene Burnouf at the College de France, that the old Abbe was still living and in full activity as Directeur des Missions Etrangeres, and I doubt whether even Burnouf himself was aware of his existence in Paris. The Abbe belongs really to the eighteenth century, but as there is much to be learnt even from such men as Roberto de Nobili, who went to India in 1606, from H. Roth, who was much consulted by Kircher in his *China Illustrata* (1667), and others, so again the eighteenth century was by no means devoid of eminent students of Sanskrit, of Indian religion, and Indian subjects in general.

It is true that in our days their observations and researches possess chiefly a historical interest, but they are by no means to be neglected. They make us see how the acquaintance of European scholars with India began, and under what circumstances the first steps were taken by these pioneers, chiefly missionaries, towards acquiring a knowledge of the ancient language of India, Sanskrit, and through it, towards gaining an acquaintance with one of the most interesting peoples and one of the richest and most original literatures of the world. The reports sent from India by Pere Coeurdoux (1767), and published by Barthelemy in the *Memoirs of the French Academy*, the letters of Pere Calmette (1733), and of Pere Pons (1740), are full of curious information, anticipating on many points the later discoveries of Sir William Jones and other members of the Asiatic Society of Bengal. It should be remembered also that the first Sanskrit grammar was published at Rome in 1790 by Paolino de S. Bartolommeo, four years before the death of Sir William Jones (1746-1794).

Abbe Dubois, though born about 1770 and therefore considerably the junior of Sir William Jones belonged by his place in the history of Sanskrit scholarship to the period that came to an end with the beginnings of the Asiatic Society of Bengal, which had been founded by Sir William Jones in 1784. Nor must it be forgotten that while the real revival of Sanskrit studies took place in Bengal, Abbe Dubois spent the whole of his life in the Deccan and in Madras Presidency. He was, therefore, as may be seen by his translation of the *Panchatantra*, under the title of *Le Pantchatantra ou les cinq ruses*, Fables du Brahme Vichnou-Sarma; *Aventures de Paramarta et autres contres*, le tout traduit pour la premiere fois, Paris, 1826, a Tamil far more than a Sanskrit scholar, and well acquainted with Tamil literature, which hitherto has been far too much neglected by students of Indian literature, philosophy, and religion.

Though little is known of Abbe Dubois' life beyond the fact that he lived retired from the world, and retired even from his fellow-workers, and a stranger, it would seem, to the researches which were carried on all around him by the devoted and enthusiastic scholars of Sanskrit literature in France, England, and Germany, his principal book, *Description of the Character, Manners, and Customs of the People of India, and of their Institutions, Religious and Civil,* published both in French and in English, has always continued to be read and to be quoted with respect, as containing the views of an eye-witness, of a man singularly free from prejudice, and of a scholar with sufficient freedom from prejudice and of a scholar with sufficient knowledge, if not of Sanskrit, yet of Tamil, both literary and spoken, to be able to enter into the views of the natives, to understand their manners and customs, and to make allowance for many of their supersitious opinions and practices, as mere corruptions of an originally far more rational and intelligent form of religion and philosophy.

New men who were real scholars have hitherto undertaken to tell us what they saw of India and its inhabitants during a lifelong residence in the country, and in spite of the great opportunities that India offers to intelligent and observant travellers, we know far less of the actual life of India than of that of Greece and Rome. **There are few men now left who, like Abbe Dubois, have actually been present at the burning of widows, or who can give us, as he does, the direct reports of eye-witnesses who saw a king burnt with two of his queens** joining hands on the burning pyre over the corpse of their husband. In the South these Suttees were far less frequent than in Bengal, where in the year 1817 no less than 706 cases of Suttee had been officially reported, and where this practice had at last to be put down by the law during the Governor-Generalship of Lord William Bentinck (1825-1835), thanks chiefly to the active exertions and the moral influence of Ram Mohun Roy.

As a trustworthy authority on the state of India from 1792 to 1823 Abbe Dubois' work will always retain its value, and in its final and complete form now offered to the public, it will be welcome not only to Sanskrit scholars, but to all who take an intelligent interest in that wonderful country. As the Abbe went to India as a missionary, and was a man remarkably free from theological prejudices, missionaries in particular will read his volume with interest and real advantage.

# Abbe Dubois and His Book

## Henry K. Beauchamp

In the Library of the Madras Literary Society and Auxiliary of the Royal Asiatic Society may be seen, in a conspicuous position above one of the doorways, a striking portrait in oil-colours. This portrait at a distance one takes to be that of some Hindu, clothed in white, wearing a white turban, and holding in one hand, the bamboo staff that tradition assigns to a Hindu pilgrim. A closer inspection, however, shows that in reality it is the portrait of a European, a face that literally speaks to you from the canvas.

This portrait is that of Abbe J.A. Dubois, a Christian missionary who laboured for some thirty-one years in India, striving to fulfil the task which his sense of religious duty imposed upon him. Merely in this respect one can claim for him no special merit. His special claim to recognition will be found elsewhere, in the wonderful record which he compiled of the manners, customs, institutions, and ceremonies of the people among whom he lived and moved.

In his day, it must be remarked, there were no royal roads to such knowledge. There were no text-books to prepare the way by their critical analyses of the sacred Hindu writings. Such knowledge had to be gained at first hand, and by the more laborious method of personal inquiry in situ.

'I had no sooner arrived amongst the natives of India,' the Abbe himself tells us, 'than I recognized the absolute necessity of gaining their confidence. Accordingly, I made it my constant rule to live as they did. I adopted their style of clothing, and I studied their customs and methods of life in order to be exactly like them. By such conduct I was able to ensure a free and hearty welcome from people of all castes and conditions, and was often favoured of their own accord with the most curious and interesting particulars about themselves.'

Major Mark Wilks, the accomplished historian of Mysore, who in those days was British Resident in that province, in introducing the Abbe's work to the notice of the Government of Fort St. George, remarked: 'Of the history and character of the author, I only know that he escaped from one of the fusillades of the French Revolution and has since lived amongst the Hindus as one of themselves; and of the respect which his irreproachable conduct inspires, it may be sufficient to state that when travelling, the house of a Brahmin is uniformly cleared for his reception, as a spontaneous mark of deference and respect.'

The Abbe was ordained in the diocese of Viviers in 1792, at the age of twenty-seven, and left France in the same year. On reaching India he was attached to the Pondicherry Mission. He must have quickly made for himself a name, for on the fall of Seringapattam, he was specially invited to visit the capital of Mysore in order to reconvert and reorganize the Christian community which had been forcibly converted to Mahomedanism by Tippu Sultan. I may mention that, through the influence of the Abbe in Mysore, not a single priest of the Missions Etrangeres was persecuted by Tippu. He once more gathered the lost sheep, and established on a permanent basis the Roman Catholic Church in the province of Mysore. **He met the problem of the poverty of the people committed to his care by founding agricultural colonies and he used his influence to such good effect in preventing epidemics of small-pox by promoting vaccination**—then, a comparatively novel idea—that he was afterwards granted a special pension by the East India Company.

The French MS. of the work which the Abbe compiled has a somewhat remarkable history. In its original form it was placed in the hands of Major Wilks in the year 1806, when the Abbe had been some fourteen years in the country. Major Wilks studied it for more than a year and then forwarded it to the Government of Fort St. George with a letter of warm recommendation. This judgement was heartily endorsed by Sir James Mackintosh, and also by Mr. W. Erskine, of Bombay, a man of distinguished talents and an acknowledged authority in everything connected with the mythology, literature, customs and institutions of the people of India. Major Wilks had no difficulty in persuading Lord William Bentinck, who was then at Madras, to purchase the MS. on behalf of the East India Company.

The purchase of the MS. was reported by the Madras Government to the Board of Directors in 1807 as 'an arrangement... of great public importance'; and the MS. itself was transmitted to London at the same time for translation and publication. It was not until 1816, however, that the English translation was actually published.

As to the intrinsic value of the Abbe's work, I have no hesitation in saying that it is as valuable to-day as ever it was, even more valuable in some respects. It is true that a mass of learned literature on the religious and civil life of the Hindus has accumulated since the Abbe's days, but the fact is that the Abbe's work, composed as it was in the midst of the people themselves, is of a unique character, for it combines, as no other work on the Hindus combines, a recital of the broad facts of Hindu religion and Hindu sociology with many masterly descriptions, at once comprehensive and minute.

There is one other matter which I feel bound to refer to before concluding, and that is the impression he derived after three decades of Mission labour as to the possibility of converting India to Christianity. I have no wish to renew the bitter controversy which ensued on the publication of his *Letters on the State of Christianity in India* soon after his return of France; the purport of those *Letters*, as I understand them, was to assert that, **under existing circumstances, there is no human possibility of converting the Hindus as a nation to any sect of Christianity.**

He refers to the collapse of the Church, with its hundreds of thousands of converts, many of them of high caste. The Abbe completely despaired of the higher castes ever becoming Christians, though he was ready to acknowledge that there was a harvest-field among the low castes and outcastes. On his own attempts to convert the Hindus he remarks: 'For my part I cannot boast of my successes. During the long period I have lived in India in the capacity of a missionary, I have made with the assistance of a native missionary, in all between two and three hundred converts of both sexes. Of this number two-thirds were Pariahs or beggars; and the rest were composed of Sudras, vagrants, and outcastes of several tribes, who being without resource, turned Christians in order to form connexions, chiefly for the purpose of marriage or with some other interested views.'

It may be mentioned that in the agricultural settlement of reconverted Christians the inhabitants retained their Hindu caste distinctions; and the following observations in Mr. V.S. Narasimha Iyengar Mysore Census Report (1891) are noteworthy:

'Roman Catholicism is able to prevail among the Hindus by reason of its policy of tolerating among its converts the customs of caste and social observances, which constitute so material a part of the Indian social fabric. They still pay worship to the Kalasam at marriages and festivals, call in the Brahmin astrologer and purohita, use the Hindu religious marks, and conform to various other amentities.'

The last years of the Abbe's life were spent at the headquarters of the Missions Etrangeres at Paris. He left India on January 15, 1823. On his return to Paris he was at once made Director of the Missions Etrangeres, and from 1836 to 1839 he filled the post of Superior. During his leisure he found time to translate into French the whole of the *Panchatantra*, the famous book of Hindu fables, and also a work which he entitled *The Exploits of the Guru Paramarta*. He died in 1848 at the patriarchal age of eighty-three.

*Madras, Sept.1897*

Authorspeak

# Authentic Records

Though Europeans have possessed settlements in India for more than three centuries, it is only within recent times that authentic details have been obtained with respect to the people who dwell in this vast country and whose ancient civilization, methods of government, manners, creeds and customs, are nevertheless so well worthy of notice. **It is impossible to doubt for a moment at an epoch when our most civilized countries of the West were still plunged in the dark abyss of ignorance, the various forms of their institutions, both political and social; their knowledge of mathematics, especially of astronomy; their systems of metaphysics and ethics: all of these had long ago made the people of India famous far beyond their own borders; while the renown of Hindu philosophers had reached even Europe.**

The many ill-informed and often contradictory narratives about India which have been published in present times have deservedly fallen into discredit. Yet it must be admitted, some good work has been done by certain literary societies that have of recent years been established in India. Yet, it must be confessed, the information which we possess about the people of India is very meagre. The ancient history of their country is, for one thing, enshrouded in chimera and fable, that it is not too much to presume that we shall never succeed in throwing proper light on all this mass of absurdities.

My readers will see in the following pages to what extremes the people of India carry their belief in and love for the marvellous. Their first historians were in reality poets, who seem to have decided that they could not do better than compose their poems in the spirit of the people for whom they were writing. The Indian muse of history thus became a kind of magician whose wand performed wonders.

While waiting for inquirers more skilful than myself, to find a way through this labyrinth, which to me is absolutely inextricable, I offer to the public a large number of authentic records which I have carefully collected and which, for the most part, contain particulars that are either unknown or only partially known. I believe, that they will be acknowledged to contain some useful materials for future savants who may undertake a complete and methodical treatise on the people of India.

In this new edition the contents of my first MS. have been carefully revised and corrected. They have, moreover, been considerably augmented by many curious details which did not appear in the original document. During my long sojourn in India I never let slip any opportunity of collecting materials and particulars of all sorts. My information has been drawn partly from the books which are held in highest estimation amongst the people of India, and partly from such scattered records as fell by chance into my hands and contained facts upon which I could thoroughly rely. But in regard to the majority of the materials, I am chiefly dependent on my own researches, having lived in close and familiar intercourse with persons of every caste and condition of life.

In publishing these records of my researches I have no wish to aspire to literary fame. I have noted down just what I saw, just what I heard, just what I read. I have aimed only at simplicity and accuracy.

# Contents

# 1

# Caste: A Civilising Factor

The word caste is derived from the Portuguese, and is used in Europe to designate the different tribes or classes into which the people of India are divided.[1] The most ordinary classification, and at the same time the most ancient, divides them into four main castes. The first and most distinguished of all is that of Brahmana, or Brahmins; the second in rank is that of Kshatriyas, or Rajahs; the third the Vaisyas, or Landholders and Merchants; and the fourth the Sudras, or Cultivators and Menials.

The functions proper to each of these four main castes are: for Brahmins, priesthood and its various duties; for Kshatriyas, military service in all its branches; for Vaisyas, agriculture, trade, and cattle-breeding; and for Sudras, general servitude. Each of the four main castes is subdivided into many others, the number of which it is difficult to determine because the subdivisions vary according to locality, and a sub-caste existing in one province is not necessarily found in another.

1. The Sanskrit word is Varna = colour, thus showing that upon the difference of colour between the Aryan Brahmins and the aboriginal inhabitants the distinction of caste was originally founded. —Pope

Amongst the Brahmins of the south in particular for example, there are to be found three or four principal divisions, and each of these again is subdivided into at least twenty others. The lines of demarcation between them are so well defined as to prevent any kind of union between one sub-caste and another especially in the case of marriage.

The Kshatriyas and Vaisyas are also split up into many divisions and sub-divisions. In Southern India neither Kshatriyas nor Vaisyas are very numerous; but there are considerable numbers of the former in Northern India.

The Sudra caste is divided into most sub-castes. Nobody in any of the provinces where I have lived has ever been able to inform me as to the exact number and names of them. It is a common saying, however, that there are 18 chief sub-castes, which are again split up into 108 lesser divisions.

The Sudras are the most numerous of the four main castes. They form, in fact, the mass of the population, and added to the Pariahs, or Outcastes, they represent at least nine-tenths of the inhabitants. When we consider that the Sudras possess almost a monopoly of the various forms of artisan employment and manual labour, and that in India no person can exercise two professions at a time, it is not surprising that the numerous individuals who form this main caste are distributed over so many distinct branches.

However, there are several classes of Sudras that exist only in certain provinces. Of all the provinces that I lived in, the Dravidian, or Tamil, country is the one where the ramifications of caste appeared to me most numerous. There are not nearly so many in Mysore or the Deccan. Nowhere in these latter provinces have I come across castes corresponding to those which are known in the Tamil country under the names of Moodelly, Agambady, Nattaman, Totiyar, Udaiyan, Valeyen, Upiliyen, Pallen, and several others.[1]

It should be remarked, however, that those Sudra castes which are occupied exclusively in employments indispensable to all civilized societies are to be found everywhere under names varying with the languages of different localities. Of such I may cite, amongst others, the gardeners, the shepherds, the weavers, the Panchalas (the five castes of artisans, comprising the carpenters, goldsmiths, blacksmiths, founders, and in general all workers in metals), the manufacturers and vendors of oil, the fishermen, the potters, the washermen, the barbers, and some others. All these form part of the great main caste of Sudras; but the different castes of cultivators hold the first rank and disdainfully regard as their inferiors all those belonging to the professions just mentioned, refusing to eat with those who practise them.

In some districts there are castes which are not to be met with elsewhere, and which may be distinguished by peculiarities of their own. I am not aware, for example, that the very remarkable caste of Nairs, whose women enjoy the privilege of possessing several husbands, is to be found anywhere but in Travancore, though they enjoy the privilege of changing their husbands, they do not entertain more than one husband at a time. Amongst these same people, again, is another distinct caste called Nambudiri, which observes one revolting custom. The girls of this caste are usually married before the age of puberty; but if a

1. *Moodelly*, 'chief man' or highly respectable trader. *Agambady*, he who performs rgenial offices in temples or palaces. *Nattaman*, a caste of cultivators. *Totiyar*, a caste of labourers. *Udaiyan*, a potter. *Valeyen*, a fisherman. *Upiliyen*, salt manufacturer. *Pallen*, agriculturist. —Ed.

girl who has arrived at an age when the signs of puberty are apparent, happens to die before having had intercourse with a man, caste custom rigorously demands that the inanimate corpse of the deceased shall be subjected to a monstrous connexion. For this purpose the girl's parents are obliged to procure by a present of money some wretched fellow willing to consummate such a form of marriage: for were the marriage not consummated the family would consider itself dishonoured.[1]

The caste of Kullars, or robbers, who exercise their calling as an hereditary right, is found only in the Marava country, which borders on the coast, or fishing districts. The rulers of the country are of the same caste. They regard a robber's occupation as discreditable neither to themselves nor to their fellow castemen, for the simple reason that they consider robbery a duty and a right sanctioned by descent. This caste is looked upon in the district of Madura, where it is widely diffused, as one of the most distinguished among the Sudras.

There exists in the same part of the country another

---

1. Whatever may have been the case in the days of the Abbe, these customs no longer exist. In regard to this, Mr. W. Logan, in his *Manual of Malabar*, writes thus: 'To make tardy retribution—if it deserves such a name—to women who die unmarried, the corpse, it is said, cannot be burnt till a tali string (the Hindu equivalent of the wedding ring of Europe) is tied round the neck of the corpse, while lying on the funeral pile, by a competent relative. Nambudiris are exceedingly reticent in regard to their funeral ceremonies and observances, and the Abbe Dubois' account. Abbe must have misunderstood his informant in regard to the practice. What is done is merely to perform the religious rites, usually associated with Hindu marriages, over the dead body of the woman before the corpse is cremated.

—Ed.

caste, known as the Totiyars, in which brothers, uncles, nephews, and other near relations are all entitled to possess their wives m common.

In Eastern Mysore there is a caste called Morsa-Okkala-Makkalu, in which, when the mother of a family gives her eldest daughter in marriage, she is obliged to submit to the amputation of two joints of the middle finger and of the ring finger of the right hand. And if the bride's mother be dead, the bridegroom's mother, or in default of her the mother of the nearest relative, must submit to this mutilation.[1]

Generally speaking, there are few castes which are not distinguished by some special custom quite apart from the peculiar religious usages and ceremonies which the community may prescribe to guarantee or sanction civil contracts. In the cut and colour of their clothes and in thc style of wearing them, in the peculiar shape of their jewels and in the manner in which they are displayed on various parts of the person, the various castes have many rules, each possessing its own significance. Some observe rites of their own in their funeral and marriage ceremonies; others possess ornaments which they alone may use, or flags of certain colours for various ceremonies, which no other caste may carry. Yet they arouse neither contempt nor dislike in members of other castes which do not admit them. The most perfect toleration is the rule in such matters.

The various classes of Sudras who dwell in the hills of the Carnatic observe amongst their domestic regulations a practice as peculiar as it is disgusting. Both men and women pass their lives in a state of uncleanness and never wash their clothes. This habit

---

1. This custom is no longer observed; instead of the two fingers being amputated, they are now merely bound together and thus rendered unfit for use. —Ed.

is most religiously observed, and, If anybody were so rash as to wash but once in water the cloths with which he or she is covered, exclusion from caste would be the inevitable consequence. This custom, however, may be due to the scarcity of water, for in this part of the country there are only a few stagnant ponds, which would very soon be contaminated if all the inhabitants of a village were allowed to wash their garments in them.

Independently of the divisions and sub-divisions common to all castes one may further observe in each caste close family alliances cemented by intermarriage. Hindus of good family avoid as far as possible intermarriage with families outside their own circle. They always aim at marrying their children into the families which are already allied to them, and the nearer the relationship the more easily are marriages contracted. A widower is remarried to his deceased wife's sister, an uncle marries his niece, and a first cousin his first cousin. Persons so related possess an exclusive privilege of intermarrying, upon the ground of such relationship; and if they choose, they can prevent any other union and enforce their own preferential right, however old, unsuited, infirm, and poor they may be.[1]

In this connexion, however, several strange and ridiculous distinctions are made. An uncle may marry the daughter of his sister, but in no case may he marry the daughter of his brother. A brother's children may marry a sister's children, but the children of two brothers or of two sisters may not intermarry. Among descendants from the same stock the male line always has the right of contracting marriage with the female

---

1. This custom is gradually giving way now amongst the higher castes.

—Ed

line, but the children of the same line may never intermarry.

This rule is universally and invariably observed by all castes, from the Brahmin to the Pariah. It is obligatory on the male line to unite itself with the female line. Agreeably to this a custom has arisen which so far as I know is peculiar to the Brahmins. They are all supposed to know the *gotram* or stock from which they spring: that is to say, they know who was the ancient *Muni* or devotee from whom they descent, and they always take care, in order to avoid intermarriage with a female descendant of this remote priestly ancestor, to marry into a *gotram* other than their own.

Hindus who cannot contract a suitable marriage amongst their own relations are nevertheless bound to marry in their own caste, and even in that subdivision of it to which they belong. In no case are they permitted to contract marriages with strangers. Furthermore, persons belonging to a caste in one part of the country cannot contract marriages with persons of the same caste in another part, even though they may be precisely the same castes under different names. Thus the Tamil Yedeyers and the Canarese Upparerru would never consent to take wives from the Telugu Gollavaru and the Tamil Pillay, although the first two are, except for their names, identical with the second two.

## The Four Divisions

The most distinguished of the four main castes into which the Hindus were originally separated by their first legislators is, that of the Brahmins. After them come the Kshatriyas, or Rajahs. Superiority of rank is at present warmly contested between the Vaisyas, or merchants, and the Sudras, or cultivators. The former appear to have almost entirely lost their superiority except in the Hindu books, where they are invariably placed before the Sudras. In ordinary life the latter hold themselves to be superior to the Vaisyas, and consider themselves privileged to mark their superiority in many respects by treating them with contumely.

Even the Brahmins do not hold the highest social rank undisputed. The Panchalas, or five classes of artisans already mentioned, refuse, in some districts, to acknowledge Brahmin predominance, although these five classes themselves are considered to be of very low rank amongst the Sudras and are everywhere held in contempt. Brahmin predominance is also still more warmly contested by the Jains.

As to the particular subdivisions of each caste it is difficult to decide the order of hierarchy observed amongst them. Sub-castes which are despised in one district are often greatly esteemed in another, according as they conduct themselves with greater propriety or follow more important callings. Thus the caste to which the ruler of a country belongs, however low it may be considered elsewhere, ranks amongst the highest in the ruler's own dominions, and every member of it derives some reflection of dignity from its chief.

In general it will be found that those castes are most honoured who are particular in keeping themselves pure by constant bathing and by abstaining from animal food, who are exact in the observance of marriage regulations, who keep their women shut up and punish them when they err, and who resolutely maintain the customs and privileges of their order.

Of all the Hindus the Brahmins strive most to keep up appearances of outward and inward purity by frequent ablutions and severe abstinence not only from meat and everything that has contained the principle of life, but also from several natural products of the earth which prejudice and superstition teach them to be impure and defiling. It is chiefly to the scrupulous observance of such customs that the Brahmins owe the predominance of their illustrious order, and the reverence and respect with which they are everywhere treated.

Amongst the different classes of Sudras, those who permit widow remarriage are considered the most abject, and, except the Pariahs, I know very few castes in which such marriages are allowed to take place openly and with the sanction of the caste.[1]

The division into castes is the paramount distinction amongst the Hindus; but there is still another division, that of sects. The two best known are those of Siva and Vishnu, which are again divided into a large number of others. There are several castes, too, which may be distinguished by certain marks painted on the forehead or other parts of the body.

## The Sects

The first three of the four main castes, that is to say the Brahmins, Kshatriyas, and Vaisyas, are distinguished by a thin cord hung across from the left shoulder to the right hip. But this cord is also worn by the Jains and even by the Panchalas.

There is yet another division more general than any I have referred to yet, namely, that into Right-hand and Left-hand factions. This appears to be but a modern invention, since it is not mentioned in any of

1. Remarriage of virgin widows is one of the foremost planks in the platform of social reform, but it is opposed violently by the orthodox. –Ed

the ancient books of the country; and have been assured that it is unknown in Northern India. This has turned out to be the most direful disturber of the public peace. It has proved a perpetual source of riots, and the cause of endless animosity amongst the natives.

Most castes belong either to the Left-hand or Right-hand faction. The former comprises the Vaisyas or trading classes, the Panchalas or artisan classes, and some of the low Sudra castes. It also contains the lowest caste, namely, the Chucklers or leather-workers, who are looked upon as its chief support.

To the Right-hand faction belong most of the higher castes of Sudras. The Pariahs are its chief support, as a proof of which they glory in the title Valangai-Mougattar, or friends of the Right-hand. In the disputes and conflicts which so often take place between the two factions it is always the Pariahs who make the most disturbance and do the most damage. The opposition between the two factions arises from certain exclusive privileges to which both lay claim. But as these alleged privileges are nowhere clearly defined and recognized, they result in confusion and uncertainly, and are with difficulty capable of settlement. In these circumstances one cannot hope to conciliate both parties; all that one can do is to endeavour to compromise matters as far as possible.

When one faction trespasses on the so-called rights of the other, tumults arise which spread gradually over large tracts of territory, afford opportunity for excesses of all kinds, and generally end in bloody conflicts. The Hind, ordinarily so timid and gentle in all other circumstances of life, seems to change his nature completely on occasions like these.

I have several times witnessed instances of these

popular insurrections excited by the mutual pretensions of the two factions and pushed to such an extreme of fury that the presence of a military force has been insufficient to quell them. I have sometimes seen these rioters stand up against several discharges of artillery without exhibiting any sign of submission. And when at last the armed force has succeeded in restoring order it is only for a time. At the very first opportunity the rioters are at work again, regardless of the punishment they have received.[1]

The rights and privileges for which the Hindus are ready to fight such sanguinary battles appear highly ridiculous. Perhaps the sole cause of the contest is the right to wear slippers or to ride through the streets in a palanquin or on horseback during marriage festivals. Sometimes it is the privilege of being escorted on certain occasions by armed retainers, sometimes that of having a trumpet sounded in front of a procession, or of being accompanied by native musicians at public ceremonies. Perhaps it is simply the particular kind of musical instrument suitable to such occasions that is in dispute; or perhaps it may be the right of carrying flags of certain colours or certain devices during these ceremonies.[1]

## Advantages Resulting from Caste

Many persons study so imperfectly the spirit and character of the different nations that inhabit the earth and the influence of climate on their manners, customs, predilections, and usages, that they are astonished to find how widely such nations differ from

---

1. These faction fights have gradually disappeared under the civilizing influences of education and good government; and if they ever occur at all, are confined to the lowest castes and never spread beyond the limits of a village. The distinction between the two factions, however, still exist. —Ed.

each other. Trammelled by the prejudices of their own surroundings, such persons think nothing well regulated that is not included in the polity and government of their own country. They would like to see all nations of the earth placed on precisely the same footing as themselves. Everything which differs from their own customs they consider either uncivilized or ridiculous.

I have heard some persons, sensible enough in other respects, but imbued with all the prejudices that they have brought with them from Europe, pronounce what appears to me an altogether erroneous judgement in the matter of caste divisions amongst the Hindus. In their opinion, caste is not only useless to the body politic, it is also ridiculous, and even calculated to bring trouble and disorder on the people. For my part, having, lived many years on friendly terms with the Hindus, I have been able to study their national life and character closely, and I have arrived at a quite opposite decision on this subject of caste. **I believe caste division to be in many respects the *chef-d' aevvre*, the happiest effort of Hindu legislation. I am persuaded that it is simply and solely due to the distribution of the people into castes that India did not lapse into a state of barbarism, and that she reserved and perfected the arts and sciences of civilization, whilst most other nations of the earth remained in a state of barbarism.** I do not consider caste to be free from many great drawbacks; but I believe that the resulting advantages, in the case of a nation constituted like the Hindus, more than outweigh the resulting evils.

To establish the justice of this contention we have only to glance at the condition of the various races of men who live in the same latitude as the Hindus, and to consider the past and present status of those among them whose natural disposition and character have not been influenced for good by the purifying doctrines of Revealed Religion. We can judge what the Hindus would have been like, had they not been held within the pale of social duty by caste regulations, if we glance at neighbouring nations west of the Peninsula and east of it beyond the Ganges as far as China. In China itself a temperate climate and a form of government peculiarly adapted to a people unlike any other in the world have produced the same effect as the distinction of caste among the Hindus.

After much careful thought I can discover no other reason except caste which accounts for the Hindus not having fallen into the same state of barbarism as their neighbours and as almost all nations inhabiting the torrid zone. **Caste assigns to each individual his own profession or calling; and the handing down of this system from father to son, from generation to generation, makes it impossible for any person or his descendants to change the condition of life which the law assigns to him for any other.** Such an institution was probably the only means that the most near-sighted prudence could devise for maintaining a state of civilization amongst a people endowed with the peculiar characteristics of the Hindus.

We can picture what would become of the Hindus if they were not kept within the bounds of duty by the rules and penalties of caste, by looking at the position of the Pariahs, or outcastes of India, who, checked by no moral restraint, abandon themselves to their natural propensities. Anybody who has studied the conduct and character of the people of this class—which, by the way, is the largest of any in India[1]—will agree

1. This is true only of Southern India, where the Pariahs number 5,000,000. They form one-seventh of the total population.

with me that a State consisting entirely of such inhabitants could not long endure, and could not fail to lapse before long into a condition of barbarism. For my own part, being perfectly familiar with this class, and acquainted with its natural predilections and sentiments, I am persuaded that a nation of Pariahs left to themselves would speedily become worse than the hordes of cannibals who wander in the vast waste of Africa, and would soon take to devouring each other.

I am no less convinced that if the Hindus were not kept within the limits of duty and obedience by the system of caste, and by the penal regulations, attached to each phase of it, 'they would soon become just what the Pariahs are, and probably something still worse. **The whole country would necessarily fall into a state of hopeless anarchy, and, before the present generation disappeared, this nation, so polished under present conditions, would have to be reckoned amongst the most uncivilized of the world. The legislators of India, whoever they may have been, were far too wise and too well acquainted with the natural character of the people for whom they prescribed laws** to leave it to the discretion or fancy of each individual to cultivate what knowledge he pleased, or to exercise, as seemed best to him, any of the various professions, arts, or industries which are necessary for the preservation and well-being of a State,

They set out from that cardinal principle common to all ancient legislators, that no person should be useless to the commonwealth. At the same time they recognized that they were dealing with a people who were indolent and careless by nature, and whose propensity to be apathetic was so aggravated by the climate in which they lived, that unless every individual had a profession or employment rigidly imposed upon him, the social fabric could not hold together and must quickly fall into the most deplorable state of anarchy. These ancient lawgivers, therefore, being well aware of the danger caused by religious and political innovations, and being anxious to establish durable and inviolable rules for the different castes comprising the Hindu nation, **saw no surer way of attaining their object than by combining in an unmistakable manner those two great foundations of orderly government, religion and politics.** Accordingly, there is not one of their ancient usages, not one of their observances which has not some religious principle or object attached to it. Everything, indeed, is governed by superstition and has religion for its motive. The style of greeting, the mode of dressing, the cut of clothes, the shape of ornaments and their manner of adjustment, the various details of the toilette, the architecturc of houses, the comers where the hearth is placed and where the cooking pots must stand, the manner of going to bed and of sleeping, the forms of civility and politeness that must be observed: all these are severely regulated. It is for this reason that the IIindus hold all their customs and usages to be inviolable, for, being essentially religious, they consider them as sacred as religion itself.

The wisest and most famous of all lawgivers, Moses, availed himself of the same institution, as being the one which offered him the best means of governing the intractable and rebellious people of whom he had been appointed the patriarch. The division of the people into castes existed also amongst the Egyptians. With them, as with the Hindus, the law assigned an occupation to each individual, which was handed down from father to son. It was forbidden to any man to have two professions, or to change his own. Each caste had a special quarter assigned to it, and people of a different caste were prohibited from settling there.

Nevertheless, there was this difference between the Egyptians and the Hindus: with the former all castes and all professions were held in esteem; all employments, even of the meanest kind, were alike regarded as honourable; and, although the priestly and military castes possessed peculiar privileges, nobody would have considered it anything but criminal to despise the classes whose work, whatever it happened to be, contributed to the general good[1]. With the Hindus, on the other hand, there are professions and callings to which prejudice attaches such degradation that those who follow them are universally despised by those castes which in the public estimation exercise higher functions.

It must here be remarked, however, that the four great professions without which a civilized nation could not exist, namely, the army, agriculture, commerce, and weaving, are held everywhere in the highest esteem.

These same caste distinctions observable amongst Hindus exist likewise, with some differences, amongst the Arabs and Tartars. Probably, indeed, they were common to the majority of ancient nations. Cecrops, it will be remembered, separated the people of Athens into four tribes or classes, while their great lawgiver, Solon, upheld this distinction and strengthened it in several ways. Numa Pompilius, again, could devise no better way of putting an end to the racial hatred between Sabines and Romans, that by separating the body of the people into different castes and classes. The result of his policy was just what he had desired. Both Sabines and Romans, once amalgamated in this manner, forgot their national differences and thought only of those of their class or caste.

Those who instituted the caste system could not but perceive that with nations in an embryonic stage the more class distinctions there are the more order and symmetry there must be, and the more easy it is to exercise control and preserve order. This, indeed, is the result which caste classification amongst the Hindus has achieved. The shame which would reflect on a whole caste if the faults of one of its individual members went unpunished guarantees that the caste will execute justice, defend its own honour, and keep all its members within the bounds of duty. For, be it noted, every caste has its own laws and regulations; or rather, we may say, its own customs, in accordance with which the severest justice is meted out, just as it was by the patriarchs of old.

Thus in several castes adultery is punishable by death. This of course is no longer allowed by law. Girls or widows who succumb to temptation, are made to suffer the same penalty as those who have seduced them. The largest temple of the town of Conjeeveram, in the Carnatic, an immense building was constructed, so it is said, by a rich Brahmin who had been convicted of having had illicit intercourse with a low-casts Pariah woman.

Another advantage resulting from the caste system is the hereditary continuation of families and that purity of descent which is a peculiarity of the Hindus, and which consists in never mixing the blood of one family or caste with that of another. Marriages are confined to parties belonging to the same family or at any rate the same caste.

## Arts and Industries

Further, one would be justified in asserting that it is to caste distinctions that India owes the preservation of her arts and industries. For the same reason she would have reached a high standard of perfection in them had not the avarice of her rulers prevented it. It was chiefly to attain this object that the Egyptians were divided into castes, and that their laws assigned the particular place which each individual should occupy in the commonwealth. Their lawgivers no doubt considered that by this means all arts and industries would continue to improve from generation to generation, for men must needs do well that which they have always been in the habit of seeing done and which they have been constantly practising from their youth.

This perfection in arts and manufactures would undoubtedly have been attained by so industrious a people as the Hindus, if, the cupidity of their rulers had not acted as a check. As a matter of fact, **no sooner has an artisan gained the reputation of excelling in his craft than he is at once carried off by order of the sovereign, taken to the palace, and there confined for the rest of his life, forced to toil without remission and with little or no reward.** Under these circumstances, which are common to all parts of India under the government of native princes, it is hardly surprising that every art and industry is extinguished and all healthy competition deadened. **This is the chief and almost the only reason why progress in the arts has been so slow among the Hindus, and why in this respect they are now far behind other nations who did not become civilized for many centuries after themselves.**

Their workmen certainly lack neither industry nor skill. In the European settlements, where they are paid according to their merit, many native artisans are to be met with whose work would do credit to the best artisans of the West. Moreover, they feel no necessity to use the many European tools, whose nomenclature alone requires special study. One or two axes, as many saws and planes, all of them so rudely fashioned that a European workman would be able to do nothing with them—these are almost the only instruments that are to be seen in the hands of Hindu carpenters. The working materials of a journeyman goldsmith usually comprise a tiny anvil, a crucible, two or three small hammers, and as many files. With such simple tools the patient Hindu, thanks to his industry, can produce specimens of work which are often not to be distinguished from those imported at great expense from foreign countries. To what a standard of excellence would these men have attained if they had been from the earliest times subjected to good masters!

## Political Advantages

I will venture to express one other remark on the political advantages resulting from caste distinctions. In India parental authority is but little respected: and parents, overcome doubtless by that apathetic indifference which characterizes Hindus generally, are at little pains, to inspire those feelings of filial reverence which constitute family happiness by enchaining the affections of the children to the authors of their existence. **Outward affection appears to exist between brothers, and sisters, but in reality it is neither very strong nor very sincere. It quickly vanishes after the death of their parents, and subsequently, we may say, they only come together to fight and to quarrel** Thus, as the ties of blood relationship formed so insecure a bond between different members of a community, and guaranteed no such mutual assistance and support as were needed, it became necessary to bring families together in large caste communities, the individual members of which had a common interest in protecting, supporting, and defending each other. It was thus that the links of the Hindu social chain were so strongly and ingeniously forged that nothing was able to break them.

This was the object which the ancient lawgivers of India attained by establishing the caste system, and they thereby acquired a title to honour unexampled in the history of the world. Their work has stood the test of thousands of years, and has survived the lapse of time and the many revolutions to which this portion of the globe has been subjected. The Hindus have often passed beneath the yoke of foreign invaders, whose religions, laws, and customs have been very different from their own; yet all efforts to impose foreign institutions on the people of India have been futile, and foreign occupation has never dealt more than a feeble blow against Indian custom. Above all, and before all, it was the caste system which protected them.

# 2

# The Origin of Caste

Apparently there is no existing institution older than the caste system of the Hindus. Greek and Latin authors who have written about India concur in thinking that it has been in force from time immemorial and certainly the unswerving observance of its rules seems to me an almost incontestable proof of its antiquity.

Dr. Muir, in *Old Sanskrit Texts*, Vol, 1, p. 159, reviewing the texts which he had cited on this subject, says:- 'First, we have the set of accounts in which the four castes are said to have sprung from progenitors who were separately created; but in regard to the manner of their creation, we find the greatest diversity of statement. The most common story is that the castes issued from the mouth, arms, thighs, and feet of Purusha, or Brahma. The oldest extant passage in which this idea occurs, and from which all the later myths of a similar tenor have no doubt been borrowed, is to be found in the Purusha Sukta; but it is doubtful whether in the form in which it is there represented, this representation is anything more than an allegory. In some of the texts from the Bhagavata Purana traces of the same allegorical character may be perceived; but in Manu and the Puranas the mystical import of the Vedic text disappears, and the figurative narration is hardened into a literal statement of fact. In the chapters of the Vishnu, Vayu, and Markandeya

Puranas, where castes are described as coeval with creation, and as having been naturally distinguished by different gunas, or qualities, involving varieties of moral character, we are nevertheless allowed to infer that those qualities exerted no influence on the classes in which they were inherent, as the condition of the whole race during the Krita age is described as one, of uniform perfection and happiness; while the actual separation into castes did not take place, according to the Vayu Purana, until men had become deteriorated in the Treta age.

'Second, in various passages from the Brahmanas epic poems, and Puranas, the creation of mankind is described without the least allusion to any separate production of the progenitors of the four castes. And whilst in the chapters where they relate the distinct formations of the castes, the Puranas assign different natural dispositions to each class, they elsewhere represent all mankind as being at the creation uniformly distinguished by the quality of passion. In one text men are said to be the offspring of Vivasat; in another his son Manu is said to be their progenitor, whilst in a third they are said to be descended from a female of the same name. The passage which declares Manu to have been the father of the human race explicitly affirms that men of all the four castes were descended from him. In another remarkable text the Mahabharata categorically asserts that originally there was no distinction of classes, the existing distribution having arisen out of differences of character and occupation. In these circumstances, we may fairly conclude that the separate origination of the four castes was far from being an article of belief universally received by Indian antiquity.'

The following is the categorical assertion in the Mahabharata (Santi Parvan) above referred to. It occurs in the course of a discussion on caste between Bhrigu and Bharadwaja. Bhrigu, replying to a question put by Bharadwaja, says: 'The colour (Varna) of the Brahmins was white; that of the Kshatriyas red; that of the Vaisyas yellow; and that of the Sudras black.' Bharadwaja here rejoins, 'If the caste (varna) of the four classes is disunguished by their colour (varna), then a confusion of all the castes is observable......' Bhrigu replies, 'There is no difference of castes: this world, having been at first created by Brahma entirely Brahmanic, became (afterwards) separated into castes as the consequence of work. Those Brahmins (twice-born men) who were fond of sensual pleasure, fiery, irascible, prone to violence, who had forsaken their duty and were red limbed, fell into the condition of Kshatriyas. Those Brahmins who derived their livelihood from kine, who were yellow, who subsisted by agriculture, and who neglected to practise their duties, entered into the state of Vaisyas. Those Brahmins who were addiction to mischief and falsehood, who were covetous, who lived by all kinds of work, who were black and had fallen from punty, sank into the condition of Sudras.'

The Hindu legislators of old had the good sense to give stability to these customs and regulations by associating with them many outward ceremonies, which, by fixing them in the minds of the people, ensured their more faithful observance. These ceremonies are invariably observed, and have never been allowed to be ignored without grave consequences. Failure to perform a single one of them, however unimportant it might appear, would never go unpunished.

One cannot fail to remark how very similar some of these ceremonies are to those which were performed long ago amongst other nations. Thus the Hindu precepts about cleanness and uncleanness, as also the means employed for preserving the one and effacing the other, are similar in many respects to those of the ancient Hebrews. The rule about marrying in one's caste, and even in one's family, was specifically imposed upon the Jews in the laws which Moses gave them from God. This rule, too, was in force a long time before that, for it appears to have been general amongst the Chaldeans. We find also in the Holy Writ that Abraham espoused his niece, and that the holy patriarch sent into a far country for a maiden of his own family as a wife for his son Isaac. Again, Isaac and his wife Rebecca found it difficult to pardon their son Esau for marrying amongst strangers, that is, amongst the Canaanites; and they sent their son Jacob away into a distant land to seek a wife from amongst their own people. In the same way Hindus residing in a foreign country will journey hundreds of leagues to their native land in search of wives for their sons.

Again, as to the caste system, Moses, as is well known, established it amongst the Hebrews in accordance with the commands of God. This holy lawgiver had, during his long sojourn in Egypt, observed the system as established in that country, and had doubtless recognized the good that resulted from it. Apparently, in executing the divine order with respect to it he simply adapted and perfected the system which was in force in Egypt.

The Indian caste system is of still older origin. The Hindu sacred writings record that the author of it was God Brahma. It is easy to understand the allegorical signification of this legend, in which one can distinctly trace the relative degrees of subordination of the different castes. The Brahmins, destined to fulfil the high functions of spiritual priesthood and to show the way of salvation to their fellowmen, issue from the head of the Creator; the Kshatriyas, endowed with physical force and destined to undergo the fatigues of war, have their origin in the shoulders and arms of Brahma; the Vaisyas, whose duty it is to provide the food, the clothing, and other bodily necessities of man, are born in the belly of the god; and the Sudras, whose lot is servitude and rude labour in the fields, issue from his feet.

Besides this traditional origin of the different castes, known to all Hindus, there is another to be found in their books, which traces the institution back to the time of the Flood. For, It should be noted, this terrible world-renovating disaster is as well known to the Hindus as it was to Moses. A celebrated personage, reverenced by the Hindus, and known to them as escaped the calamity in an ark, in which were also the seven famous Penitents of India. After the Flood, according to Hindu writers, this saviour of the human race divided mankind into different castes: as they exist at the present day.

The many subdivisions into which these four great original castes were broken up undoubtedly from later times. They were due to the absolute necessity of assigning to each person in a special manner his particular place in the social organization. There are some Hindu authors who assert that the individuals composing the first ramifications of the large Sudra caste were the bastard offspring of the other higher castes, and owed their origin to illicit intercourse with the widows of the four great caste divisions. It is said that these bastard children, born of a Brahmin father and a Kshatriya mother, or of a Vasiya father and a Sudra mother, etc., were not recognized by any of the four primary castes, and so they were placed in other caste categories and were assigned special employments, more or less humble, according to their extraction.

A few of these many subdivisions are said to be of quite recent origin. For instance, the five artisan classes are said to have originally formed only one class, as also the barbers and washermen, the Gollavarus and Kurubas, and a large number of other who in recent times have split up into new-castes.

# 3

# The Brahmins at the Head

The real origin of the Brahmins is wrapped in mystery and one can only hazard conjectures on the subject, or put belief in myths. The story most generally accepted says that they were born from Brahma's head, which accounts for their name. One would suppose that as all castes were born from this same father they would be privileged to bear the same name; but as the Brahmins were the first-born, and issued from the noblest part of the common parent, they claimed special privileges from which all others were rigorously excluded. They have another theory to bear out the accepted belief that no one else is entitled to the illustrious name of Brahmin. They say that no one knows anything about Brahma's attributes and virtues beyond what they themselves choose to teach mankind, and that this knowledge in itself gives them the right to bear his name.

The great difference between their caste and all others is that a Brahmin only becomes a Brahmin after the ceremony of the triple cord. Until this essential ceremony has been performed, he ranks only as a Sudra. By mere birth he is no different from the rest of his race; and it is for this reason that he is called *Dvija* (*Bis genitus*, or Twice-born). His first birth only gives him his manhood, whereas the second raises him to the exalted rank of Brahmin, and this by means of the ceremony of the triple cord. Indeed, two out of the seven famous Penitents, or Rishis, or Munis, who are supposed to have been the original founders of the various sects of Brahmins of the present day, did not originally belong to this caste at all; but by reason of the length and austerity of their term of penance, they were rewarded by having their state of penitent Kshatriyas changed to that of penitent Brahmins by the investiture of the triple cord. These seven Penitents of Hindu history are the most celebrated personages recognized by the people of India. Their names are Kasyapa, Atri, Bharadwaja, Gautama, Viswamitra, Jamadagni, and Vasishta.

The last-named and Viswamitra are those who were considered worthy of being admitted into the high caste of Brahmins. These far-famed Rishis must be of great antiquity, for they existed even before the Vedas, which allude to them in several places. They were the favoured of the gods, and more especially of Vishnu, who at the time of the Deluge made them embark on a vessel which he piloted, and thereby saved them from destruction. Even the gods were called to account for having offended these holy men, who did not hesitate to curse the deities who committed infamies.

The seven Penitents, after setting a virtuous example on earth, were finally transited to heaven, where they occupy a place amongst the most brilliant constellations. They are to be recognized in the seven stars that form the Great Bear, which, according to Hindu tradition, are neither more nor less than the seven famous Rishis themselves. They are, according to Hindu legend, by ancestors of the Brahmins in reality and not by metamorphosis, and it is believed that without ceasing to shine in the firmament they can, and occasionally do, revisit the earth to find out what is occurring there.

Are there any families in Europe which can, not withstanding the mythical origins which heraldic science professes to discover, pride themselves on the possession of such ancestors? And seeing that in our own aristocracy a man with a noble lineage is not above assuming an air of extreme hauteur and exclusiveness, we ought not to be surprised at a Brahmin's vanity or at the contempt with which he treats anyone belonging to an inferior caste. This idea of handing down to posterity the names of their great men by immortalizing them, and assigning to them a place among the constellations, appears to have been an almost universal practice amongst ancient races.

Astronomy has played an important part in the history of almost all idol worshipping nations; and of all creeds such as it certainly is the least unreasonable, and has survived the longest. The religious and political lawgivers of these races were clever enough to perceive that the worship of the stars had taken a great hold upon mankind, and that the simplest and most effectual way of perpetuating the memory of their heroes would be to transform them into outward objects that were always before the eyes of the people. It was thus that the Greeks and Romans consecrated the memory of their divinities and demigods; and no doubt the Hindu lawgivers were prompted to immortalize their seven Rishis by means of the brightest stars in the sky because they realized that Hindu imagination is only appealed to through the visible, and therefore that was the best way to prepetuate the veneration due to these illustrious beings.

But whatever may have been the claims of Brahmins to a celestial origin, it is a well-authenticated fact that neither their caste nor any other existed in the countries to the north-east of Bengal four or five centuries ago. About that time the inhabitants of those parts, thinking that it might be to their advantage to adopt the customs of their neighbours, began to clamour for Brahmins. Accordingly, some were made to order out of the youths of the country, who, after conforming to the customs and rites of the Brahmins, were incorporated into their caste by the investiture of the triple cord. The descendants of these ready-made Brahmins have ever since been considered on an equality with the rest. The southern Brahmins do not care to be reminded of the fact yet they are obliged to admit it, as well as that two of the Rishis were originally Kshatriyas. An objection which people often put to them is that if nothing but the investiture of the triple cord can make Brahmins of them, then their wives, who do not go through the ceremony, really belong to thc Sudras; and this means that all Brahmins are obliged to marry out of their caste and by so doing, violate their most sacred principles. The reply they invariably make to this, as to other embarrassing, questions, is that they are but following time-honoured customs and institutions.

## Subdivisions

Brahmins are subdivided into seven sects, each of which has for its patron one of the celebrated Penitents already mentioned. Besides this, they are split up into four classes, each class recognizing one of the four Vedas as its own. Thus there are Brahmins of the Yajur-Veda, of the Sama-Veda, of the Rig-Veda, and of the Atharva-Veda. Some are of opinion that this fourth class is extinct; but, as a matter of fact, it still exists, although there are but few representatives left, who are even more exoteric than the other castes, because they allow bloody sacrifices to be offered up. Added to this, they teach a belief in witchcraft, and anyone who is supposed to possess the art earns the odious reputation of being a sorcerer. When the *yajnam* sacrifice takes place, it is customary for Brahmins of all four Vedas to be present. The prayers which are offered up at the sandhya are quoted from the four Vedas, each Brahmin repeating those of his own particular Veda, which accounts for the slight differences.

Under ordinary circumstances the Brahmins do not appear to be very strict about these minor distinctions, or to prefer one Veda to another. Nor is this altogether surprising, considering that the author of the famous Indian poem Bhagavata declares that originally the four Vedas were one and the same. According to him, it was the Penitent Vyasa who divided them into four books, and at the same time added introductions an commentanes to render them more intelligible. Indeed, owing to inherent fault, or to the mistakes made by ignorant and inattentive copyists, the Vedas are so obscure that even men of learning find it hard to fathom them.

To Vyasa is also attributed the authorship of the eighteen Puranas.[1] These are eighteen poems, containing most minute accounts of Hindu mythology with its gods and heroes. The fables contained in them are responsible for the gross forms of idolatry practised by the Hindus.

Brahmins are also distinguishable by their sect, by their names, by the marks which they trace on their foreheads and other parts of the body, and also by the

1. The names are Brahma-purana. Padma-purana, Siva-purana, Bhagavata, Bavirhotra-purana. Naradia, Markandeya-purana, Brahmaveyverta-purana, Linga-purana, Varaha-purana, Skanda-purana, Vamana-purana, Vayu-purana, Kurma-purana, Matsya-purana, Garuda-purana, Brahmanda-purana.

high priest to whose jurisdiction they are subject. The four principal sects of Brahmins south of the Kistna are: the Vaishnavites, the Smarthas, the Tatvavadis, and the Utrassas. The distinctive mark of the Vaishriavite Brahmins is the *namam*: Their *simhasana*, that is, the place where their high priest resides and their chief school, is at Hobbala in the Northern Carnatic. The Smartha Brahmins trace three horizontal lines on the forehead with sandalwood paste. Their *simhasana* is at Sringeri in North-west Mysore. Besides these horizontal lines on the brow, the Tatvavadi Brahmins have ineffaceable marks branded on certain parts of their bodies with a red-hot iron. Their *simhasana* is at Sravenur. The Utrassa Brahmins draw a perpendicular line from the top of the forehead to the base of the nose.

There are also Brahmins known as Cholias, who are looked down upon by the rest. They appear or be conscious of their own inferiority, for they hold themselves aloof from other Brahmins. All menial work connected with the temples is performed by them, such as washing and decorating the idols, preparing lighted lamps, incense, flowers, fruits, rice, and other similar objects of which sacrifices are composed. In many temples even Sudras are allowed to exercise these functions, and men of this caste are always chosen for the office of sacrifices in pagodas where rams, pigs, cocks, and other living victims are offered up. No Brahmin would ever consent to take part in a sacrifice where blood has to be shed. It is perhaps on account of the work they condescend to do that the Cholia Brahmins have fallen into such contempt. According to the general view of the Brahmins, to do any work which can be left to the lowest amongst the Sudras is to put themselves on their level, and consequently to degrade themselves. In any case the work of a pujari is not thought much of, and by some it is considered absolutely degrading. However, some Brahmins have to accept this task on account of their poverty, but they only do so with extreme reluctance. It is a common proverb amongst them that *for the sake of one's belly one must play many parts.*[1]

There are other Brahmins who are derisively called meat Brahmins and fish Brahmins. For instance, there are the Konkani Brahmins, who come from Konkana, who eat fish and eggs without the slightest compunction, but will not touch meat. And there are many Brahmins from the northern provinces who make no secret of the fact that they eat meat. People tell me, though I can hardly believe it, that such conduct does not lessen the esteem in which they are held in their own country by those of their own caste who abstain from such forbidden food. Anyhow, when these degenerate Brahmins visit Southern India, and their ways become known, all the other Brahmins keep them at a distance and refuse to have any dealings with them. I wonder whether the first Hindu lawgivers forbade the eating of meat and of all other substances containing the germ of life. Do the southern Brahmins observe a rule strictly laid down, and do the northern Brahmins therefore break a law common to the whole caste? It is probable that the northern Brahmins, feeling the want of more substantial food, freed themselves from a custom which was not found irksome by their southern brethren in a hotter climate.

It is certain that from the earliest times learning was cultivated by the Hindus. The Brahmins have always been, as it were, its depositories, and have always considered it as belonging exclusively to

1. In Sanskrit: *Udara nimittan bahu krita vesham*, which literally means, 'For the belly's sake many roles are played.' —Ed

themselves. They saw well enough what a moral ascendency knowledge would give them over the other castes, and they therefore made a mystery of it by taking all possible precautions to prevent other classes from obtaining access to it.

The question arises: Have they themselves systematically cultivated learning? Have they made any appreciable progress in its pursuit? This we must answer in the negative, if at least we are to compare what has come down to us from their ancient authors with the present conditions of instruction and learning amongst them. **I do not believe that the Brahmins of modern times are, in any degree, more learned than their ancestors of the times of Lycurgus and Pythagoras.** During this long space of time many barbarous races have emerged from the darkness of ignorance have attained the summit of civilization, and have extended their intellectual researches almost to the utmost limits of human intelligence; yet all this time the Hindus have been perfectly stationary. We do not find amongst them any trace of mental or moral improvement and any sign of advance in the arts and sciences.

Every impartial observer must, indeed, admit that they are now very far behind the peoples who inscribed their names long after them on the roll of civilized nations. The learning which won for them so much respect and reverence from their fellow-countrymen, and which rendered them so famous in the eyes of foreign nations, among whom ignorance and superstition then prevailed, was connected with astronomy, astrology, and magic. Several authors have given details of their astronomical system, and it is fully explained in the *Asiatic Researches*. Moreover, Father Pons, a former Jesuit missionary in the Carnatic, had, long before this, discussed it in a highly interesting treatise published in the *Memoires de l' Academie des Sciences*, and likewise we find it discussed in the *Histoire Generale de Tous les Peuples* by the Abbe Lambert. It is from these sources that the famous astronomer Bailly derived almost all that he has written on Hindu astronomy. The accuracy of the investigations of the learned Jesuit missionary in this direction has been since confirmed; but in the same work he speaks of the schools and of what he calls the 'academies' of India.

As a matter of fact, no comparison whatever can be drawn between schools in India and those in Europe. The system pursued in the former of causing everything to be learnt by rote is, in my opinion, essentially wrong and tends to prolong indefinitely the course of study. Moreover, there is no regular plan of instruction, and there is no public institution which is, properly speaking, devoted to the diffusion of knowledge. It is true that in certain large towns, or in the precincts of some of the more important temples, Brahmins impart the knowledge which they possess—some gratuitously and others for payment; still, for all this, instruction is carried on without any definite system or any attempt at discipline.

Let a youth learn who has a mind to do so, and as long as he chooses: this seems to be their guiding principle. There is nothing in these institutions which is calculated to stimulate the teachers or to encourage the pupils. There are no public examinations to undergo, no degrees to aspire to, no prizes to be won; in fine, no special privilege or advantage of any importance is held out to students who distinguish themselves by their attainments.

The Hindu system of astronomy being, sufficiently well known, I shall refrain from repeating here what others have said on the subject. But I shall dwell at some length on the other two branches of their scientific knowledge, namely, astrology and magic.

## Astrology

Astrology, together with the notions which originate from it, has at all times exercised a great influence over the nations of the world, civilized as well as uncivilized. In Europe the appearance of a comet or a total eclipse formerly spread the greatest terror in the minds of the multitude, who looked upon these celestial phenomena as the forerunners of some public calamity; and even at the present day these chimerical fears still exercise some influence over the imagination of the ignorant and superstitious.

The influence of the stars, scrutinized with the eyes of reason, need not be looked upon altogether as an idle imagining; and there is doubtless a happy medium to be observed between the widely divergent opinions of authors concerning the action, more or less direct, more or less limited, exercised by the stars over the vegetable and animal kingdoms of this earth of ours. Be this as it may, however, **no other nation appears to have carried its astrological notions to such extremes as the Hindus.**

Each planet in turn is supposed to exercise its influence during the space of a year. The ruling planet is attended by another, which plays the part of a minister. The latter assumes in the following year the supreme functions of the former, and so on year after year.

Some of these planets are beneficent, others the reverse. The Moon, Mercury, Jupiter, and Venus are of the former order. Under their sway everything thrives: men live happily and are blessed with abundance; the fertile fields yield rich harvests, and the fruitful trees bear abundantly. The Sun, Mars, and Saturn, on the other hand, have a tendency to cause evil to animate as well as to inanimate nature. Their reign is, therefore, almost always disastrous. Men are oppressed with sickness, they attain success m nothing; they experience only troubles and disappointments; moreover, the rains hold off, the soil becomes unfruitful, famine and misery everywhere prevail. When, however, an unpropitious planet has for its attendant minister planet of an opposite character, and vice versa, the good one counteracts and counterbalances at least to a certain degree the evil influence of the other. Thus one can expect to enjoy unalloyed happiness only during those years when two benign planets hold their sway at one and the same time. Similarly, one must dread continual misfortunes when both planets have an evil inclination to harass unfortunate mankind.

There are four principal clouds which yield rain, and each in its turn discharges this duty for the space of one year. Their names are Samvarta, Avarta, Pushkala, Drona. The first and the last are favourably disposed towards mankind, and yield copious showers. Avarta and Pushkala, on the other hand, produce nothing but storms and hurricanes, and are sparing of the rain which refreshes and fertilizes the soil.

The frequency of rain depends also to a great extent on the good or bad will of seven elephants. Each of these is known by its own name, and each in turn is charged with the annual duty of carrying water to the clouds. Four of them display great activity in the discharge of their duty, and supply the clouds with an sample provision of rain. But the other three acquit themselves very carelessly of their duty during their terms of service; consequently, the ground remains parched up, and scarcity prevails.

Seven snakes, each also bearing a particular name, exercise in turn for the space of one year supreme authority over all species of snakes. The snake Ananta, the first one, is the most powerful of all, and supports the earth on its head. The year of its reign is considered unhappy, inasmuch as snakes are then extremely venomous and their bite invariably proves fatal. The reign of the snake Karkataka is equally unhappy. The remaining five are by no means equally mischievous. It is seldom that persons are bitten by snakes while these are in power; and should a person be bitten, the bite does not prove fatal. The snake Maha-Padma particularly is the friend of men; it not only prevents other snakes from harming them, but also comes to their aid by sending the physician Dhanvantari to cure such as may have been accidentally bitten.

By the combination of the twelve signs of the Zodiac with the planets and with the star which is in the ascendant on each day of the moon, Hindu astrologers believe themselves capable of telling the secrets as well as the future events of life. The Sun remains thirty days in each of the signs of the Zodiac; the Moon, two days and a quarter; Mars and Mercury, a month and a half; Jupiter, one year Venus, two years and a half; Saturn, one year and a half. Each sign of the Zodiac has, besides, two stars and a quarter, which are assigned to it from among the twenty-seven constellations or stars of the lunar month.

By comparing all these phenomena, and by joining in regular order, certain words with the different signs of the Zodiac, they are enabled to know the past, the present, and the future, and to recover things that have been lost or stolen. The coincidence of these words is, for this purpose, combined with the sign of the Zodiac, the planet, the star, and the time of the day or night at which the astrologer is consulted.

By the same means it is possible to find out, not only the place wherein a stolen article is secreted, but also the sex and the caste of the thief. They are also able to ascertain whether or not the stolen or lost article will be recovered, according as the sign, the planet, and the star which correspond to the time at which the consultation takes place are favourable or the reverse. They discover in the same way whether a person who has been long absent is dead or alive; whether he is sick or in good health; whether he is at liberty or in prison; whether he will return or not.

But one of the most important combination calculated is that relating to birth. In fact, according to the Hindus, the future lot of men is supposed to depend on the sign of the Zodiac and the star under which they are born. This is what they call *lagnam*. It is supposed that each of the twelve signs prevails over daily occurrences during a fixed interval of time. Thus, for Instance, the sign Aries (the Ram) prevails for two hours; Taurus (the Bull) for two hours and a quarter; Gemini (the Twins) for two hours and a half; and so on. Again, the sign which corresponds to the moment of birth is termed Janma-lagnam; and by combining it with the planet and the star of the day, they ascertain beyond a doubt whether the child is born to be happy or unhappy.

Of the seven days of the week, three are held to be unlucky, namely, Sunday, Tuesday, and Saturday. On these days no important business ought to be undertaken, no journey begun.

Of the twenty-seven stars of each lunar month, seven are reputed to be more or less unlucky; and everything undertaken on the days on which these appear is attended with disastrous results. The rest of the science is based on similar considerations.

## Magic

Magic, that art which gives shrewd people influence over fools, seems to have found a favourite abode in the Peninsula of India. Certainly, in this respect, India has no reason to be envious of the ancient Thessaly or of the city of Colchis famous for the enchantments of Circe and Medea. Nothing in this country happens by chance or from natural causes. Obstacles of every kind, disappointments, unlucky incidents, diseases, premature deaths, barrenness of women miscarriages, diseases among cattle; in fine, all the scourges to which human beings are exposed are attributed to the occult and diabolical machinations of some wicked enchanter hired by an enemy. Should a Hindu, at the time he is visited by any calamity happen to be at variance with anyone of his neighbours, the latter is immediately suspected and accused of having had recourse to magic to harm him. The accused of course, never puts up patiently with an imputation invidious. Anger is engendered, and the flame of discord grows hotter and hotter, until some serious consequences result from this new development.

At every step one meets with batches of these soothsayers and sorcerers distributing good luck to all comers, and for a consideration unfolding to the view of the rich and of the poor the secrets of their destinies. But these sorcerers of the lowest rank, whose whole stock-in-trade consists of a large fund of impudence, are not held in much dread. Others there are whose diabolical art knows no bounds, and who are initiated into the most profound secrets of magic. To inspire love or hatred; to introduce a devil into the body of any one, or to expel it; to cause the sudden death of an enemy, or to bring on him an incurable disease; to produce contagious diseases among cattle, or to preserve them against such contagion; to lay bare the closest secrets; to restore stolen or lost articles, etc.; all these are mere bagatelles to such men. The very sight of a person who is reputed to be gifted with such enormous power inspires terror.

These professors of magic are often consulted by persons who wish to avenge themselves on some enemy by means of witchcraft. Their help is also sought by sick folk who are persuaded that their disease has been caused by the casting of some magical spell upon them, and who wish to recover their health by throwing a counter-spell upon those who caused the disease by such means.

The Hindus have several books which treat ex professo of all these follies of the magic art. The principal and most ancient of them is the fourth Veda, called the Atharva-Veda[1]. The Brahmins would have it believed that this book has been lost; but it is known that it still exists, and that they keep it in concealment with even greater care than they do the other three. In fact, the magicians being everywhere dreaded and hated, the Brahmins have good reason to conceal everything that may lead to the suspicion of their being initiated in the secret dealings of these impostors. It

---

1. Atharva-Veda is a collection of formulae to avert the consequences of mistakes or mishaps in sacrifices. Atharva, Brahma's eldest son, identified with Angirasa, is the author of this Veda, which belongs to a later period than the other three Vedas. This Veda is a collection of original hymns mixed up with incantations. It has no direct relation to mere rituals or sacrifices. The recitation of this Veda is considered to confer longevity, or cure diseases, to obtain success in love or gaming, to effect the ruin of enemies, and to secure the reciter's own prosperity. —Ed.

is, however, certain that magic occupies one of the first places in the list of sciences of which these great men profess to be the sole inheritors.

It should be remarked that if the Hebrews and the various other peoples, whom Holy Writ represents as being addicted to these superstitions did not actually borrow them from the Hindus, they must both at least have copied the system from the same sources. We are aware of the extensive reputation enjoyed by magicians and soothsayers among the children of Israel, who were strictly warned by God, through Moses, against consulting such men. Saul, who had vainly tried to exterminate or expel them, was weak enough to have recourse to the enchantments of the witch of Endor.

There can be no doubt that their ancestors cultivated the art from timc immemorial; and it is not likely that the successors would have neglected so good an example, and allowed the practice to fall into disuse. Many Brahmins moreover, in spite of the restrictions imposed upon them, are known to have made a special study of this mysterious book. Besides, do not their religions of sacrifices and their mantrams bear a great resemblance to magical formulae and conjurings?

I happen to have come across a Hindu book treating of the subject in hand, which perhaps few Europeans have yet heard of. It is called the *Agrushada Parikshai*. The passages which I will here extract from it will never make anybody a sorcerer, but it strikes me that they may not be wholly uninteresting to those who like to meditate on the aberrations of the human mind.

The author begins by investigating the extent of a magician's power. Such power is enormous. A magician is the dispenser of both good and evil; but is more frequently inclined by natural malevolence to do evil rather than good. Nothing is easier for him than to afflict anybody with sicknesses, such as fever, dropsy, epilepsy, palsy, madness, and, in fine, diseases of all species. But all this is a mere trifle compared with what his art can otherwise do! It is capable of completely destroying an army beseiging a city, and also of causing the sudden death of the commander of a beseiged fortress and of all its inhabitants, and so forth.

The Mahomedans in India, being quite as superstitious as the natives of the country, are no less infatuated with the power of magic, It is a well-known fact that the last Mussalman prince who reigned in Mysore, the fanatical and superstitious Tippu Sultan, during has last war, in which he lost his kingdom and his life, engaged the service of the most celebrated magicians of his own country and of neighbouring provinces, in order that they might employ all the resources of their art in destroying by some efficacious operation the English army which was then advancing to beseige his capital, and which he found himself utterly incapable of repelling by force of arms. In this they acknowledged their powerlessness; and to save the reputation of their craft they were obliged to maintain that their magical operations, so potent when directed against every other enemy, were utterly ineffectual against Europeans[1].

But if magic teaches the means of doing evil, it also affords the means of counteracting its pernicious effects. There is no magician so skilful but that others can be found more skilful than he, to destroy the evil effects of his enchantments, and cause them to recoil with all their force upon himself or upon his clients. Apart from the direct influence exercised by

---

1. It is generally believed by the Hindus that such sorcerers and magicians are powerless against Governments—an ingeneous admission of force majeure! —Ed.

themselves, the magicians also possess an ample collection of amulets and talismans, which are looked upon as efficacious against all sorcery and spells, and which are largely distributed, not without payment of course amongst those who consult them. For instance, there are certain glass beads made magical by *mantrams*, different kinds of roots, and thin plates of copper engraved with unknown characters, strange words and uncouth figures. These amulets are always worn by Hindus who, when protected by such talismans, believe themselves quite safe from all kinds of evil.

Secret remedies for inspiring illicit passion, for rekindling the flame of extinct love, and for reviving impaired virility, also fall within the province of these professors of magic, and form by no means the least lucrative part of their trade. It is to such men, that a wifc always applies when she wishes to reclaim her faithless husband or to prevent him from becoming so. Debauched gallants and lewd women also seek the help of love potion to seduce or captivate the object of their passion.

I was not a little surprised to find in the book which I am now describing mention made of *incubi*. But these demons of India are much more mischievous than those of whom the Jesuit Delrio speaks in his *Disquisitiones Magicae*. By the violence and persistence of their embraces they so tire out the women whom they visit at night under the form of a dog, a tiger, or some other animal, that the unfortunate creatures die of sheer lassitude and exhaustion.

But another speaks at great length of the means best suited to enchant weapons. The effects which weapons so treated have the virtue of producing are in no way inferior to those caused by the famous Durandal (Orlando's enchanted sword) and by the spear of Argail, which in ancient times routed so many miscreants. The Hindu gods and giants in their wars against each other used no other weapons but these. Is there anything, for instance, that can be compared with the Arrow of Brahma or the Arrow of the Serpent Capella? The former is never shot without causing the destruction of a whole army; and the latter, launched in the midst of enemies, has the effect of causing them to drop down in a state of lethargy—an effect which, as one may well suppose, made singularly short work of those who were subjected to it.

There is not a secret of magic which this book does not teach us. It puts us in possession of the means of acquiring wealth and honour; of rendering barren women fruitful; of discovering, by merely rubbing the hands and eyes with some enchanted mixtures, treasures buried in the ground or hidden elsewhere; of acquiring invulnerability and the most formidable powers in war by means of bones carried on the person. Strange to say, the only thing which it does not reveal is the means of rendering oneself immortal.

It is not by entering into compact with the devil, as our magicians were erstwhile supposed to have done, that the magicians of India obtained the power of performing so many prodigies. These latter, indeed, are not the kind of people to run the risk of having their necks twisted in evil company of this sort. It is quite sufficient for a Hindu to become an expert in the black art if he receives a few private lessons from the *guru*, or master, of the adepts. It is this guru who guides him in the right way, who confers his powers upon him, and to whom he owes obedience. Should a god, a demon, or a spirit be so stubborn as to disregard the orders of the newly initiated disciple, the latter has simply to repeat his injunction in the name and from the feet of his guru.

Brahma, Vishnu, and Siva themselves are subject to the commands of the magicians. There are, however, certain divinities who are invoked by preference. Among these the planets occupy the first place. The term *graha*, by which they are designated signifies the act of seizing, that is, of laying hold of those whom they are enjoined by magical enchantments to torment. The next in order are the *bhoothams*, or the element, each of which contains a destructive principle. Then come the *pretas* or spirits of dead bodies, the Pisachas a term by which the Native Christians designate the devil; the female deities called Sakti; Kali, the goddess of destruction; and Marana Devi, the goddess of death.

In order to call all these spirits into action, the magician has recourse to various mysterious ceremonies, mantrams and sacrifices.The magician must be stark naked while he offers up the sacrifices to Lakshmi, the wife of Vishnu; while, on the other hand, he must be decorously clad 'when such sacrifices are offered to Rama. The flowers offered to the god invoked must be red; and, when the object is to produce the death of any person, the boiled rice offered up must be stained with blood, for which purpose a human victim, a young girl for choice, is sometimes slain.

We know the. virtue of mantrams, but it is especially in connexion with magic that they are most effective. Mantrams have such an influence over the gods, even of the very first rank, that they are quite unable to resist doing, that the heavens, or in the air, or on earth, all that the magician requires of them. Among the mantrams there are some, called the fundamentals, whose effects are decisive and irresistible. They are composed of various strange monosyllables, harsh of sound and difficult to pronounce; such as *h'hom, h'rhum, sh'hrum, sho'hrum, ramaya, namaha*. This last word signifies 'respectful greeting'.

The magician sometimes repeats these mantrams in a humble and supplicatory manner, loading with praises the god whom he invokes; but he quickly resumes his imperious tone, and exclaims as though in a vehement rage, 'Grasp it! Grasp it!' or 'Begone!

Begone! If thou art willing to do what I ask of thee, well and good; if not, I command thee to do it in the name of such and such a god, in the name of the feet of my guru!' Whereupon the god cannot do otherwise than comply with the magician's demands without a murmur!

From the haughty and indecorous manner in which the Hindu magicians treat their good-natured deities, as it may be judged that they are not the men to allow themselves to be frightened as easily as were the poor witches of Horace, Canidia and Sagana, who, it will be remembered, were put, to terrified flight by a commonplace sound, resembling the bursting of an inflated bladder, made by the God of the Gardens, who had been troubled by the enchantments which they came to perform every night in the place entrusted to his keeping.

It is impossible to enumerate the various drugs, ingredients, and utensils that go to make up the stock-in-trade of an Indian magician. There are certain incantations, in the performance of which it is necessary to use the bones of sixty-four different animals—neither more nor less—and amongst them may be mentioned those of a man born on a Sunday which happens to be new-moon day, of a woman born on a Friday, the feet-bones of a Pariah, of a cobbler, of a Mahomedan, and of a European. If all these bones are mixed together, enchanted by mantrams, consecrated by sacrifices, and then buried in the house, or at the threshold of an enemy on a night that the stars show to be propitious, they will infallibly cause the enemy's death.

In the same way, should the magician, in the silence of the night, bury these bones at the four cardinal points of a hostile camp, and then, retiring cardinal to some distance, repeat seven times the mantram of defeat, the result will be that within seven days the whole encamped army will either disperse of itself or perish to the last man. Thirty-two weapons, consecrated by the sacrifice of a human victim, will spread such dismay among a beseiging army that a hundred of their opponents will appear to it as a thousand.

Sometimes a quantity of mud collected from sixty-four filthy places is kneaded together with hair, parings of nails, bits of leather, etc., and is then moulded into small figures, on the breasts of which the name of one's enemy is written. Certain words and mantrams are then repeated over these figures, which are also consecrated by sacrifices. No sooner is this done than the grahas or planets take possession of the person against whom such incantations are directed, and afflict him with a thousand ills.

These figures are sometimes pierced through and through with an awl, or are mutilated in various ways with the intention of killing or mutilating in the same manner the person who is the object of vengeance. At all times and in all places the same barbarous means have sufficed to excite the imagination of the vulgar, the ignorant, and the superstitious. They were, are, and will be the same throughout the world.

*Devovet absentes, simulacraque cerea fingit, Et miserum tenues in iecur urget acus.*

The two witches of Horace, who have just been mentioned, also had, among their other magical apparatus, two figures, one of wool and the other of wax. Sixty-four roots of different kinds of noxious plants are known among the magicians, and, when duly prepared with mantrams and sacrifices, become powerful weapons for covertly dealing fatal blows to obnoxious persons.

It must here be remarked that the profession of a magician is not altogether free from danger. If the Hindus themselves are revengeful, their gods are also passably so. Again, the gods do not obey without some feeling of anger the orders given to them by a miserable mortal, and they sometimes punish in a very cruel and brutal manner the person who ventures to command them. Woe to him who commits the smallest error, or makes the slightest omission in the innumerable ceremonies that are obligatory under such circumstances! He is immediately crushed with the full weight of the mischief which he was preparing for others.

The fanatical Leaguers of France in the sixteenth century carried their superstitious practices to such extremes that they caused wax figures to be made representing Henry III and the King of Navarre. They pierced the different parts of these figures with thorns in the space of forty days, and on the fortieth day they struck them about the region of the heart, believing that they would thereby cause the death of the princes whom the images represented. In the year 1751 a pretended sorcerer named Trois-echelles, who was executed on the Place de Greve, declared during his examination that there existed in France three hundred thousand persons practising the same profession as himself. Possibly he exaggerated, but at all events, if historians eliminated from their records all the follies of men, they would certainly not have much left to relate.

Then again, a magician is in constant danger from rivals who exercise the same trade, especially when his rivals are as skilful as himself, or maybe more so. For these may succeed in counteracting his charms, and in bringing upon his own head, or upon the heads of his clients, the whole weight of his evil machinations. Accordingly there exists, in appearance or in reality, an inveterate mutual hatred amongst this crowd of men who pretend to be the interpreters of destiny. Occasionally they are seen to bid defiance to each other, and to enter the lists in the presence of witnesses and arbitratars, whom they call upon to decide which of the two is the more skilful in his art.

The test consists, for example, in having to lift from the ground a spell-bound object, such as a piece of straw, a wand or a piece of money. The two antagonists, placing themselves at either side of and at an equal distance from the aforesaid object, pretend to approach it; but the mantrams which they utter, at the enchanted ashes which they sprinkle upon each other, have the effect of arresting their course. An invisible and irresistible force seems to drive them back; they try again and again to advance towards the object, but often have to draw back. They redouble their efforts; convulsive movements agitate them; the sweat pours from them; they spit blood. At last one of them succeeds in getting hold of the spell-bound object, and he is proclaimed the victor.

Sometimes, again, one of the combatants is thrown violently upon the ground by the force of the mantrams of his antagonist. He then rails about like one possessed, and finally remains for some time motionless, feigning unconsciousness. At last, however, he recovers the use of his senses, gets up apparently much fatigued and exhausted, and retires covered with shame and confusion. A sickness of several days is supposed to be the immediate result of his strenuous yet futile efforts.

It will, doubtless, be easily guessed that these fooleries are the outcome of a premeditated understanding between the charlatans who practise them. But the multitude who pay for being treated to a spectacle of this kind, and who look upon the actors with fear and admiration, are fully persuaded that all their contortions are due to supernatural causes. It must, however be admitted that these men go through their parts with really admirable skill and precision. On many an occasion they have been seen to perform sleight-of-hand tricks with such rare skill as to astonish persons of a much less credulous turn of mind than the Hindus.

# 4

# The Sudras and Tribes at the Bottom

Amongst the immense number of classes of which the Sudra caste is composed, it is impossible to give precedence to any one class in particular; the natives themselves not being agreed on that point, and the social scale varying in different parts of the country. There are certain classes, however, who, owing to the depth of degradation into which they have fallen, are looked upon as almost another race of beings, altogether outside the pale of society; and they are perfectly ready to acknowledge their own comparative inferiority. The best known and most numerous of these castes is the Parayer (one that beats the drum) as it is called in Tamil, the word from which the European name Pariah is derived. The particulars which I am about to give of this class will form striking contrasts with those I have related about the Brahmins, and will serve to demonstrate how incapable the Hindus are of showing any moderation in their caste customs and observances.

## The Pariahs

Their contempt and aversion for these social outcastes are as extreme, on the one hand, as are the respect and veneration which they pay, on the other, to those whom their superstitions have invested with god-like attributes. Throughout the whole of India the

Pariah are looked upon as slaves by other castes, and are treated, with great harshness. Hardly anywhere are they allowed to cultivate the soil for their own benefit, but are obliged to hire themselves out to the other castes, who in return for a minimum wage exact the hardest tasks from them.

Furthermore, their masters may beat them at pleasure; the poor wretches having no right either to complain or to obtain redress for that or any other ill treatment their masters may impose on them. In fact, these Pariahs are the born slaves of India.

This class is the most numerous of all, and in conjunction with that of the Chuklers, or cobblers, represents at least a quarter of the population. It is painful to think that its members, though so degraded, are yet the most useful of all. On the whole agricultural work is totally done by them[1] and they have also other tasks to perform which are still harder and more indispensable.

However, notwithstanding the miserable condition of these wretched Pariahs, they are never heard to murmur, or to complain of their low state. The idca that he was born to be in subjection to the other castes is so ingrained in his mind that it never occurs to the Pariah to think that his fate is anything but irrevocable. Nothing will ever persuade him that men are all made of the same clay, or that he has the right to insist on better treatment than that which is meted out to him.[2]

---

1. An appreciable percentage of the Pariahs has now migrated to the towns, where they serve as domestic servants in European and Eurasian households. —Ed.

2. The Christian missionaries in India have done and are doing much to elevate the condition and character of this class. In Madras city there are now Pariah associations and also a journal specially representing Pariah interests. —Ed.

They live in hopeless poverty, and the greater number lack sufficient means to procure even the coarsest clothing. They go about almost naked, or at best clothed in the most hideous rags. They live from hand to mouth the whole year round, and rarely know one day how they will procure food for the next. When they happen to have any money, they invariably spend it at once, and make a point of doing no work as long as they have anything left to live on.

In a few districts they are allowed to cultivate the soil on their own account, but in such cases they are almost always the poorest of their class. Pariahs who hire themselves out as labourers earn, at any rate, enough to live on; and their food, though often of the coarsest description, is sufficient to satisfy the cravings of hunger. But those who are their own masters, and cultivate land for themselves, are so indolent and careless that their harvests, even in the most favourable seasons, are only sufficient to feed them for half the year.

The contempt and aversion with which the other castes and particularly the Brahmins regard these unfortunate people **are carried to such an excess that in many places their presence, or even their footprints, are considered sufficient to defile the whole neighbourhood.** They are forbidden to cross a street in which Brahmins are living Should they be so ill-advised as to do so, the latter, would have the right, not to strike them themselves, because they could not do so without defilement, or even touch them with the end of a long stick, but to order them to be severely beaten by other people. **A Pariah who had the audacity to enter a Brahmin's house might possibly be murdered on the spot.** A revolting crime of this sort has been actually perpetrated in States under the rule of native princes without a voice being raised in expostulation.

Anyone who has been touched, whether inadvertently or purposely by a Pariah is defiled by that single act, and may hold no communication with any person whatsoever until he has been purified by bathing, or by other ceremonies more or less important according to the status and customs of his caste. It would be contamination to eat with any members of this class; to touch food prepared by them, or even to drink water which they have drawn; to use an earthen vessel which they have held in their hands; to set foot inside one of their houses, or to allow them to outer houses other than their own. Each of these acts would contaminate the person affected by it, and before being readmitted to his own caste such a person would have to go through many exacting and expensive formalities. Should it be proved that anyone had any connection with a Pariah woman he would be treated with even greater serverity.[1]

Nevertheless, the disgust which these Pariahs inspire is not so intense in some parts of the country as in others. The feeling is most strongly developed in the southern and western districts of the Peninsula; in the north it is less apparent. In the northern part of Mysore the other classes of Sudras allow Pariahs to approach them, and even permit them to enter that part of the house which is used for cattle. Indeed, in some places custom is so far relaxed that a Pariah may venture to put his head and one foot, but one foot

1. Even to this day a Pariah is not allowed to pass a Brahmin street in a village, though nobody can prevent, or prevents, his approaching or passing by a Brahmin's house in towns. The Pariahs, on their part, will under no circumstances allow a Brahmin to pass through their *parcherries* (collections of Pariah huts), as they firmly believe that it will lead to their ruin. —Ed.

only, inside the room occupied by the master of the house; it is said that still further north the difference between this and other Sudra castes gradually diminishes, until at last it disappears altogether.

The origin of this degraded class can be traced to a very early period, as it is mentioned in the Puranas. The Pariahs were most probably composed, in the first instance, of all the disreputable individuals of different classes of society, who, on account of various offences, had forfeited their right to associate with respectable men. They formed a class apart, and having nothing to fear and less to lose, they gave themselves up, without restraint, to their natural tendencies towards vice and excess, in which they continue to live at the present day.

In very early days, however, the separation between Pariahs and the other castes does not appear to have been so marked as at present. Though relegated to the lowest grade In the social scale, they were not then placed absolutely outside and beyond it, the line of demarcation between them and the Sudras being almost imperceptible. Indeed, they are even to this day considered to be the direct descendants of the better class of agricultural labourers. The Tamil Vellalers and the Okkala-makkalu-kanarey do not disdain to call them their children. But one thing is quite certain, that if these classes share a common origin with the Pariahs and acknowledge the same, their actions by no means corroborate their words, and their treatment of the Pariahs leaves much to be desired.

Europeans are obliged to have Pariahs for their servants, because no native of any other caste would condescend to do such menial work as is exacted by their masters. For instance, it would be very difficult to find amongst the Sudras anyone who would demean himself by blacking or greasing boots and shoes, emptying and cleansing chamber utensils, brushing and arranging hair, etc; and certainly no one could be found who for any consideration whatever would consent to cook food for them, as this would necessitate touching beef, which is constantly to be seen on the tables of Europeans, who thereby show an open disregard of the feelings and prejudices of the people amongst whom they live. Foreigners are therefore obliged to have recourse to Pariahs to perform this important domestic service. If the kind of food which they do not scruple to eat lowers Europeans in the eyes of the superstitious native, much more are they lowered by the social status of the people by whom they are served, for it is a fact recognized by all Hindus that none but a Pariah would dare to eat food prepared by Pariahs.

One is bound to confess that the evil reputation which is borne by this class is in many respects well deserved, by reason of the low conduct and habits of its members. A great many of these unfortunate people bind themselves for life, with their wives and children, to the ryots, or agricultural classes, who set them to the hardest labour and treat them with the greatest harshness. The village scavengers, who are obliged to clean out the public latrines, to sweep the streets, and to remove all rubbish, invariably belong to this class. These men, known in the south by the name of *totis*, are, however, generally somewhat more humanely treated than the other Pariahs, because, in addition to the dirty work above mentioned, they are employed in letting the water into the tanks and channels for irrigating the rice fields; and on this account they are treated with some consideration by the rest of the villagers.

Amongst the Pariahs who are not agricultural slaves there are some who groom and feed the horses of private individuals, or those used in the army; some are in charge of elephants; others tend cattle; others are messengers and carriers; while others, again, do ordinary manual work. Within recent times Pariahs have been allowed to enlist in the European and Native armies, and some of them have risen to high rank, for in point of courage and bravery they are in no way inferior to any other caste.

Pariahs, being thus convinced that they have nothing to lose or gain in public estimation, abandon themselves without shame or restraint to vice of all kinds, and the greatest lawlessness prevails amongst them, for which they do not feel the least shame. **One might almost say that, in the matter of vice, they outstrip all others in brutality,** as the Brahmins do in malice. Their habits of uncleanliness are disgusting. Their huts, a mass of filth and alive with insects and vermin, are, if possible, even more loathsome than their persons. Their harsh and forbidding features clearly reveal their character, but even these are an insufficient indication of the coarseness of their minds and manners.

They are much addicted to drunkenness, a vice peculiarly abhorrent to other Hindus. They intoxicate themselves usually with the juice of the palm-tree, called toddy, which they drink after it has fermented, and it is then more spirituous, In spite of its horrible stench they imbibe it as if the nauseous liquid were nectar. Drunken quarrels are of frequent occurrence amongst them, and their wives are often sufferes, the unhappy creatures being nearly beaten to death, even when in a state of pregnancy. It is to this brutality and violence of their husbands that I attribute the frequent miscarriages to which Pariah wives are subject, and which are much more common amongst them than amongst women of any other caste.

What chiefly disgusts other natives is the revolting nature of the food which the Pariahs eat. Attracted by the smell, they will collect in crowds round any carrion, and contend for the spoil with dogs, jackals, crows, and other carnivorous animals. They then divide the semi-putrid flesh, and carry it away to their huts where they devour it, often without rice or anything else to disguise the flavour. That the animal should have died of disease is of no consequence to them, and **they sometimes secretly poison cows or buffaloes that they may subsequently feast on the foul, putrefying remains.** The carcasses of animals that die in a village belong by right to the *toti* or scavenger, who sells the flesh at a very low price to thc other Pariahs in the neighbourhood. When it is impossible to consume in one day the stock of meat thus obtained, they dry the remainder in the sun, and keep it in their huts until they run short of other food. There are few Pariah houses where one does not see festoons of these horrible fragment hanging up; and though the Pariahs themselves do not seem to be affected by the smell, travellers passing near their villages quickly perceive it and can tell at once the caste of the people living there. This horrible food is, no doubt, the cause of the greater part of the contageous diseases which decimate them, and from which their neighbours are free.

The condition of the Pariahs, which is not really slavery as it is known amongst us, resembles to a certain extent that of the serfs of France and other countries of Northern Europe in olden times. This state of bondage is at its worst along the coast of Malabar, as are several other customs peculiar to the country. The reason is that Malabar, owing to its position, has generally escaped the invasions and revolutions which have so often devastated the rest of India, and has thus managed to preserve unaltered many ancient institutions, which in other parts have fallen into disuse.[1]

Of these the two most remarkable are proprietary rights and slavery. These two systems are apparently inseparable one from the other; and indeed, one may well say, *no land without lord.* All the Pariahs born in the country are serfs for life, from father to son, and are part and parcel of the land on which they are born. The landowner can sell them along with the soil, and can dispose of them when and how he pleases.

## Malabar Coast Tribes

This proprietary right and this system of serfdom have existed from the remotest times, and exist still amongst the Nairs, the Coorgs, and the Tulus, the three aboriginal tribes of the Malabar coast. This is, I believe, the only province in India where proprietary right has been preserved intact until the present day. Everywhere else the soil belongs to the ruler and the cultivator is to him or taken away from him according to the will of the government for the time being.

On the Malabar coast, however, the lands belong to those who cultivated it and who posses the right of handing them down to their descendants. Here the lands may be alienated, sold, given away, or disposed of according to the will of the owners. In a word, the *jus utendi et abutendi*, which is the basis of proprietary right, belongs entirely to them. Every landed proprietor in that country possesses a community of Pariahs to cultivate his fields, who are actually his slaves and

1. Things in this respect have, of course, changed a great deal for the better since the Abbe wrote. —Ed.

form an integral part of his property. All children born of these Pariahs are serfs by birth, just as their parents were; and their master has the right, if he chooses, to sell or dispose of parents and children in any way that he pleases.

If one of these Pariahs escapes and takes service under another master, his real master can recover him anywhere as his own property. If a proprietor happens to possess more slaves than he requires for cultivating his land, he sells some to other landlords who are less fortunate than himself. It is by no means uncommon to see a debtor, who is unable to pay his debts in hard cash, satisfy his creditors by handing over to them a number of his Pariah slaves. The price of these is not exorbitant. A male still young enough to work will fetch three rupees and a hundred *seers* of rice, which is about the value of a bullock. But the landed proprietors do not usually sell their slaves except in cases of great emergency; and even then they can only sell them within the borders of their own country. In no case have they the right to export them for sale to foreigners.

Each landowner in the province of Malabar lives in a house that is isolated in the middle of his estate. Here he dwells, surrounded by his community of Pariah serfs, who are always remarkably submissive to him. Some landowners possess over a hundred of them. **They treat them usually in a humane manner. They give them only such work as their age or strength permits; feed them on the same level that they themselves eat;** give them in marriage when they come of age; and every year provide them with cloth in four or five yards of cloth for the women and a coarse woolen blanket for the men.

In Malabar it is the Cherumars who are condemned to perpetual slavery; but then there are no free men among them. All are born slaves from generation to generation. They have not even the right to buy their own freedom; and if: they wish to secure their independence they can only do so by escaping secretly from the country. All the same, I have not heard that they often resort to this extremity. They are accustomed from father to son to this state of servitude; they are kindly treated by their masters; and they have no notion of what freedom or independence means, and are happily resigned to their lot. They look upon their master as their father, and consider themselves to belong to his family. As a matter of fact, their physical condition, which is the only thing that appeals to their senses, is much better than that of their brethren who are free. The slaves of Malabar are certain of a living, the supreme requirement of nature, whereas the free Pariahs of other provinces live for half his time in actual want of the meanest subsistence, and is often exposed to death from starvation.

About half of my various congregations consisted of Pariah Christians. On reaching the hut to which my duty led me, I was often obliged to creep in on my hands and knees, so low was the entrance door to the wretched hovel. When once inside, I could only partially avoid the sickening smell by holding to my nose a handkerchief soaked in the strongest vinegar. I would find there a mere skeleton, perhaps lying on the bare ground, though more often crouching on a rotten piece of matting, with a stone or a block of wood as a pillow. The miserable creature would have for clothing a rag tied round the loins, and for covering a coarse and tattered blanket that left half the body naked. I would seat myself on the ground by his side, and the first words heard would be: 'Father, I am dying of cold and hunger.' I would spend a quarter of an hour or so by him and at last leave this sad spectacle with my heart torn asunder by the sadness and hopelessness of it all, and my body covered in every part with insects and vermin. Yet, after all, this was the least inconvenience that I suffered, for I could rid myself of them by changing my clothes and taking a hot bath. The only thing that really afflicted me was having to stand face to face with such a spectacle of utter misery of affording any save the most inadequate remedies.

**As for myself, for the first ten or twelve years that I was in India, I lived in such abject poverty that I had hardly sufficient means to procure the bare necessaries of life;** but even then I was as happy and contented as I will now that I am better off. Besides the consolations which my religion gave me under these trying circumstances, my reason found me others in the reflection that nineteen-twentieths of the people among whom I was living were bearing far greater trials of all kinds than any that I was called on to endure.

## Othe Classes

Bcsides the Pariahs, who are to be found all over the Peninsula, there are in certain provinces other classes composed of individuals who equal and even surpass them in depravity of mind and customs, and in the contempt in which they are held. Such, for instance, is the caste of Pallers, who are only found in Madura and in the neighbourhood of Cape Comorin. The Pallers consider themselves superior to the Pariahs, in as much they do not eat the flesh of the cow; but the Parihas look on them as altogether their inferiors, because they are the scum of the Left-hand faction, whilst they themselves are the mainstay of the Right-hand.

These two classes will never agree, and wherever they are found in fairly equal numbers, the disputes and quarrels amongst them are interminable. They lead the same sort of life, enjoy an equal share of public opprorium, and both are obliged to live far apart from all other classes of the inhabitants.

Amongst the forests on the Malabar coast there lives a tribe which, incredible as it may seem, surpasses the two of which I have just spoken in degradation and squalid misery. They are called Puliahs, and are looked upon as below the level of the beasts which share this wild country with them. They are not even allowed to build themselves huts to protect themselves from the inclemencies of the weather. A sort of lean-to, supported by four bamboo poles and open at the sides, serves as a shelter for some of them, and keeps off the rain, though it does not screen them from the wind. Most of them, however, make for themselves what may be called nests in the branches of the thickestfoliaged trees, where they perch like birds of prey for the greater part of the twenty-four hours. They are not even allowed to walk peaceably along the high roads. If they see anyone coming towards along they are bound to utter a certain cry and to go a long way round to avoid passing him. A hundred paces is the very nearest they may approach anyone of a different caste. If a Nair who always carries arms, meets one of these unhappy people on the road, he in entitled to stab him on the spot. The Puliahs live so absolutely savage life, and have no communication whatever with the rest of the world.

The Chucklers, or cobblers, are also considered inferior to the Pariahs all over the Peninsula, and, as a matter of fact, they show that they are of a lower grade by their more debased ideas, their greater ignorance and brutality. They are also much more addicted to drunkenness and debauchery. Their orgies take place principally in the evening, and their villages resound, far into the night, with the yells and quarrels which result from their intoxication. Nothing will persuade them to work as long as they have anything to drink; they only return to their labour when they have absolutely no further means of satisfying their ruling passion. Thus they spend their time in alternate bouts of work and drunkenness. The women of this wretched class do not allow their husbands to outshine them in any vice, and are quite as much addicted to drunkenness as the men. Their modesty and general behaviour may therefore be easily imagined. The Pariahs refuse to have anything to do with the Chucklers, and do not admit them to any of their feasts.

There is one class amongst the Pariahs which rules all the rest of the caste. These are the Valluvas these are sometimes physicians and astrologers. They are called the *Brahmins of the Pariahs* in mockery. They keep themselves quite distinct from the others, and only intermarry in their own class. They consider themselves as the gurus, or spiritual advisers, of the rest. It is they who preside at all the marriages and other religious ceremonies of the Pariahs: they predict all the mentioned events in the Hindu almanac, such as lucky and unlucky days, favourable or unfavourable moments for beginning a fresh undertaking, and other prophecies of a like nature. But they are forbidden to meddle with anything pertaining to astronomy, such as the foretelling of eclipses, changes of the moon, etc.; this prerogative belonging exclusively to the Brahmms.

There are other classes, too, which, though a trifle higher in the Hindu social scale, are for all that not treated with much more respect. Firstly, amongst the Sudras there are those who follow servile occupations, or at least occupations dependent on the public; secondly, those who perform low and disgusting offices, which expose them to frequent defilements; and, thirdly, there are the nomadic tribes, who are always wandering about the country, having no fixed abode.

Amongst the first I place the barbers and the washermen. There are men belonging to these two employments in every village, and no one exercising the same profession can come from another village to work in theirs without their express permission. Their employments are transmitted from father to son, and those who pursue them form two distinct castes.

The barber's business is to trim the beard, serve the head, pare the nails on hands and feet, and clean the ears of all the inhabitants of his village. In several of the southern provinces the inhabitants have all the hair on different parts of their bodies shaved off, with the exception of the eye-brows; and this custom is always observed by Brahmins on marriage days and other solemn occasions.[1] The barbers are also the surgeons of the country. Whatever be the nature of the operation that they are called on to perform, their razor is their only instrument, if it is a question of amputation; or a sort of stiletto, which they use for paring nails, if they have to open an abscess, or the like. They are also the only accredited fiddlers, and they share with the Pariahs the exclusive right of playing wind instruments.

As to the washermen, their business is much the same here as everywhere else, except for the extreme filthiness of the rags that are entrusted to be

1. This custom of shaving the hair from all parts of the body, for ceremonies where absolute purity is required, is not peculiar to the Brahmins; it was also common amongst the Jews, for the same reason, and was part of their ceremonial law (Numbers viii. 6, 7).

cleaned. Those engaged in these two occupations are in dependent position that they dare not refuse to work for anyone who chooses to employ them. They are paid in kind at harvest time by each inhabitant of their village. No doubt the contempt in which they are held by men of other castes, who look upon them as materials, is due partly to this state of subjection, and also to the uncleanness of the things which they are compelled to handle.

The potters also are a very low class, being absolutely uneducated. The five castes of artisans, and also, as a rule, all those employed in mechanical or ornamental arts, are very much looked down upon and despised.

The Mochis, or tanners, though better educated and more refined than any of the preceding classes, are not much higher in the social scale. The other Sudras never allow them to join in their feasts; indeed, they would hardly condescend to give them a drop of water to drink. This feeling of repulsion is caused by the defilement which ensues from their constantly handling the skins of dead animals.

## The Arts

As a rule, the mechanical and the liberal arts, such as music, painting, and sculpture, are placed on very much the same level, and those who follow these professions, which are left entirely to the lower castes of the Sudras, are looked upon with equal disfavour.[1]

As far as I know, only the *Mochis* take up painting as a profession. Instrumental music, and particularly

1. Those who follow these liberal arts are treated with more respect in these days. At all events, they are not looked upon with disfavour. There are, now many Brahmins in Southern. India who are professional musicians, though they play on certain instruments only. —Ed.

that of wind instruments, is left exclusively, as I have already mentioned, to the barbers and Pariahs. The little progress that is made in these arts is no doubt due to the small amount of encouragement which they receive. As for painting, one never sees anything but daubs. The Hindus are quite satisfied if their artists can draw designs of stinky figures painted to the most vivid colours. Our best engravings, if they are uncoloured or our finest miniatures or landscapes, are quite valueless in their eyes.

Though the Hindus much enjoy listening to music, and introduce it freely into all their public and private ceremonies, both religious and social, yet It must be admitted that this charming art is here still in its infancy. I should say Hindus are no further advanced in it now than they were two or three thousand years ago. They do not expect their musicians to produce harmonious tunes when they play at their feasts and ceremonies, for their dull ears would certainly not appreciate them. What they like is plenty of noise and plenty of shrill piercing sounds.

Why is it, it may well be asked, that it should be considered shameful to play on wind instruments in India? I suppose it is on account of the defilement which the players contract by putting such instruments to their mouths after they have once been touched by saliva, which, is the one excretion from the human body for which Hindus display invincible horror. There is by no mean the same feeling with regard to stringed instruments. In fact, you may often hear Brahmins singing. In accompanying themselves on a sort of lute which is known by the name of *vina*. This instrument has a rather agreeable tone, and would be still more pleasing if the sounds extracted from it were more varied. It has always been a favourite amongst the better classes.

## Nomads

I will now turn to the nomadic castes, which swell the number of wretched and degraded beings among the nation I am describing. Without any fixed abode, wandering about from one country to another, the individuals of which these vagabond tribes are composed pay little or no attention to the various customs which are obligatory on every respectable Hindu; and this is why they are so cordially detested.

One of the largest of these casts is that which is known in the south by the name of Kuravers or Kurumarus. This is subdivided into two branches, one of which carries on trade in grains. Gangs of men bring this article from the coast and distribute it in the interior of the country, using asses, of which they posses considerable numbers as their means of commodity, they reload the asses with different kinds of grain, for which there is a ready sale on the coast, and start off again at once. Thus their whole lives are spent in hurrying from one country to another without settling down in any place.

The occupation of the second branch of these Kuravers is to make baskets and mats of grasses and bamboo, and other similar utensils which are used in Hindu households. They are obliged to be perpetually moving from one place to another to find work, and are without any fixed abode.

The Kuravers are also the fortune-tellers of the country. They speak a language peculiar to themselves, which is unintelligible to any other Hindu. Their manners and customs have much in common with those of the wandering tribes that are known in England as Gypsies, and in France as Egyptians, or Bohemians. Their women tell the fortunes of those who consult them and are willing to pay them. The person who wishes to learn his fate seats himself in front of the soothsayer and holds out his hand, while she beats a little drum, invokes all her gods or evil spirits, and gabbles aloud a succession of fantastic words. These preliminaries over, she studies with the most scrupulous attention the ones on the hand of the simple-minded person who is consulting her, and finally predicts the good or evil fortune that is in store for him.

The Kuraver women also tattoo the designs of flowers and animals which decorate the arms of most young Hindu women. The tattooing is done by first delicately tracing the desired objects on the skin, then pricking the outline gently with a needle, and immediately after rubbing in the juice of certain plants, whereby the design becomes indelible.

The Kurumarus are much addicted to stealing, and from this tribe come the professional thieves and pickpockets known by the name of Kallabantrus. These people make a study of the art of stealing, and all the dodges of their infamous profession are instilled into them from their youth. To this end their parents teach them to lie obstinately, and train them to suffer tortures rather than divulge what it is in their interest to hide. Far from being ashamed of their profession, the Kallabantrus glory in it, and when they have nothing to fear they take the greatest pleasure in boasting of the clever thefts they have committed in various places. Those who, caught in the act, have been badly hurt, or who have been deprived by the magistrates of noose, ears, or right hand, show their scars and mutilations with pride, as proofs of their courage and intrepidity; and these men are usually the chosen heads of their caste.

They always commit their depredations at night. Noiselessly entering a village, they place sentients along the different roads, while they select the houses that can be entered with the least risk. These they creep into, and in a few minutes strip them of all the metal vessels and other valuables they can find, including gold and silver ornaments which the sleeping women and children wear round their necks. They do not break open the doors of the houses, for that would make to much noise and so lead to their detection. Their plan is too pierce the mud wall of the house with a sharp iron instrument specially made for the purpose, with which they can in a few moments easily make a hole large enough for a man to creep through. They are so clever that they generally manage to carry out their depredations without being seen or heard by anyone. But if they happen to be surprised, the Kallabantrus make a desperate resistance and do their best to escape. If one of their number is killed in the scrimmage, they will run any to obtain possession of the corpse. They then cut off the head and carry it away with them to avoid discovery.

In the provinces which are governed by native princes, these villains are, to a certain extent, protected by the authorities, who countenance their depredations in return for a stipulated sum, or on condition that they pay the value of half the booty that they steal to the revenue collector of the locality. But as such an understanding could not possibly be anything more than tacit in any civilized country, this infamous arrangement is kept secret. The culprits, therefore, can expect no compensation to be publicly awarded them by the magistrates for the wounds and mutilations which they may suffer in the course of their nocturnal raids; but these same magistrates will do their best to screen or palliate their offences, the profits of which they share, and will always protect their clients from the well-deserved punishment when they appeal before them in Court.

The last Mussulman prince who governed Mysore had a regular regiment of Kallabantrus in his service, but to be employed, not to fight amongst his troops, steal the despoil, carry off any valuables they could find amongst the officers' baggage, spike the enemy's guns and act as spies. They were paid according to their skill and success. In times of peace they were sent into neighboring States to pilfer for the benefit of their master, and also to report on the proceedings of the rulers. The minor native princes called Poligars always employ a number of these ruffians for the same purposes.

In the provinces where these Kallabantrus are countenanced by the government, the unfortunate inhabitants have no other means of protecting themselves from their depredations than by making an agreement with the head of the gang to pay him an annual tax of a quarter of a rupee and a fowl per house, in consideration of which he becomes responsible for all the thefts committed by his people in villages which are thus, so to say, insured.

Besides the Kallabantrus of the Kurumaru caste, the province of Mysore is infested by another caste of thieves, called Kanojis, who are no less dreaded than the others.

But of all the nomadic castes which wander about the country, the best known and most detested is the Lambadis, or Sukalers, or Brinjaris. No one knows the origin of this caste. The members of it have different manners and customs, and also a different religion and language from all the other castes of Hindus. Certain points of resemblance, however, which are to be found between them and the Mahrattas, lead one to believe that they must have sprung from these people in the first instance, and have inherited from them their propensities for rapine and theft and their utter disregard for the rights of property when they think they are stronger than their victims and are safe from retributory justice. However, the severe sentences that the magistrates have latterly passed on them in several cases have exercised a salutary influence. They no longer dare to rob and steal openly. But the lonely traveller who meets them in some lonely spot had better beware, especially if they have reason to think that he would be worth plundering.

In times of war they attach themselves to the army where discipline is least strict. They come swarming in from all parts, hoping, in the general disorder and confusion, to be able to thieve with impunity. They make themselves very useful by keeping the market well supplied with the provision that they have stolen on the march. Thcy were thus employee, to the number of several thousands, by the English, who, however, had occasion to regret having taken these untrustworthy and ill-disciplined people into their service, when they saw them ravaging the country through which they passed and causing more annoyance than the whole of the enemy's army. The frequent and severe punishments that were inflicted on their chiefs had no restraining effect whatever on the rest of the horde. They had been attracted solely by the hope of plunder and thought little of the regular wages and other inducements which had been promised them.

In times of peace these professional brigands occupy themselves in trading in grain and salt which they convey from one part of the country to the other on their bullocks; but at the least whisper of war, or the slightest sign of coming trouble, they are at once on the look-out, ready to take advantage in the first moment of confusion of any opportunity for pillaging.

In fact the unfortunate inhabitants of the country fear an invasion of a hostile army far less than they do a sudden irruption of these terrible Lambadis.

Of all the castes of the Hindus this particular one is acknowledged to be the most brutal. The natural proclivities of its members for evil are clearly indicated by their ill-favoured, wild appearance and their coarse hard-featured countenances, these characteristics being as noticeable in the women as in the men. In all parts of India they are under the special supervision of the police, because there is only too much reason for mistrusting them.

Their women are, for the most part, very ugly and revoltingly dirty. Amongst other glaring vices they are supposed to be much addicted to incontinency; and they are reputed to sometimes band themselves together in search of men whom they compel by force to satisfy their lewd desires.

The Lambadis are accused of the still more atrocious crime of offering up human sacrifices. When they wish to perform this horrible act, it is said, they secretly carry off the first person they meet. Having conducted the victim to some lonely spot, they dig a hole in which they bury him up to the neck. While he is still alive they make a sort of lump of dough made of flour, which they place on his head. This they fill with oil, and light four wicks in it. Having done this, the men and women join hands, and, forming a circle, dance round their victim, singing and making a great noise, till he expires.

Amongst other curious customs of this odious caste is one that obliges them to drink no water which is not drawn from springs or wells. The water from rivers or tanks being thus forbidden, they are obliged in a case of absolute necessity to dig a little hole by the side of a tank or river and take the water that filters through, which by this means is supposed to become spring water.

Another nomadic caste is that of the Wuddars, whose trade is to dig wells, tanks, and canals, and to repair dykes. They, too, have to travel about in search of work. This caste is also much despised. The manner of the individuals composing it are as low as their origin, and their minds as uncultivated as their manners. Their extreme uncouthness may, perhaps, account for the low estimation in which they are held.

In Mysore, and in the north-west of the Carnatic, another caste of nomads is to be met with, known as part of the caste of Gollavarus, or shepherds, and were agriculturists. They took to their present kind of life about a hundred and fifty years ago, and like it so much that it would be impossible to persuade them to change it for any regular occupation. The cause of their secession from the rest of their caste was that one of their headmen was grievously insulted by the governor of the province in which they lived. As they never received any redress at all commensurate with the affront, they determined to avenge themselves by deserting their homes in a body, and thus bringing all the agricultural work of the country to a standstill. From that time to this they have never attempted to return to their former mode of life, but are always wandering from place to place without settling anywhere.

Some of their headmen, with whom I have conversed, have told me that they number about two thousand families, half of whom wander through the Telugu country and the rest through Mysore. The headmen meet from time to time to settle the differences which frequently arise amongst the members. However, the Pakanattis are the quietest and best behaved of all the wandering tribes. They are kept in excellent order; and though they always go about in bands, theft and pillage are unknown amongst them and if any of them are found guilty of either, they are severely punished by the rest. They are all most miserably poor; the better off possess a few buffaloes and cows, the milk of which they sell but the greater number of them are professional herbalists. They collect plants, roots, and other things in the different countries that they wander through such as are used for medicine or dyes, or for salves, etc., for horses and cattle. These they sell in the bazaars, and the little money that they thus earn helps them considerably. They supplement their livelihood by hunting, fishing, begging, and charlatanry.

## Isolated Living

All these tribes live entirely isolated from the rest of the world, with whom they hold no communication, except in order to obtain the bare necessities of life. They lead for the most part a pastoral life, and their headmen occasionally possess considerable heads of cattle, consisting of bullocks, buffaloes, and asses. They travel in bands of ten, twenty, thirty, or more families. They shelter themselves under bamboo or mats, which they carry everywhere with them. Each family has its own mattent, seven or eight feet long, four or five feet broad, and three or four feet high, in which father, mother, children, poultry, and sometimes even pigs, are housed, or rather huddled together, this being their only protection against bad weather.

They always choose woods or lonely places as sites for their camps, so that none can see what goes on amongst them. Besides their mattents and the other necessaries for camping, they always take care to be provided with small stores of grain, as well as with the household utensils necessary for preparing and cooking their food, Those who possess beasts of burden make them carry the greater part of their goods and chattels, but the unfortunate wretches who have no other means of transport are compelled to carry all their worldly possessions, that is to say, the necessaries for housing and feeding themselves. I have seen the husband carrying on his head and shoulders the tent, the provisions, and some earthen vessels, whilst the wife, her body half uncovered, carried an infant on her back, hanging behind her in the upper part a for cotton garment; on her head was the mortar for husking the rice; while following her came a child bending under the weight of the rest of the household chattels.

I have often seen this sad spectacle, and always with deep feelings of pity. Such is the kind of life which many Hindus are accustomed to, and which they bear without murmuring or complaining, and without even appearing to envy those whose lives are spent in pleasant places.

Each one of these nomadic tribes has its own habits, laws, and customs; and each forms a small and perfectly independent republic of its own, governed by such rules and regulations as seem best to them. Nothing is known by the outside world of what happens amongst them; and chiefs of each caste are elected or dismissed by a majority of votes. They are commissioned, during the time that their authority lasts, to enforce the caste rules to settle disputes, and to punish all misdemeanour and crime. But however heinous the offences may be, they never involve the penalty of death. The guilty person has only either to pay a fine, or suffer a severe flogging or some other corporal punishment. Travelling ceaselessly from one country to another, these vagrant families pay no tax to any government; the majority possess nothing, and they have consequently no need of the protection of a prince to guard them against spoliation.

Further, they have no claims to take before the courts, since they administer justice themselves; and being without any ambition, they ask neither pardon nor favour from any prince. All these nomadic tribes stink in the nostrils of other Hindus, owing to the kind of life which they lead, to the small esteem in which they hold the religious practices observed by other castes, and, lastly, to the vulgar vices to which they are enslaved. But the heaviest indictment against them is their excessive intemperance in eating and drinking. With the exception of cow's flesh, they eat indiscriminately of every kind of food, even the most revolting, such as the flesh of foxes, cats, rats, snakes, crows, etc. Both men and women drink to excess toddy and arrack, i.e., the spirit of the palm or other trees, and they will consume every kind of liquor and enervating drug which they can procure.

The majority of these vagabonds live in a state of extreme poverty. When no other resource remains to them they beg, or else send their women to earn their livelihood by prostitution.

Among the degraded beings who form the dregs of society in India must be classed the jugglers, the charlatans, mountebanks, conjurers, acrobats, rope-dancers, etc., There are two or three castes which practise these professions, travelling from country to country to find patrons or dupes. It is not surprising with a people so credulous and endued with such a love of the marvellous as the Hindus, that such impostors should abound. They are regarded as magicians and sorcerers, as men versed in witchcraft and all the occult sciences, and are viewed with fear and distrust; while the hatred in which they are held is much greater than is accorded in Europe to people of the same description. Some of these charlatans carry on a trade with a credulous public in quack medicines and universal panaceas. They may often be heard in the street haranguing the multitude and extolling their wares. They even surpass our own quacks in effrontery and barefaced imposture. Others are conjurers or acrobats, and both one and the other perform really astonishing feats of legerdemain and agility. European jugglers would certainly have to lower their colours before them.

The best known of these castes is that of the Dombers or Dombarus. To the earnings which the men make by their industry the women also add the sums that they gain by shameless immorality; their favours, if such a word be applicable, are accorded to any one who likes to pay for them. However, in spite of all this, the Dombers lead a wretched life, and their extreme poverty is caused by their boundless intemperance. They always spend in eating and drinking much more than they actually possess, and when all their means are exhausted, they have recourse to begging.

Other troops of vagabonds of the same class adopt the profession of travelling actors. I once met a large party who were representing the ten Avatars or incarnations of Vishnu, on which subject they had composed as many sacred plays. The greater number of them however play obscene and funny farces in the streets, with boards and trestles for their stage; or else they exhibit manonettes, which they place in disgusting postures, making them give utterance to the distinguishable and filthy nonsense. These shows are exactly suited to the taste and comprehension of the stupid crowd which forms the audience.

Some Hindu jugglers turn their attention to snake-charming, especially with cobras, the most poisonous of all. These they teach to dance, or to move in rythym to music; and they perform what appear to be the most alarming tricks with these deadly reptiles. In spite of all their care and skill it sometimes happens that they are bitten; and this would infallibly cost them their lives, did they not take the precaution to excite the snake every morning, forcing it to bite may rid itself of the venom that re-forms daily in its fangs. They also pose as possessors of the secret of enhanting snakes, pretending that they can attract them with the sound of their flutes.

This craft was practised elsewhere in the very earliest times, as may be gathered from a passage in Holy Scripture, where the obstinacy of a hardened sinner is likened to that of a deaf adder that shuts its ears to the voice of the charmer. Be that as it may, I can vouch for it that the pretended power of Hindu snake-charmers is a mere imposture. They keep a few trained tame snakes, which are accustomed to come to them at the sound of a flute, and when they have settled the amount of their reward with the persons who think, or have been persuaded, that there are snakes in the vicinity of their houses, they place one of these tame reptiles at their corner, taking care not to be observed.

One of the conditions on which they always insist is that any snake which they charm out of a hole shall not be killed but shall be handed over to them. This point settled, the charmer seats himself on the ground and begins to play on his flute, turning first to one side, then to the other. The snake, on hearing these familiar sounds comes out of its hidingplace, and crawls toward its master, gliding quietly into the basket in which it is usually shut up. The charmer then takes his reward and goes off in search of other dupes.

## Wild Tribes

I will now give some particulars about the wild tribes which inhabit the jungles and mountains in the south of India. They are divided into several castes, each of which is composed of various communities. They are fairly numerous in many places in the Malabar hills, or Western Ghats, where they are known by the generic name of Kadu-Kurumbars. These savages live in the forests, but have no fixed abode. After staying a year or two in one place, they move on to another. Having selected the spot for their temporary sound they surround it with a kind of hedge, and each family chooses a little patch of ground, which is dug up with a sharp piece of wood hardened in the fire. There they sow small seeds, and a great many pumpkins, cucumbers, and other vegetables; and on these they live for two or three months in the year. They have little or no intercourse with the more civilzed inhabitants of the neighbourhood. The latter indeed prefer to keep them at a distance from their houses, as they stand in considerable dread of them, looking upon them as sorcerers or mischievous people, whom it is unlucky even to meet. If they suspect a Kadu-Kurumbar of having brought about illness or any other mishap by his spells, they punish him severely, sometimes even putting him to death.

During the rains these savages take shelter in miserable huts. Some find refuge in caves, holes in the rocks, or in the hollow trunks of old trees. In fine weather they camp out in the open. At night each clan assembles at a given spot, and enormous fires are lit to keep off the cold and to scare away wild beasts. Men, women and children all sleep huddled together anyhow. The poor wretches no clothes a wear woman's only covering being a few leaves sewn together and tied round the waist. Knowing only of the simple necessities of existence, they find enough to satisfy their wants in the forest. Roots and other natural products of the earth, snakes and animals that they can snare or catch, honey that they find on the rugged rocks or in the tops of trees, which they climb with the agility of monkeys; all these furnish them with the means of satisfying the cravings of hunger. Less intelligent even than the natives of Africa, these savages of India do not possess bows and arrows, which they do not know how to use.

It is to them that the dwellers in the plains apply when they require wood with which to build their houses. The jungle tribes supply them with all materials of this kind, in exchange for a few valueless objects,—grain as copper or brass bangles, small quantities of grain or a little tobacco to smoke. Both men and women occupy themselves in making reed or bamboo mats, baskets, hampers, and other household articles, which they exchange with the inhabitants of more civilized parts for salt, pepper, grain, etc.

According to the people of the plains, these savages can, by means of witchcraft and enchantments, charm the tigers, elephants, and venomous snakes which share the forests with them, so that they need never fear their attacks.

Their children are accustomed from their earliest infancy to the hard life to which nature appears to have condemned them. The very day after their confinement the women are obliged to scour the woods with their husbands in order to find the day's food. Before starting they suckle the new-born child, and make a hole in the ground in which they put a layer of teak leaves. The leaves are so rough that if they rub the skin even gently they draw blood. In this hard bed the poor little creature is laid, and there it remains till its mother returns in the evening. On the fifth or sixth day after birth they begin to accustom their infants to eat solid food; and in order to harden them at once to endure inclement weather, they wash them every morning in cold dew, which they collect from the trees and plants. Until the infants can walk, they are left by themselves from morning till night, quite naked, exposed to sun, wind, rain, and air, and buried in the holes which serve them for cradles. The whole religion of these savages seems to consist in the worship of bhootams, or evil spirits, which worship they perform in a way peculiar to themselves. There pay no regard whatever to the rest of the Hindu deities.

Besides the Kadu-Kurumbars there is another tribe of savages living in the forests and mountains of the Carnatic, and known by the name of Irulers, or in some places Soligurus. Their habits are identical with those of the Kadu-Kurumbars. They lead the same kind of life, have the same religion, customs, and prejudices; in fact, onc may say that the difference between the two tribes exists only in name.

In several parts of Malabar a tribe is to be found called the Malai-Kondigaru, which, though as wild as those mentioned above, has perhaps a little more in common with civilized humanity. They live in the forest, and their principal occupation is to extract the juice of the palm-tree, part of the which they during the rest sell. The women climb the trees to obtain it, and they do so in a surprisingly agile manner. These people always go about naked. The women only wear a little rag, which flutters about in the wind and most imperfectly covers that portion of their bodies which it is supposed to hide.

During one or the expeditions which the last Sultan of Mysore made into the mountains, he met a horde of these savages, and was much shocked at their state of nudity; for, however depraved Mahomedans may be in their private life, nothing can equal the decency and modesty of their conduct in public. They are horrified at word of look that even verges on indecency or immodesty, especially on the part of their women. The Sultan therefore caused the headmen of the Malai-Kondigarus to be brought before him, and asked them why they and their women did not cover their bodies more decently. They excused themselves on the plea of poverty, and that it was the custom of their caste. Tipu replied that he must require them to wear clothing like the other inhabitants of the country, and that if they had not the means wherewith to buy it, he would every year provide them gratuitously with the cotton cloths necessary for the purpose. The savages, however, though urged by the Sultan, made humble remonstrances and begged hard to be allowed to dispense with the encumbrance of clothing. They finally told him that if they were forced to wear clothing, they would all leave the country and live wherey the would be allowed to follow their custom unmolested. The Sultan was accordingly obliged to give way.

In and around Coorg is another tribe of savages known by the name of Yeruvaru. It is akin to Pariah caste, and is composed of several communities scattered about in the jungles. These people, however, work for their living, and make themselves useful to the rest of the population. They leave their homes to get food from the more civilized inhabitants of the neighbourhood, who, in return for a small quantity of rice given as wages, make them work hard in agricultural pursuits. The indolence of these savages is such, however, that as long as there is a handful of rice in their huts they absolutely refuse to work, and will only return to it when their supply of grain is entirely exhausted. Nevertheless, the other inhabitants are obliged to keep on good terms with them, because they perform all the hardest manual labour, and because if one of them was affronted or thought himself as ill-treated, all the rest of the clan would take his part, and leave their usual abode and hide in the forest. The civilized inhabitants, to whom they are thus indispensable, would not be able to persuade them to resume their work until they had made friendly overtures and agreed to pay damages. These wild yet simple-minded people find it so difficult to procure the bare necessaries of life that they never even think of small luxuries which most other Hindus are so fond of, such as betel, tobacco, oil to anoint their heads, etc. They do not even appear to envy those who employ them, and are satisfied If they can get a little salt and pepper to flavour the tasteless vegetables and roots which form the principal part of their food.

All these wild tribes are gentle and peaceable by nature. They do not understand the use of weapons of any sort, and the sight of a stranger is sometimes sufficient to put to flight a whole community. No doubt the climate in which they live is in a great measure responsible for their timid, lazy, and indolent character. They are very unlike the savages who people the vast forests of America or Africa, in as much as they do not know what war means, and appear to be quite incapable of returning evil for evil. For, of course, no sane person believes the accusation brought against them that they can injure their neighbours by means of that they enchantments. Hidden in thick forests, or in dens and caves in the rocks, they fear nothing in the world so much as the approach of a civilized being, and far from envying the happiness which the latter boasts of having found in the society of his fellow-men, they shun any intercourse with him fearing lest he should try to rob them of their liberty and independence, and lest they should be condemned to submit to a civilization which to them is only another term for bondage.

At the same time, these wild tribes of Hindus retain a few of the customs of their fellow-countrymen. For instance, they are divided into castes, they never eat beef, they have similar ideas about defilement and purification, and they keep the principal regulations relating to them.

# 5

# Marriage

To a Hindu marriage is the most important and most engrossing event of his life; it is a subject of endless conversation and of the most prolonged preparations. An unmarried man is looked upon as having no social status and as being an almost useless member of society. He is not consulted on any important subject, and no work of any consequence may be given to him. A Hindu who becomes a widower finds himself in almost the same position as a bachelor, and speedily remarries.

Though marriage is considered the natural state for the generality of men, those who from pious motives remain unmarried are looked up to and treated with the utmost respect. But it is only those persons who have renounced the world, and have chosen to lead a life of contemplation, who can take vows of celibacy. In any other case marriage is the rule, and everyone is under the obligation of discharging the great debt to his ancestors, namely, that of begetting a son[1]. No doubt it will be asked whether the Hindu devotees who take vows of celibacy do really remain as chaste as they are supposed to be. I should say without hesitation,

1. The Sanskrit word for son, *putra*, means literally, 'one who saves from *put* or hell'—the hell into which parents without sons fall. —Ed.

No. Many have concubines under various pretexts, and many give themselves up in secret to vices which would disgust the most shameless libertine. Among this latter class are the greater number of the gurus and sannyasis, who wander about the country and live on the credulity of the public. Others shut themselves up in seclusion and lead idle and easy-going lives, their sole occupation being to receive the abundant offerings flowing in from the ignorant and foolish who believe in the false reputation for holiness which such people have acquired.

Montesquieu says that our natural human tendency is to prefer in the cause of religion anything that presupposes effort. So in the matter of morality, we incline theoretically to anything that bears the impress of asceticism. Celibacy, for instance, has taken the greatest hold on those to whom it seems most unsuited, and on whom it might have the most disastrous results.

But this privilege which men possess of remaining single, and giving themselves up to a life of contemplation, is not shared by women. They at all events cannot, under any circumstances, take vows of celibacy. Subjected on all sides to the moral ascendancy of man, the very idea that they could possibly place themselves in a state of independence and out of men's power is not allowed to cross their minds. The opinion is firmly established throughout the whole of India, that women were only created for the propagation of the species, and to satisfy men's desires. All women therefore are obliged to marry, and marriages are carefully arranged before they arrive at a marriageable age.

Polygamy is tolerated amongst persons of high rank, such as rajahs, princes, statesmen, and others. Kings are allowed five legitimate wives, but never more. None the less this plurality of wives amongst the great is looked upon as an infraction of law and custom, in fact, as an abuse. But in every country in the world those in power have always been able to twist the law in their own favour, however definitely it may be laid down. The principal Hindu gods had only one wife. Brahma had only Sarasvati; Vishnu, Lakshmi; and Siva, Parvati. It is quite true that under their different forms these venerable personages committed frequent breaches of their marriage vow; but this only serves to prove that from the earliest times marriage was looked upon by the Hindus as a legal union between two persons of opposite sexes.

If in the present day any person of inferior rank cohabits with several women only one of them bears the name and title of wife; the others are merely concubines. In several castes the children of the latter are illegitimate, and if the father dies without having previously settled some of his property upon them, they have no share when it comes to be divided. I only know of one case in which a man can legally marry a second wife, his first being still alive; and that is when, after he has lived for a long time with his wife, she is certified to be barren, or if she has only borne female children; for in the latter case the debt to one's ancestors, that is to say, the birth of a son-is considered to have been imperfectly paid. But even in this case, before a man contracts a second marriage, it is necessary that he should obtain the consent of the first; and she is always regarded as the chief wife and retains all her prerogatives.

It may be remembered that for the same reason Abraham took Hagar to be his wife during the lifetime and with the consent of Sarah, his lawful wife. One may also remember what dissensions arose in the family of the holy patriarch as the result of this marriage with two women. It is exactly the same in

Hindu families where there are two legal wives. Consequently the majority of Hindu husbands prefer, under such circumstances, to give up the hope of having a son, rather than be subjected to the numberless troubles which are the invariable result of the remedy permitted by law.

A celebrated statesman of the last century, Burke, speaking on this subject from a political point of view, said that the Christian religion, by bringing marriage back to its primitive and only legitimate state, had contributed more by that alone to the general peace, happiness, stability, and civilization of the human race, than it would have been possible for it to do in any other department of divine providence.

The indissolubility of the marriage tie is also an essential principle which it seems to me is not less firmly established amongst the Hindus than that which limits this important act to the legal union of one man with one woman. A Hindu can only put away his legitimate wife for one cause, and that is adultery. If this rule is violated it is only among the most degraded of the lower castes. A marriage can also be annulled if it has been contracted in violation of the prohibitory degrees which are laid down by custom, and which of themselves are sufficient to nullify the union.

**I have never yet heard of a divorce being permitted on account of incompatibility of temper, nor have I ever heard of a man being allowed to put away his wife, however vicious she might be, simply in order to marry another woman.** Hindus, put too serious a value on this solemn contract to allow it to be thus degraded to a state which would be nothing more or less than concubinage. A Hindu, and especially a Brahmin, would hardly be inclined to repudiate his wife even for adultery, unless her guilt were very notorious. As a general rule, when the wife of a

Brahmin gives occasion, by injudicious behaviour, for remarks of a kind damaging to her character, her friends and relatives do their utmost to excuse her conduct and to hush up all scandal about her, so as to avoid the necessity of such an extreme measure as a divorce, the disgrace of which reflect on the whole caste).

## Ceremonies

I will now give a detailed account of the principal ceremonies which take place both before and at the time of a wedding. A young Brahmin should, ordinarily speaking, be married when he is about sixteen years of age, but the ceremony is often postponed till he is older than this. The wife chosen for him is generally five, seven, or at the utmost nine years old.

The Jews also married their children at an early age. A youth who was not married before he was eighteen was considered by them to be sinning against the command of the Creator, which says: 'Increase and multiply.' He was free to marry as soon as he had attained the age of thirteen. Their daughters were betrothed in childhood, and were married as soon as they had arrived at a suitable age, which was usually fixed by them at twelve.

This custom of marrying girls in their early childhood, and as soon as possible, though common to all castes, is most strictly observed by the Brahmins When once a girl has passed the marriageable age, it is very difficult for her to find a husband. In this caste there is often an enormous difference in age between the husband and the wife. It is no uncommon thing to see an old man of sixty or more, having lost his first wife, marry for the second time a little child five or six years old, and even prefer her to girls of mature age. What is the result of this? The husband generally dies long before his wife, and often even before she has attained the age which would allow him to exercise his rights as a husband. So the poor girl becomes a widow before she has even become a wife, and as by the custom of her caste she may not marry again, she is oftentimes tempted to lead a dissolute life, thereby reflecting discredit on the whole caste. Everybody recognizes these abuses but the idea of remedying them by allowing a young widow to break through the stern rule of custom and marry again would never even enter the head of a Hindu, more especially of a Brahmin[1]. It is true that the strange preference which Brahmins have for children of very tender years would make such a permission almost nominal in the case of their widows.

Amongst the Jews it was permissible for widows to marry again; but those who voluntarily, out of respect and affection for their dead husbands, refrained from marrying again, were looked up to with very great respect.

The expenses of a wedding are so considerable that in all castes one often sees young men, who are without the necessary means, using the same expedient to procure a wife that Jacob employed with Laban. Just like the holy patriarch a Hindu without means will enter the-service of one of his relations, or of some other person of the same caste who has daughters to marry, and will engage himself to serve for a certain number of years without wage, on condition that, at the end of that time, he is to receive one of the daughters in marriage. When the time agreed upon has expired the father fulfils his promise, undertakes the whole expense of the marriage, and then allows

1. Hindu social reformers are now agitating for virgin-widow remarriages, and in a few instances such marriages have been brought about.—Ed.

the young couple to go away and live where they please. At their departure he gives them a cow, a pair of oxen, two copper vessels (one for drinking, the other for food), and enough rice to feed them for the first year of their married life. It is very remarkable that in India the term which a man has to serve for his wife is the same as that for which Jacob bound himself to Laban, namely, seven years.

The inclinations of the persons about to be married are never consulted. In fact, it would be ridiculous to do so amongst the Brahmins, seeing the age at which they marry their daughters. But even the Sudras, who often do not marry their daughters until they have attained full age, would never dream of consulting the tastes and feelings of their children under these circumstances. The choice is left entirely to the parents. That which chiefly concerns the young man's family is the purity of the caste of his future wife. Beauty and personal attractions of any kind count for nothing in their eyes. The girl's parents look more particularly to the fortune of their future son-in-law, and to the character of his mother, who after the marriage becomes the absolute mistress of the young wife.

A Sanskrit verse, commonly quoted, says: 'The girl courts beauty; the mother, riches; the father, knowledge; relatives, good lineage; other people, sumptuous marriage-feasts.'

The same months are chosen for a wedding as are selected for the ceremony of the Upanayana, that is to say, the months of March, April, May and June, and especially the two last. However, it is possible in a case of urgency for a marriage to take place in November or February. But in both these months there are so many precautions to be observed, so many calculations to be made according to the signs of the

Zodiac, the phase of the moon, and other things, that it is far from easy to find a day on which all the auspices are propitious.

There are four different ways of arranging the preliminaries of a marriage. The first, the most honoured and respected of all, is for the father of the bride not only to refuse to receive the sum of money to which he is entitled from the young man's parents, but to undertake to bear all the expenses of the ceremony, to purchase all the jewels and other ornaments which it is customary to give a girl on this occasion, and also to make handsome presents to the son-in-law and his parents. But this can only be done by the rich and people of high position.

The second way is for the parents of both the contracting parties to agree to share all the expenses. The third method is that usually adopted by people of all castes who are not rich. The parents of the girl insist not only on the youth's parents bearing all the expenses of the wedding and of the jewels, but they also exact payment of a sum of money in return for their daughter, the amount of which is laid down by caste custom. This method is the commonest of all, for to marry and to buy a wife are synonymous expressions in India. The wife is never given up to her husband until he has paid the whole of the sum agreed upon. It was the custom also among the Jews for the husband to give the wife her dower.

This custom is an endless source of quarrels and disputes. If a poor man, after the marriage has taken place, cannot pay the stipulated amount, his father-in-law sues him for it, and takes his daughter away hoping that the desire to have her back again will induce the man to find the money. Sometimes this succeeds, but it pretty often happens that the son-in-law, being always unable to pay the debt, leaves his wife for years as a pledge with his father-in-law, and at last the latter, convinced that by this means he will get nothing, and fearing lest his daughter should succumb to the temptations to which her youth exposes her, withdraws his demands. A compromise is effected and the husband at length regains his wife.

The fourth method, to which none but the very poorest have recourse, is very mortifying to the girl's parents, for they go themselves and hand her over to the tender mercies of the young man's parents, leaving it to them to do what they will with her, to marry her when and how they like, to spend as little or as much as they choose on the wedding, and begging them at the same time to pay them something for their daughter.

As soon as the parents have discovered a suitable girl, and have ascertained if the family are likely to assent, they choose a day when all the auguries are favourable, and go to formally ask for her. They provide themselves with a new cloth, such as is worn by women, a coconut, five bananas, some vermilion, and some powdered sandalwood. While on the way, they pay great attention to any omens that they may notice. If they consider them to be unfavourable they retrace their steps, and postpone the business till another day. Thus, for instance, if a snake crosses their path, or a cat, or a jackal, or if they should happen to see anything that is regarded as an evil omen, they decide that the best thing to do is to return to their home.

All Hindus are full of these superstitions. No matter how important the business may be that they are about to undertake, they will never hesitate for a moment to put it off, if they catch sight of one of these objects or one of these animals. I have several times seen labourers take their oxen back to their sheds, and remain idle all day, simply because when leaving the village in the morning, a snake had crossed their path.

If nothing of this sort has disturbed them on the way they present themselves at the house of the girl's parents and make known the object of their visit. The latter, before giving any answer, look steadfastly towards the south, and wait till one of those little lizards which one sees running about the walls of a house has uttered a certain sharp cry, such as these reptiles often-make. Then when the Lizard of the South has spoken, the parents of the girl give their consent to the marriage, and accept the present which has been brought by the other parties.

In the evening of the same day, about dusk, they call together a few relatives and friends, and summon a Purohita in order to consult him about the marriage. Whilst the men, seated on mats or carpets, are talking together, the women purify a part of the house; that is to say, they rub the floor well with cow-dung mixed with water, and then draw lines of red and white upon it. As soon as they have finished, they bring in the god Vigneshwara, to whom they do puja, and for naiveddya they offer peas, sugar, a coconut, and a sweet beverage called Paramanna. All present worship this god, and pray him to remove any obstacles which might interfere with the projected marriage. If during this ceremony the Lizard of the South again utters his cry they think it a favourable omen.

After this ceremony, the Purohita fixes on a lucky day on which to begin to celebrate the marriage. The parents of the girl then definitely give their permission, and in token of their promise they offer betel to all those who are present. These preliminaries ended, they begin to think of making preparations far the wedding. Gold and silver ornaments are ordered for the couple, and form the subject of endless discussion.

The wedding garments are also got ready, a large number of cloths, such as are worn by both men and women, are bought to be given away as present to relations and friends, a large store is laid in of rice, wheat flour, liquefied butter, oil of sesamum, peas of all kinds, dried and fresh vegetables, fruits, groceries, pickles, and in fact every sort of edible that a Brahmin is permitted to use. They also provide saffron, or turmeric, vermilion, antimony, sandalwood powder, incense, quantities of flowers, akshatas, or coloured rice, betel, areca-nut, etc., etc.; also a great quantity of small silver and copper coins. Further, they buy new baskets, and above all, plenty of new earthen vessels of all shapes and kinds; for these vessels may never be used a second time, and are immediately broken after being once used, no matter to what purpose they have been put.

## Gifting the Girl

When everything is ready, they begin to put up a pandal or canopy. The god Vigneshwara is carried into it, and to him they do puja, entreating him to ward off any hindrance or misfortune which might happen during the celebration of the marriage. The Purohita who presides at the ceremony must be one of the first to take up his place under the pandal; he must be provided with some darbha grass, small pieces of wood from the seven sacred trees, and a few other indispensable objects for the sacrifices he is about to offer up.

In the first place, due honour is paid to the household gods. To this end all the Brahmins present, both men and women, anoint their heads with oil of sesamum, and then bathe. The women, after preparing the various dishes for the feast, take a portion from each, which they place on a metal dish, and proceed, singing songs and accompanied by all the guests to offer it as naiveddya to these gods, having first, of course, done puja to them. They even go so far as to place to the right of them pickles, to give a relish to their rice, while on their left they place a cup full of the sweet drink called Paramanna, with which to quench their thirst. The master of the house then performs the Samkalpa and offers sandalwood, akshatas, flowers, and lustral water to his guests, who ought, when receiving all this, to think of the household gods, in whose honour the feast immediately following is spread, great pains having been taken to make it bountiful and magnificent. Betel is distributed at the termination of the repast, after which the guests disperse.

The second day, nine Brahmins specially chosen for the purpose perform the sacrifice of Homam and another to fire, in honour of the nine planets, as at the ceremony of the upanayana. Two women take the consecrated fire and carry it, singing the while, to the centre of the pandal, placing it on the raised dais of earth. Each of the women then receives a present of a new cloth, and a little bodice called Ravikai. All present then walk round the brazier of hot coal reciting mantrams, scattering darbha grass and bowing to the ground. Presents are given to the nine Brahmins who have sacrificed to the planets, and, as usual, the meeting ends with a feast.

The third day the father of the bridegroom, having made his ablutions, takes some akshatas in a cup, and goes out early to call together relatives and friends. As soon as all are assembled under the pandal, a pure cloth or carpet is spread on the raised earthen dais, and the future husband and wife are seated thereon facing the east. The married women then approach them and rub their heads with oil, singing the while, and then proceed with the important ceremony known as Nalangu, which consists in smearing the naked parts of their bodies with powdered saffron, and immediately after pouring a great quantity of warm water over their heads. The women never cease singing the whole time, and are accompanied by musical instruments. After the Nalangu is over the women array the young couple in new clothes, as the Upanayana. The evening of the same day, at the moment when the lamps are being lighted, the guests return to assist at the following ceremony:— the married women, singing all the time, take a wooden cylinder which they cover with lime and then paint with red longitudinal stripes. On this they tie small twigs of the mango tree. They next sprinkle a great quantity of powdered saffron over the cylinder, which they immediately afterwards dip into a new earthen vessel. This they carry with much solemnity, singing the while, to the centre of the pandal, where they offer it a sacrifice of incense, and offer some betel for Naiveddya. Every person present makes a profound obeisance to the vessel. No other saffron but what is thus consecrated is used during the whole ceremony.

All these proceedings are merely preparatory to the marriage ceremony itself, which lasts for five days. The first day is called Muhurta, that is to say, the great day, or the happy and auspicious day. It is on this day that the most important and solemn ceremonies take place. The head of the family goes out early to invite his guests, while the women busy themselves with purifying the house and the pandal, which they decorate all round with wreaths of mango leaves. The guests having arrived stand in a row, and first adorn their foreheads with akshatas and sandalwood. They next anoint their heads with the oil of sesamum which is provided for them, and then they go and perform their ablutions. On their return the Purohita performs the Samkalpa and invokes all their gods, beginning with Brahma, Vishnu, Rudra, Nevendra, and then the twelve Adityas, the eight Vasus, the nine Brahmas, the eleven Rudras, the Gandharvas, the Siddhas, the Saddhyas, the Naradas, the seven great Rishis, the nine planets; in fact, every deity whose name occurs to his memory. With low obeisance he invites them all to come to the marriage-feast, makes many flattering speeches to them, and begs them to remain under the pandal, and to preside over the ceremony during the five days that it lasts.

Then comes the invocation of ancestors. The couple about to be married are seated on the earthen dais in the centre of the pandal, having on each side of them their fathers and mothers, all with their faces turned towards the east. The father of the bride rises, places the sacred amulet on the ring-finger of his right hand, performs the Samkalpa, and puts a certain quantity of rice in a metal dish, and on this rice a coconut dyed yellow, three areca-nuts in their shells, and five others without their shells.

Then, taking one of the nuts in one hand and the metal dish in the other, he repeats three times in a loud voice the names of his father, his grandfather, and his great-grandfather. Each time he pronounces their names he raps the copper dish three times with the areca-nut, and at last, again invoking them by name he says: 'O my ancestors, you who dwell in the Pitraloka (or paradise of ancestors), deign to come to this pandal, bringing with you all the other ancestors who preceded you. Be present, I beseech you, during the five days of this marriage-feast, preside at the festivity, and grant to it a happy termination!' He then gives the rice, the coconut, and the areca-nut which were on the dish to the Purohita.

This done, the married women bring some fire on a new earthen chafing-dish, and, singing, place it in the centre of the pandal. The Purohita then consecrates it by scattering all round it some darbha grass. To the north of it he places some small pieces of the sacred fig-tree, by the side of which are placed three small earthen vessels and one of copper. The first contains milk, the second liquefied butter, the third curds, and the fourth a certain quantity of cooked and uncooked rice mixed together. To the south of the brazier are spread nine portions of rice on a large banana leaf. These are tactfully arranged in squares, each portion being destined for one of the nine planets. Puja is done to each of these nine planets individually, and offerings of bananas and betel are made to them as *naiveddya*, after which they receive the same invitation as the gods and the ancestors.

The Purohita places on the east side of the brazier another banana leaf, on which he spreads darbha grass and akshatas. This is an offering to Brahma, to whom is presented a *naiveddya* of raw sugar and betel. Then follows the invocation of the Ashta-dik-palakas, or the eight divine guardians of the eight corners of the world; and puja is offered them on the same banana leaf. Then comes the inauguration of the ishta-devata or tutelary deity, and the deification of the five little pots in the manner that has already been described for the Upanayana.

These ceremonies ended, the father of the girl performs the homam in honour of Brahma, Vishnu, and Rudra, of the eight gods who guard the eight compass-points of the world, of the eight Vasus, and of Indra, taking care to mention all these gods by name, and also to repeat mantrams suitable to the occasion.

He again does homam to the nine planets, makes a sacrifice to fire, and offers the latter some liquefied butter as naiveddya.

A new earthen chafing-dish is then brought, to which they fasten a piece of saffron thread, and on it is placed the consecrated fire. Women carry this fire away to a place apart, singing, of course, the while. Great care is taken not to let the fire go out till the end of the festivity. It would be considered a terribly bad omen if, through negligence or any other cause, it should be extinguished.

Now comes the muhurta, that is to say, the most essential ceremony of the marriage. To begin with, a sacrifice is offered to Vigneshwara. The bride and bridegroom are seated on the earthen dais, their faces towards the east, and the married women proceed, singing the while, with the young people's toilette, which is of the most elegant and sumptuous description. When attired the bridegroom rises, performs the Samkalpa, prays to the gods to pardon all the sins he has committed since he received the triple cord; and, to be the more sure of this pardon, he recites a mantram, and gives fifteen fanams to a Brahmin as alms. He then dresses himself up as a pilgrim, and makes all preparations as if he were really going to take a long journey, announcing that he is going to start on a holy pilgrimage to Kasi, that is, Benares. He leaves the house accompanied by the married women singing in chorus, and by his parents and friends, and preceded by instruments of music. After passing the outskirts of the village he turns his steps to the east.

But here his future father-in-law meets him, and asks him where he is going, and on learning the object of his journey, begs him to give it up. He tells him that he has a young virgin daughter, and that if he wishes it he will give her to him in wedlock. The pilgrim accepts the proposal with joy, and returns with his escort to the place whence he set out. On his return the women perform the ceremony of the Aratti.

The bride and bridegroom having again taken their places on the dais, and the Samkalpa having been performed, they then begin the important ceremony called Kankana-dharana, the wearing of the Kankana. For this purpose they obtain two pieçes of saffron or turmeric, round which they tie a double thread. They place on a metal dish two handfuls of rice, and on this rice a coconut painted yellow, and on the coconut the two pieces of saffron. Prayers are offered to all the gods collectively, who are implored to come and place themselves on this Kankana, and to remain there till the five days of the marriage ceremony have been accomplished. The bridegroom then takes one of the pieces of saffron and ties it on his wife's left wrist, who in her turn ties the other piece on his right wrist. The rice and coconut on which the Kankana has been lying are then given to the Purohita.

Then follows the procession of the tutelary deity. The mother of the bride, accompanied by the other women and the Brahmins who are present, go and fetch the copper vase which represents the Ishta-devata. The women begin to sing and the musicians to play, and forming a procession they march to the end of the street, where, after choosing a clean spot, they pour out some of the water contained in the vase. They do puja to the deity while it rests on the ground, and then it is taken back with the same pomp to the place whence it came. Then follows the most important ceremony of all, which is called Kanyadana, or the gift of the virgin. This is what takes place. The bridegroom being seated facing the east, his father-in-law performs the Samkalpa, places himself in front of him, and looks at him fixedly for some time without speaking. He is supposed to imagine that he sees in his son-in-law the great Vishnu; and with this in his mind, he offers him a sacrifice of arghya, padya, achamana, akshatas, sandalwood, and flowers. A new copper vessel is then brought. In this the young man places his feet, which his father-in-law washes first with water, then with milk, and then again for the third time with water, while reciting suitable mantrams.

He performs the great Samkalpa, which consists in adding to the ordinary Samkalpa the names and attributes of the Bharata Varsha, the Salivahana, the seven islands, the seven seas, the seven puras or cities, the seven Penitents, the seven mountains, the sacred places (punyasthalas), and the holy cities (punya puras).

He next thinks of his father, his grandfather, and great-grandfather. Pronouncing their names aloud, he prays that these and the twenty-one other ancestors, who have preceded them, may attain moksha or paradise. Then, holding betel in one hand and taking his daughter's hand in the other, he says a prayer to Vishnu, begging him to look with a gracious eye on this gift that he is making of his virgin daughter. He then places her hand in that of her future husband, pours a little water over it, and gives him some betel, the usual token of a gift.

The gift of the virgin is followed by three other gifts, namely, the go-dana, bhu-dana, and salagrama-dana, which mean the gift of cows, the gift of land, and the gift of salagramas, or small stones, to which they attach a superstitious value.

Then follows the ceremony called Mangalashta, the eight marriage blessings, which concludes with the throwing of coloured rice over the couple by way of blessing them. The bride and bridegroom are seated facing each other, and a sheet of silk is suspended in front of them. This is held by twelve Brahmins, and hides them from the other guests, who successively invoke in a loud voice Vishnu and his wife Lakshmi, Brahma and Sarasvati, Siva and Parvati, the Sun and his wife Chhaya, the Moon and his wife Rohini, Indra and Sachi, Vasishta and Arundhati, Rama and Sita, Krishna and Rukmani, and several other pairs of gods and goddesses.

As soon as the Mangalashta is finished, they fasten on the Tali, that is, the little gold ornament which all married women wear round their necks; the Tali is strung on a little cord which is dyed yellow with saffron water, and composed of 108 very fine threads closely twisted together. Other little ornaments of gold are also added, round which are fastened flowers and fine black seeds. Two handfuls of rice are placed in a metal pot, on the rice is laid a coconut dyed yellow, and on the top of the coconut the Tali, to which they offer a sacrifice of sweet perfumes. The Tali is then taken round to all the guests, both men and women, who touch it and bless it[1].

Four large metal lamps, each with four wicks, are brought in and placed on a stand, which must also be of the same metal. Above are set other lamps fashioned out of a paste composed of ground rice, and these are filled with oil. They are lighted, and four women take them in their hands. At the same time all round the pandal a great number of other lamps are lighted. Then ensues a tremendous din. The women sing, the musicians play, bells are rung, cymbals are clashed, and anything and everything within reach from which sound can be extracted is seized on, each one striving

1. Old ladies whose husbands are alive are specially requested to touch and bless the Tali, to ensure the couple a long married life. —Ed.

to outdo the other in creating noise, which is intended to drown any sounds or weeping, sneezing, quarrelling, etc., which are considered bad omens.

In the midst of this hubbub the husband advances towards his young wife, who is seated facing the east, and while reciting mantrams he fastens the Tali round her neck, securing it with three knots. The husband and wife, sitting side by side, then offer each other betel. Two married women approach them, give them the blessing, and place akshatas, which have been consecrated by mantrams, on their heads, and finally perform the ceremony of arati.

Fire is then brought on a new earthen brazier, and the Purohita consecrates it with mantrams, surrounds it with darbha grass, and does homam to it. The fire is surrounded by lighted lamps, and near it is placed a small stone called the sandalwood stone, no doubt because it has been smeared with sandalwood oil. Then the husband, holding his wife's hand, walks three times round the sacred fire, and each time he makes the circuit he takes his wife's right foot in his right hand, and makes her touch the sandalwood stone with it, touching the stone with his own foot at the same time. Whilst performing this action the thoughts of both husband and wife should be directed to the great mountain of the North called Saptakula Parvata or the mountain of the seven castes, the original home of their ancestors, the mountain being represented by this sandalwood stone.

These are the various ceremonies which compose the muhurta. As soon as they are finished, two bamboos are planted in the centre of the pandal side by side, and at the foot of each of them is placed a bamboo basket. The bride and bridegroom then stand up, each in a basket, and two other baskets full of rice are brought. They take handfuls of this rice and shower it over each other in turn. This they continue to do many times, until they are tired, or are told to stop.

In some castes the guests perform this ceremony, which is called Sesha, for the newly married pair. Princes and very rich people have been known to use for the Sesha, instead of rice, pearls and precious stones mixed together. After the Sesha the couple return to their usual seat. Akshatas consecrated by mantrams are then distributed to the guests. The husband throws over his right shoulder a piece of new and clean cloth, one end of which he unfolds before the assembled brahmins, from whom he receives a blessing, while they also recite a mantram and place a portion of the akshatas they have just received on the cloth. He takes these in his hand and puts one portion on his own head, and the rest on his wife's head, after which the women again perform Aratti to the newly married couple.

It is easy to see the allegorical meaning of most of the ceremonies which have just been described, and which are the most solemn and important of the whole proceedings. The Kanya-dana, for instance, typifies the handing over of the girl by the father to the son-in-law and the renunciation of parental authority over her. The son-in-law for his part fastens the Tali round his wife's neck to show that he accepts the gift, and that from henceforth she is his property. The sacrifice of the homam and the thrice-repeated circuit of the newly married couple round the fire are a mutual ratification of the contract they have just made with one another, for there is no more solemn engagement than that entered into in the presence of fire, which Hindus look upon as the purest of their gods, and which for this reason they always prefer to any other when they wish to make an oath specially binding. The ceremony of the Mangalashta is to call down divine blessings on the newly married couple. That of the Sesha is the outward expression of the wish that they may enjoy an abundance of this world's goods, or that their union may be fruitful, or perhaps both.

## Feast

When all these ceremonies are ended, sandalwood powder, akshatas, and betel are given to all the Brahmins present, both men and women. All must then go and perform their ablutions and return for the feast which on this day must be specially magnificent. Before sitting down to eat, they never fail to carry with due solemnity to the household gods their share of the food which has been prepared.

All the guests being seated in a row upon the ground, the men quite apart from the women, so that the latter are out of sight, a large banana leaf is placed before each person, and a helping of boiled rice is placed on it, and on one side two other leaves, folded in the form of cups, one containing melted butter and the other a strongly spiced sauce. The second course consists of dried peas, green vegetables, and roots of various kinds. The third course consists of fritters, puddings boiled in water, others fried in butter, others sweetened and spiced, curdled milk, and salt pickles. Bananas, jack and other fruits make up the fourth course. Then follows the khilavanta, which consists of four different dishes all highly flavoured, and composed of various ingredients mixed with rice. To finish the repast a beverage is handed round composed of lime-juice, sugar, cardamom, and aniseed mixed with water. The whole meal takes place in absolute silence.

When all the guests have feasted they turn their attention to the meal for the newly married couple, not forgetting the necessary ceremonies connected with it. First of all the sacred fire is brought and placed before the dais on which they are sitting. The husband rises and does homam to the fire, whilst the Purohita repeats mantrams. Then the women form a procession, and singing take the fire back to its original place. The young married couple, holding each other by the hand, go to the place where the tutelary deity is reposing, and make a deep obeisance to it. The husband then does puja to it, and offers as *naiveddya* some cakes and boiled rice. They make a similar obeisance to the five little earthen vases placed near the deity, in which are sown ten kinds of seeds, and sprinkle them with water.

It is only after having gone through all these preliminaries that the young married couple are allowed to partake of the meal which has been specially prepared for them. They sit down facing one another in the centre of the pandal on two little stools, the bridegroom facing east. Before them is spread a large banana leaf, and at each of its four corners are placed four lamps made of ground rice filled with oil, which are lighted, as well as many others all round the pandal. Then the married women bring in on two metal dishes the different viands which have been prepared for the young couple, much singing and music going on the while. After they have been helped, melted butter is poured three times on to their fingers, and after swallowing this they begin to eat their food together from the same leaf. To eat in this manner is a sign of the most complete union, and is the most unmistakable proof of friendship that two persons closely united could possibly give each other. Later on the wife will be allowed to eat what her husband leaves, but never again will she be permitted to eat in company with him. This is a favour which is only granted her on her wedding-day.

Their meal finished, the newly married couple go outside, preceded by music, and accompanied by the women singing, by all the guests, and by the Purohita. The Purohita points out to them a small star called Arundhati, the wife of the Penitent Vasishta, which is to be found near the pole-star. The couple make a deep reverence to the star and return to the house in the same procession. There the women perform the ceremony of Arati. This terminates the ceremonies of the first day, called muhurta, or the great day.

I will spare my readers the details of the ceremonies which occupy the four following days, and which, as a rule, are merely a repetition of those just described. What little variety there is, is much in the same style. These ceremonies are interspersed with the most innocent games and amusements, which would appear to us funny and only suitable for little children, but which afford them the greatest pleasure and infinite amusement.

Amongst the second day's ceremonies one of the most extraordinary is when they place a sort of ornament, called Bassinam, on the forehead of both the husband and wife. The Bassinam is covered with gold-leaf or gold paper, and flowers are entwined round it. The object of the Bassinam is to avert the effect of the drishti-dosha or evil eye, the spell which is cast by the looks of jealous or ill-disposed people. Placed thus on the most conspicuous part of the body it is supposed to detract the eyes of the malevolent, and thus prevent them exercising their malign influence on the persons of the newly married couple.

Amongst the ceremonies which take place on the third day there is a peculiar one. The husband, as usual, performs the sacrifice of the homam and another to fire, and after him his wife comes up and performs the same sacrifice, only with this difference, that instead of using boiled rice, she uses parched rice. This is, I believe, the only occasion on which a woman can take an active part in any of these sacrifices, which the Brahmins hold to be most sacred and most solemn.

The only remarkable ceremony which takes place on the fourth day is the Nalangu, in which the newly married couple rub each other's legs three times with powdered saffron. I do not in the least understand the meaning of this ceremony. I fancy its only object is to kill time. Europeans under similar circumstances would spend it in drinking, often to excess, or in gambling, dancing, singing songs in honour of love and wine, sometimes even in carrying on intrigues with the object of loosening the sacred marriage tie, which it is thc object of marriage ceremonies to make secure. **The Hindus spend their wedding-days more wisely in religious observances, of which the greater number are well calculated to leave a lasting impression on the minds of those attending them.** The innocent and artless games with which they amuse themselves afford them none the less pleasure because they are so. **In the domestic festivities of the Brahmins, decency, modesty, purity, and reserve are always conspicious.** This is the more remarkable as they obey a religion whose dogmas are for the most part saturated with immorality.

The fifth day is chiefly occupied in dismissing, with all the customary formalities, the gods, the planets, the great penitents, the ancestors, and all the other divinities who have been invited to the feast. They dismiss even the Kankanam, that is to say, the two pieces of saffron attached to the wests of the newly made husband and wife. Finally, the god of the Mantapam, that is to say of the pandal, is himself dismissed. Then follows the distribution of presents, which vary in value according to the means of the host. The Purohita who has taken the most prominent part, and after him the women who have been singing the whole time from beginning to end, carry off the lion's share of these bounties. I must just mention that the songs which are sung in these ceremonies contain nothing obscene or even erotic; they are either a sort of explanation of the aim and object of each ceremony or else a long rigmarole in praise of the bride and bridegroom, in which they also give expression to the most heartfelt wishes for their future happiness.

The festivity ends with a solemn procession through the streets, which generally takes place at night by torchlight in the midst of squibs and fireworks of all kinds. The newly married pair are seated face to face in an open palanquin highly decorated. Both of them are loaded, rather than adorned, with flowers, jewels, and other ornaments, for the most part borrowed for the occasion. The procession advances slowly. Relatives and friends before whose houses it passes, come out to meet it. The women perform the ceremony of Arati to the couple, and the men give presents of silver, fruits, sugar, betel, etc. These gifts are really only a loan, for those who receive them are expected to return them on similar occasions to the givers. I have, sometimes seen wedding processions that were really beautiful, though perhaps not quite according to our taste.

Such are a Brahmin's wedding ceremonies, all of which, and many more minute observances which I have not thought it worthwhile to mention, are scrupulously performed with more or less magnificence by the rich as well as by the poor.

Sudras' marriage ceremonies are equally solemn, though much less elaborate. In every caste marriage is looked upon as the most important affair in a man's life. It is also the most expensive one, and brings many a Hindu to ruin. Some spend on it all that they possess, and a great deal more besides; while others, in order to fulfil what is expected of them, contract debts which they are never able to repay. I shall say nothing of the feasts which are given by their relatives and friends to the newly married couple, of the presents they receive, or of the ceremonies in their honour. I will only add that for a whole month the feasting and rejoicings go on.

## Bride Returns Home

When all the festivities have at length come to an end, the bride returns home with her parents, who keep her shut up till such time as she shall be able to fulfil all the duties of a wife. This also is another occasion for festivities. There is the same gathering of friends and relatives, and almost the same ceremonies, with a few exceptions, that took place at the first wedding. The father and mother of the bridegroom, on being informed that their daughter-in-law has arrived at an age when the marriage can be consummated, go and fetch her, and conduct her home in triumph. And in order that she may become accustomed by degrees to married life, her own parents come at the end of a month and take her back to her own home, and for the first few years, or until she has children, she lives alternately in her parents' and in her husband's house.

These mutual arrangements are at first a proof of the happy understanding, existing between the two families. But unfortunately this harmony rarely lasts long, for very soon, finding herself ill-treated and even beaten by her husband, and tormented in a thousand ways by an exacting mother-in-law who treats her like a slave and vents upon her all her whims and ill-temper, the poor young wife is forced to a surreptitious flight, seeking shelter and protection under her father's roof. Then, relying on promises of better treatment in future, she consents to resume her fetters; but fresh outrages soon force her to escape again. In the end, resigning herself to the inevitable, or for the sake of her children, she gives up the struggle, and meekly bows to marital authority. A real union with sincere and mutual affection, or even peace, is very rare in Hindu households. The moral gulf which exists in this country between the sexes is so great that in the eyes of a native the woman is simply a passive object who must be abjectly submissive to her husband's will and fancy. She is never looked upon as a companion who can share her husband's thoughts and be the first object of his care and affection. The Hindu wife finds in her husband only a proud and overbearing master who regards her as a fortunate woman to be allowed the honour of sharing his bed and board. If there are some few women who are happy and beloved by those to whom they have been blindly chained by their family, this good fortune must be attributed to the naturally kind disposition of their husbands, and not in any way to the training the latter have received.

A Brahmin Purohita does not usually preside at a Sudra marriage unless the contracting parties are very rich and of high position, and thus able to recompense him handsomely. Generally the ceremony is performed by one of the mendicant Brahmins who go about selling Hindu almanacs from door to door. In each caste custom differs as to the manner in which a bride is demanded, the sum of money paid for her, the quantity and the value of her jewels, the colour and price of the wedding garments, the arrangements as to who shall defray the expenses of the ceremony, the number of feasts provided for the guests, and the presents made to relatives and friends.

Amongst the Sudras the erection of the pandal is one of the most important and solemn of the ceremonies. It is set up in the street, opposite the entrance-door of the house, seven, five, or three days before the wedding festivities begin. As soon as it is put up a procession is formed, accompanied by music, to fetch the Arasani, that is to say, a green branch of the sacred fig-tree with leaves on it. This is planted in the centre of the Pandal; puja is offered to it and also votive offerings. All present walk round it in single file, making deep obeisance to it. It represents Vishnu, to whom the sacred fig-tree is specially dedicated, and it remains in the middle of the Pandal during the whole of the ceremonies as the tutelary god of the festivity. Processions round it take place at intervals, always accompanied by the same marks of respect. Another peculiarity at a Sudra wedding is that a lamp is kept alight in a prominent part of the Pandal during the three days' festivities, the wick of which is composed of 108 threads. Among the Sudras also the number of earthen cooking-pots is restricted to ten.

The Brahmin who presides at the marriage begins by breaking one or more coconuts before the Arasani, and according as the nut breaks in this or that direction, favourable or unfavourable auguries of the future of the newly married pair are determined. Almost all the other ceremonies are identical with those of the Brahmins.

At the marriage of Kshatriyas or Rajahs, the ceremonial differs very little from that of the Brahmins. A Purohita invariably presides and takes the leading part. All the Brahmins who live in the place and in the neighbourhood are invited, but as they cannot eat with people of this caste, they receive each day portions of rice, melted butter, curdled milk, peas, vegetables, and fruits, which they cook for themselves and feast upon apart. At the termination of the ceremonies they receive more or less valuable presents of cloths and other things according to their rank and in proportion to the means of the family who give the feast.

At the marriages of Kshatriyas, too, all the different kinds of weapons used in warfare are brought in with much solemnity, accompanied by the songs of the women and by instruments of music. These weapons remain hung up in the most conspicuous part of the pandal until the festivities are ended. The guests offer them sacrifices, and worship them from time to time, and similar processions are made round them to those of the Sudras round the sacred fig-branch.

The work from which I have extracted these details gives particulars of a remarkable expedient for procuring a wife sometimes adopted by the noble caste of Kshatriyas. When a young man of this caste wishes to marry, instead of going through the usual prescribed forms and humiliating proceedings with the parents of the girl that he has in view, he exercises the right of carrying off the noble lady on whom he has set his affections. To ensure success in his enterprise he collects a numerous following, unexpectedly declares hostilities against the king whose son-in-law he hopes to be, and tries to wrest his daughter from him either by force or strategy. As soon as she is in his power he conducts her to his home in triumph, and celebrates the marriage, with all due solemnity. This method of procuring a wife, says the author, is the most approved of all in the case of a Kshatriya; and, in fact, Hindu books often mention similar instances of rape, but always amongst the Rajah caste.

The ritual of the Brahmin Purohitas, after

describing in detail the ceremonies to be observed at a Kshatriya marriage, always terminates with a short sermon on the principal duties imposed on this noble caste.

'The real caste of Kshatriyas has ceased to exist,' says this same author, 'and the so-called Kshatriyas of the present time are a bastard race. Whoever pretends to be a true Kshatriya ought to know that he can only be a soldier, and nothing else, and that his one object in life is to make war. During a war he should be careful not to injure a labourer, an artisan, anyone who flees before him, who asks his assistance or who places himself under his protection, anyone who during the battle or after it lays down his arms and with supplicating hands asks for quarter. In a word, he should conduct himself in these circumstances according to the rules laid down in the Dharma-sastra. The true Kshatriya when engaged in fighting an enemy, should give up all desire to live. Far be it from him to think of retreating or taking to flight! On the contrary, let him advance bravely, resolved to conquer or to die! The happiest death for a Kshatriya, the one he should wish for most, is to die sword in hand, fighting. It procures for him the inestimable happiness of being admitted to Swarga.

Boundless ambition is the highest virtue a Kshatriya can possess. However vast his possessions may be already, he should never say that he has enough. All his thoughts should tend to enlarging and extending his territories and to making war on nelghbouring princes with a view to appropriating their possessions by force. He should show faith and piety towards the gods; he should respect Brahmins, placing the utmost confidence in them, and loading them with gifts. Truth and justice are the foundations on which all his actions should be based. His leisure moments should be given up to reading the Dhanur-veda, and other sacred works which he has the right to study, and he should regulate his conduct by the customs of his caste. Humane and generous, he must never refuse to do good to anyone whoever he may be, and it should be said of no one that he left a Kshatriya's presence unsatisfied. The best and most honourable way in which he can spend his wealth is to give abundant alms to Brahmins, to build temples with gopurams, to erect rest-houses and other buildings for public use on the high-roads, to repair those that are falling into decay, to sink wells and make reservoirs and tanks, and to establish Chutrams (almshouses for Brahmins) in many places. He should do his best to rule his country with equity, and should keep a careful watch lest he act unjustly. He must give to all his subjects their due, and never exact from them more than what rightfully belongs to him. In short, his duty is to model his conduct in everything on the rules laid down in the Dharma-sastra.

# 6

# Funeral Ceremonies

The closing moments of a Brahmin's life are associated with a number of ceremonies. One might suppose therefrom that Brahmins were eager to preserve after their death that superiority over their fellows which they boast about so much during their lifetime; and that their desire was to surpass everybody else in their practices at the period when the scythe of Father Time reduced these gods of the earth to the level of the humblest Pariah. For the rest, most Hindus observe very many formalities when their near relatives die.

As soon as the symptoms of death become manifest in a Brahmin, a spot is chosen on the ground and smeared over with cow-dung. On this darbha grass is strewn, and over this again is placed a new and ceremonially pure cloth, upon which the dying man is then laid. His loins are next girded with another ceremonially pure cloth. Then, the dying man having given his permission, the ceremony called Sarva Prayaschitta, or perfect expiation, is performed by the Purohita and the chief mourner that is to say, the person who is most nearly related to the deceased or who by common usage has the right to perform this function. Then a few coins of gold, silver, and copper are carried in on a metal salver, and on another

Akshatas, sandalwood, and Pancha-gavja. The Purohita pours a few drops of the Pancha-gavya into the mouth of the dying man, by virtue of which his body becomes perfectly purified. Then the general purification ceremonies are proceeded with. The Purohita and the chief mourner invite the sick Brahmin to recite in spirit, if he cannot articulate distinctly, certain mantrams, by virtue of which he is delivered from all his sins.

## Godana

After this a cow is brought in along with her calf; her horns are ornamented with rings of gold or brass, her neck with garlands of flowers, while her body is covered with a new piece of cloth; and she is also decorated with various other ornaments. The cow is led up to the sick person, who takes her by the tail, and at the same time the Purohita recites a mantram praying that the cow may lead the dying Brahmin by a happy road into the other world. The latter then makes a present of the animal to some other Brahmin, into whose hand he pours a few drops of water in token of the gift. This gift of a cow is called Godana, and is indispensable if one wishes to arrive without mishap in Yama-loka, or the kingdom of Yama, the kin of hell.

Bordering Yama-Ioka there is a river of fire which all men must cross after they have ceased to live. Those who have made the Godana, when they come to their last hour, will find on the banks of this river a cow which will help them to pass on to the opposite bank without being touched by the flame. After the Godana, the coins placed on the metal salver are distributed to the Brahmins, and the sum total ought to equal the price of the cow. Afterwards the Dasha-dana, or the ten gifts, are prepared. These are to be distributed at the obsequies which will subsequently take place. The gifts consist of cows, lands, gingelly seeds, gold, ghee or liquefied butter, cloth, various kinds of grains, sugar, silver, and salt. These ten articles, which are offered to the Brahmins, are supposed to be extremely acceptable to the gods, and procure for him who offers them a blessed sojourn in the Abode of Bliss after death.

A Brahmin must not be allowed to die on a bed or even on a mat, and for this reason: the soul in separating itself from the body in which it is incorporated enters into another body, which leads it to the Abode of Bliss destined for it, and if the dying Brahmin were to expire on a bed, he would be obliged to carry it with him wherever he went, which, it may easily be supposed, would be very inconvenient. Accordingly, it is necessary, in order to relieve the dying person of such a burden, to offer abundant alms and perform expensive ceremonies. This custom has suggested a curse which is very common amongst the Brahmins when they quarrel with each other. 'Mayst thou,' they will say, 'have no person near thee to place thee on the ground in the hour of death!'

As soon as the dying person has breathed his last, it is a recognized custom that everybody present must burst into tears, and that in a fashion strictly laid down for the occasion. The chief mourner then proceeds to bathe without taking off his clothes, next has his head and face shaved, and lastly goes to bathe a second time in order to purify himself from the defilement of, the barber's touch. On his return he causes to be brought to him Pancha-gavya, gingelly oil, darbha grass, raw rice, and a few other things. He places on the ring finger of the right hand the pavitram. Then he performs the Samkalpa, and offers homam in order that the deceased may obtain a place in heaven.

Then the corpse is washed, and the barber shaves off all the hair. It is washed a second time, and after that sandalwood and Akshatas are placed upon the forehead and garlands of flowers round the neck. The mouth is filled with betel-leaves and the body is apparelled in, rich raiment and jewels. It is then placed on a kind of state bed, where it remains exposed to view during the time that the preparations for the obsequies are proceeding. When these have been finished, the person who is presiding at the ceremony brings a new piece of ceremonially pure cloth in which he wraps the corpse. A strip of this cloth is torn off, and a small piece of iron, on which a few drops of gingelly oil are poured, is tied up in it. This cloth is twisted into the form of a triple cord, and must be kept for twelve days, to be used in the various ceremonies.

The litter on which the body is placed is constructed as follows. To two long parallel poles are fastened transversely seven pieces of wood with ropes of straw, and on this the body is placed. Then they bind the toes and the two thumbs together. The shroud, which until then has been merely thrown over the body, is now wrapped around it, and is bound strongly with straw ropes. If the dead Brahmin happens to leave a wife behind, his face is left uncovered. The chief mourner then gives the signal to depart, and, carrying fire in an earthen vessel, puts himself at the head of the procession. After him comes the funeral litter, ornamented with flowers, green leaves, coloured cloths, and sometimescostly stuffs. Surrounding it are the parents and friends of the deceased, all of them without turbans, and having simply a piece of cloth thrown over their heads in token of mourning. The women are never allowed to attend the funeral ceremonies out of doors[1]. They remain in the house and utter lamentable cries.

---

1. This is not true of the Brahmins, whose women always follow the procession to the cremation ground. —Ed.

## On the Pyre

On the way to the funeral pyre three halts are made. Each time the mouth of the dead person is opened, and a little raw and soaked rice is placed in it, so that hunger and thirst may at the same time be satisfied. These halts, however, have a more serious motive. Instances have been known, it is said, of persons believed to be dead having not been so in reality, or if really dead having come to life again.[1] Seeing that the spirits of the nether world or their emissaries have been known to make mistakes in their choice and to take one person for another, these halts are made to give plenty of time for the spirits to recognize any mistakes they may have made, so that no person may be thrown on the funeral pyre who is still destined to live. Each of these halts lasts about a quarter of an hour.

On arrival at the burning-ground a shallow pit is first dug, about six feet in length and three in breadth. This is then consecrated by mantrams and sprinkled with ceremonial water, while several small pieces of money are thrown into it. Then the funeral pyre is erected, and the corpse is placed upon it. The chief mourner next takes a small ball of dry cow-dung, sets fire to it, places it upon the hollow of the deceased's stomach, and performs on this lighted bratty the sacrifice of homam. Then follows extraordinary ceremony the chief mourner placing his lips successively to all the apertures of the deceased's body,

1. These halts are made to allow time for recovery, if the man is not dead, before reaching the cremation ground. For it is a firm belief that if by any chance the supposed corpse should revive after reaching the pyre, dire consequences would result to the village. He is not, under those circumstances, allowed to go back to the village, but is expelled altogether. —Ed.

addressing to each a mantram appropriate to it, kissing it, and dropping on it a little ghee. By this ceremony the body is supposed to be completely purified.

The chief mourner then places a small piece of gold money in the mouth, and everybody present in turn deposits in it a few grains of soaked rice. The near relatives then approach and deprive the corpse of all the jewels with which it is adorned, and even of its shroud; and then it is covered with small splinters of wood which are sprinkled with Pancha-gavya. The chief mourner walks round the funeral pyre three times, and pours upon It some water that is allowed to trickle from an earthen vessel which he carries on his shoulder, and which he afterwards breaks on the head of the deceased.

This last act and that which follows formally constitute him the dead man's heir.[1] Then a lighted torch is brought to him. Before he takes it, however, it

1. 'The offering to deceased fathers at the Sraddha is the key to the Hindu law of inheritance. It furnishes the principal evidence of kinship, on which the title to participate in patrimony is founded, no power of making wills being recognized in Manu, or any other authoritative code of Hindu Jurisprudence. . . . The object of such Sraddhas is two-fold, first, the re-embodying of the soul of the deceased in some kind of form after cremation of the corpse, or simply the release of the subtile body which is to convey the soul away. Secondly, the raising him from the regions of the atmosphere where he would have otherwise to roam for an indefinite period among demons and evil spirits to a particular heaven or region of bliss. There he is eventually half deified among the shades of departed kinsmen. Manu, however, is not clear as to the precise effect of the Sraddha. He merely states that its performance by a son or the nearest male kinsman is necessary to deliver a father from a kind of hell called Put, and that the spirits of the departed (Pitris) feed on the offered food.' —Monier-Williams

is customary for him to show his grief by uttering mournful cries. In displaying his grief ne rolls upon the ground, strikes his breast with his hand, and makes the air resound with his cries. Following his example, all present also weep, or pretend to do so, holding themselves clasped one to another as a sign of grief. Then, taking hold of the torch, the chief mourner sets fire to the four corners of the pile. As soon as the flames have caught hold of it everybody retires, with the exception of the four Brahmins who have carried the corpse, and who must remain on the spot until the whole pyre has been consumed.

Meanwhile, the heir goes to bathe himself without taking off his clothes; while soaked in this way, he selects a clear spot on the ground and causes rice and pulse to be cooked there in a new earthenware vessel, which he must keep carefully for the ten days following. Then directing his thoughts to the deceased, he pours a libation of oil and water on the ground, strews darbha grass over it, which he also sprinkles with the same mixture of oil and water, and, on this again he places the rice and poles after moulding them in the form of balls. A third libation is then offered, mantrams are recited, and the balls are thrown to the crows, which, as everyone knows, are very common in India. The Hindus believe these noisy and rapacious birds to be evil spirits, in fact, devils under the form of crows. This offering, therefore, is intended to render them kindly disposed towards the dead man. If they refuse to accept the food, which we are told sometimes happens, it is a very bad omen for him, and instead of being admitted into the Abode of Bliss he will find himself, despite all the mantrams and purifying ceremonies, made captive in the Yama-Ioka, that is to say, in hell.

After the corpse has been consumed, the four

Brahmins who remained near the pyre return to the place where the other people present at the ceremonies have gathered together. Three times they walk round the assembly, asking permission to take the Bath of the Ganges. Then they proceed to perform their ablutions in order to purify themselves of the pollution of having carried a corpse. The chief mourner invites all present to take the 'Bath of the Dead,' the Mrittika-snana, which is supposed to be on behalf of the deceased whose body has just been consumed by the flames. This bath, it is supposed, will refresh it after the fiery ordeal. Then a few small coins and some betel-leaves are distributed among those present, and everyone who has a right to them is presented with the Dashadana, after which all return to the door of the deceased's house, though no person enters the house because it is still defiled. Finally, everybody washes his feet and returns to his own house.

Nevertheless, for the heir another ceremony still remains, which consists in filling a little chatty with earth and sowing nine kinds of grain, namely, rice, barley, gingelly seeds, and the five kinds of pulse. He waters them so that they may quickly sprout and be used for certain ceremonies which follow. A thing of importance that he must do that day is to place in the habitation of the deceased a small vessel full of water, over which he hangs a thread tied at one end to the ceiling. This thread is intended to serve as a ladder to the Prana, that is to say, to the life-breath which animated the body of the deceased, and which by this thread is enabled to descend and drink the water during the ten days which follow. And in order that the Prana may have something to eat as well as to drink, a handful of rice is placed each morning by the side of the vessel.

It is not until all these ceremonies and formalities

have been accomplished that the people of the house are allowed to take any food. For they have neither eaten nor drunk anything since the moment that the deceased gave up the ghost. All these practices are most rigorously observed. The omission of the most minute of them would cause no less scandal than the omission of the more important. Nevertheless, poverty is allowed as an excuse for neglecting those which entail large expenditure. For instance, most Brahmins would be quite unable to make the Dasha-dana, or ten gifts.

It is to be observed that these practices, however superstitious they may appear, clearly denote that the Hindus have preserved a most distinct idea of the immortality of the soul; that they recognize the corruption of human nature and the necessity of resorting to means of purification for enabling the soul to enter the blessed state and enjoy the rights which it has forfeited through sin. And the Prana, for instance, which is regarded by the Hindus sometimes as the soul and sometimes as the breath of life, reminds us of the *spiraculum vitae* of the Holy Scriptures, by the aid of which the Creator gave life to the day out of which he formed mankind.

## Year-long Mourning

Hindu mourning lasts one year, during which a large number of ceremonies have to be observed. The principal are as follow:

On the day after the funeral the chief mourner, accompanied by his relatives and friends, goes to the place consecrated to the burning of the dead. There he recommences the ceremonies of the previous evening, without forgetting the food for the crows, and places on the ground the strip of cloth which has been torn from the pall: The Brahmins present take the Bath of the Dead (Mrittika-snana), receive betel, and depart The heir, however, keeps back one of them, and gives him two measures of rice, peas, and vegetables, wrapped in a new cloth, which he presents as well, so that he may make a good meal and be well clothed by proxy as it were for the deceased; in case the rice, the peas, the oil, and the water which have already been offered for the latter may not be sufficient to allay his hunger and quench his thirst, and so that he may not be without clothes to cover his nakedness in the next world.

On the third day, the heir again summons his relatives and friends. He erects a small Pandal in a corner of his courtyard, and has rice, seven sorts of vegetables, cakes, etc., cooked there. When these viands have been prepared, he places them on a cloth folded in four, and covers them all with another cloth. Then five small earthen pots are brought filled with Pancha-gavya, as also a measure of rice, some peas, vegetables, sandalwood, Akshatas, three small pieces of cloth dyed yellow, some flour, a small stick two cubits in length, some betel, some gingelly oil, and the ten gifts. Provided with all these and accompanied by his relatives, he returns to the burning-ground. There he performs his ablutions, puts on the ring, or pavitram, performs the Samkalpa, and then fills a new earthen pot with water, which he sprinkles over the ashes of the deceased. After that he sprinkles them with milk. He squats on his heels with his face turned to the east, performs once more the Samkalpa, stirs the ashes with the small stick above mentioned, looking for any bones that may have escaped the flames, and these he puts into an earthen pot, reciting a mantram meanwhile. Gathering up a portion of the ashes, he throws them into the water. The remainder he collects into a heap, to which he gives the rough semblance of a human figure, supposed to represent the deceased. He offers as sacrifice to it a portion of the things he has brought, sprinkles it with Pancha-gavya, and puts the whole into an earthen pot. These sad mementoes of the deceased are destined to be thrown subsequently into one of the sacred rivers.

He then raises a mound of earth twelve inches high on the exact spot where the dead body has been burnt, and taking three small stones he places one in the middle of the mound, which receives the name of the deceased; the second, which he places at the south end, is named Yama; and the third, which he places at the north end, is called Rudra. Calling these three stones by the names which he has given them, he proceeds to rub them over with gingelly oil, bathes them while he continues to recite mantrams, and clothes them in the three pieces of yellow cloth with which he has provided himself. Afterwards, putting them back in their places, he offers them puja and Naivedya, and pours a libation of oil and water in honour of each particular one. Then all the Brahmins present file in one by one, embrace the chief mourner, and weep with him. The distribution of Dasha-dana follows as on the first day.

The three stones are next placed in the earthen pot that is intended for cooking the rice and the peas, which are mixed with a fresh supply of these vegetables, and the heir carries it all to the border of the tank. After cooking the viands he offers them to the three stones, repeats his libations, and at last throws the rice and the peas to the crows. A meal and a cloth are again bestowed on a Brahmin by proxy as it were for the deceased; and the day ends in pretty much the same manner as those preceding it. It is considered of great importance to preserve carefully for ten days the three little stones, as well as the pot used for the cooking of the crows' food. If by misfortune a single one of these articles were lost, all the ceremonies would have to be begun all over again.

From the fourth to the ninth day inclusive, these ceremonies are repeated daily. The objects are (1) to prevent the deceased suffering from hunger, thirst, and nakedness; (2) to enable him to divest himself as quickly as possible of his hideous and ghastly carcass and to assume a beautiful form, so that, in a new birth, he may be neither deaf, nor blind, nor dumb, nor lame, nor afflicted with any bodily infirmity.

On the tenth day the chief mourner rises early to make his ablutions, constructs a little pandal in his courtyard, causes rice, peas, and three sorts of vegetables to be cooked there, prepares the drink called Paramanna, and some rice cakes cooked in water. He places the whole on a large plantain leaf, with three pieces of saffron on the top. In short, he prepares all the articles indispensable for the sacrifices and offerings which he is about to make.

When all is ready, the widow of the deceased, after performing her ablutions, paints her eyelids with antimony, her forehead with vermilion, her neck with sandalwood-paste, her arms and legs with saffron; she then puts on her richest garments, bedecks herself with all her jewels, twines red flowers in her hair, and hangs garlands of sweet-smelling flowers round her neck. The married women surround her, clasp her by turns in their arms, and weep with her.

The chief mourner, provided with all his sacrificial paraphernalia, and followed by his relatives and friends, as well as by the widow and her companions, returns once more to the burning-ground, where all the preparatory ceremonies are renewed just as those already described, This time he mixes some earth with water, and spreads three coats of the mud on the three stones, accompanied by mantrams, adjurations, sacrifices, offerings, etc. The women present then surround the widow once more, beating their heads and breasts in measured time and weeping and sobbing as loud as they can.

The chief mourner makes three little balls of boiled rice and peas, places them on the ground on darbha grass, pours a libation of oil and water, offers the little balls to the deceased, and then throws them to the crows. He puts back the three stones into the earthen pot which has played so important a part during these ten daya, carries them to the edge of the tank, performs Samkalpa, puts the pavitram on his finger, walks into the water up to his neck, turns to the east, and looking towards the sun, says:

'Till now, these stones have represented the dead body; may that dead body from this moment leave its hideous form and take that of the gods! May it be transported into Swarga to enjoy all its pleasures as long as the Ganges shall flow, as long as these stones shall last!'

At these words he throws the pot and the stones inside it over his head into the water. Then he performs his. ablutions, returns to the bank, performs the Samkalpa, and distributes the Dasha-dana. Then, with the permission of the Brahmins, he and his near relatives are shaved, for during these ten days of mourning shaving is not allowed. Finally, after numberless ceremonies, of which I have given only a short epitome, all repair to the edge of the tank. There a heap of earth four fingers high is made, on which is placed a little ball also of earth, which receives the name of the deceased. Then the widow, surrounded by her companions and showing no sign of grief, divests herself of her jewels and rich garments, wipes off the artificial pigments with which she had smeared different parts of her body, and finally takes off the Tali which she wears round her neck. This discarded ornament she places near the ball of earth which represents her deceased husband, uttering these words the while: 'I abandon all these to prove to thee my love and my devotion.' Then ensue fresh wailings and weepings on the part of her companions.

The Purohita appears on the scene at this moment to perform the Punjaha-vachana, that is, the consecration of holy water. He makes all the women who are participating in the mourning drink a little of this water, and sprinkles some drops on their heads. By this means they obtain purification from the defilement which they have contracted by taking part in the funeral ceremonies. The heir gives to each person present an areca-nut and a betel-leaf, and to the widow a white cloth, which she immediately puts on.

Finally, all return to the house of the deceased, where after having inspected the lamp, which ought to have been kept burning all this time on the spot where the deceased breathed his last, each one takes leave and does not enter his own house till he has washed his feet at the door. Being now left alone, the heir takes the five little earthen pots in which he had sown some seeds on the first day, offers them puja, and then throws them into the water.

On the eleventh day, as soon as his ablutions are over, he goes to summon nineteen Brahmins, to whom he first of all offers a feast to be eaten by proxy, for the deceased. Then he puts into a basket a large earthen catty containing two measures of rice, and into another basket several more earthen pots of a smaller size. He provides himself with liquefied butter, gingelly oil, darbha grass, flowers, etc., and accompanied by the Brahmins invited, goes to the edge of the tank. There he digs a small hole, blesses it with mantrams, places therein his little earthen pots, and lights a fire, At the four corners of the hole he places darbha grass and sprinkles oil all round it. He spreads some boiled rice on a plantain leaf, sprinkles it with ghee, and makes it into thirty-six little baltls, which he throws subsequently into the fire one after the other. To this fire he makes profound obeisance, beseeching it to grant the deceased access into the Abode of Bliss. He then distributes Dasha-dana and gives the Brahmins some betel. The latter then go to bathe themselves, and return to assist in the ceremony of the Deliverance of the Bull.

For this purpose a bull three years old is chosen. It must be all of one colour, either white, red, or black. After washing it they smear it with sandalwood-paste and akshatas, decorate it with garlands of flowers, and with a red-hot iron brand on the right haunch thc figure of one of Siva's weapons called Shulah. The chief mourner implores this god to consent to the Deliverance of the Bull, so that, as a reward for this good deed, the deceased may find a place in an Abode of Bliss. They then set loose the bull, which is allowed to wander about grazing without a keeper wherever it likes, and it is given as a present to some Brahmin.[1]

The nineteen Brahmin guests seat themselves in a line on small stools. The heir spreads darbha grass before them, and gives a blade of it to each, while reciting a mantram and uttering the name of the deceased. He then sprinkles some drops of oil on their heads, presents them with sandalwood-paste, gives to each a present of two pieces of cloth, offers a libation of oil and water, and again serves them with food. The repast over, he mixes some boiled rice, peas, and herbs

1. These bulls are usually dedicated to a temple, and they are used for breeding purposes. —Ed.

together, rolling them all into three balls, which he puts into an earthen pot. After sundry libations, offerings, and other formalities, he throws these three balls to the cattle and dismisses the nineteen Brahmins, who, before returning home, take good care to bathe.

On the twelfth day the heir goes to summon eight Brahmins, and makes them sit down on as many stools in front of him. He chooses one of them to represent the corpse of the dead man, and gives him, as well as the seven others, a blade of darbha grass with the usual ceremony. He then traces three squares on the ground, over which he spreads cow-dung, which he blesses with mantrams, and over this again he pours oil and spreads darbha grass. In the middle square he places the Brahmin whom he has appointed to represent the corpse, sprinkles over his feet oil and darbha grass, and then washes them with water.

Two other Brahmins step into the second square, and the five others into the third. To each of them he performs the same office. Having made them sit down, he approaches the one who represents the corpse, sprinkles on his head and hands some drops of oil, while repeating a mantram, puts earrings in his ears and a gold ring on his finger, makes him a present of two pieces of cloth, a white blanket, a brass chembu (drinking bowl), and some betel, hangs round his neck one of the rosaries called Rudrakshas, and smears him with sandalwood-paste. Each of the seven others also receives two pieces of cloth, a white blanket, and a chembu. Then they all take part in the repast prepared for them. At its conclusion the heir puts some rice and oil in a dish, and moulds four balls, which he places on the ground after performing the necessary formalities. One of these balls is intended for the deceased, a second for the deceased's father, a third for his grandfather, and the last for his great-grandfather. Taking the deceased's ball, he says:—

'Till now thou hast preserved the hideous appearance of a corpse; from this moment thou shalt clothe thyself; in the divine form of thy ancestors; thou shalt inhabit with them the Pitri-loka (abode of the ancestors) and there enjoy every sort of happiness.'

He then divides this ball into three portions and mixes one portion with each of the remaining three balls. In the same way he tears the little strip of cloth which represents the triple cord of the deceased into three pieces and puts one on each ball. To all of these he makes offerings and libations. After this, comes a further distribution of Dasha-dana. Finally, the balls and offerings are thrown to the cattle.

When all this long and monotonous ceremony is ended, the chief mourner anoints his head with oil, takes a bath, and returns home well covered up in a cloth. He embraces his relatives and friends, addressing words of consolation to each in turn. He paints his forehead with sandalwood-paste and akshatas, resumes his turban and ordinary clothes, and distributes presents according to his means.

The Purohita also recites a great many mantrams, and sprinkles all the corners of the house with holy water, by which means it is purified, together with all those who inhabit it.[1]

On the thirteenth day the heir performs homam in the accustomed manner in honour of the nine planets.

---

1. The same kind of ceremony took place amongst the Romans on the tenth day, named *denicales feriae*. As may have been observed, this is not the only feature of resemblance between the funeral ceremonies of the Romans and those of the Hindus.

A ceremony something like that of the twelfth day takes place on the twenty-seventh, but only three Brahmins take part in this, representing respectively the deceased, his father, and his grandfather. One is supposed to call himself Vasudeva, the second calls himself Yama, and the third calls himself the Sun. The heir makes the usual offerings and libations to these personages, gives each of them a piece of cloth, and has a meal served up to them, at the end of which he kneads three balls composed of rice, peas, and herbs, which are solemnly offered to the deceased and his two ancestors.

The same ceremony is repeated on the 30th, 45th, 60th, 75th, 90th, 120th, 175th, 190th, 210th, 240th, 270th, 300th, and 330th day after the death of the deceased. Further, the anniversaries of the deaths of his father and mother must be celebrated by a Hindu all his lifelong without fail; and each time most of the formalities just mentioned must be observed and liberal gifts made to Brahmins.

At each new moon it is the indispensable duty of a man to offer a libation of oil and water to his deceased father, as well as to his grandfather and to his great-grandfather.[1] I have mentioned that the pecuniary circumstances of many Brahmins do not allow of their fulfilling to the letter the costly obligations imposed upon a chief mourner. But there are a great many which are obligatory and which entail considerable expense. Conceit and vanity, which are such strong incentives in the minds of Brahmins, induce many of them to contract debts infinitely beyond their means in order to make a show on such occasions.

---

1. And also to their wives. Libations are also sometimes offered to the maternal grandfather, great-grandfather, and great-great-grandfather and their wives.

The funeral ceremony for a woman is nearly the same as that for a man. Rather less attention, however, is paid to a widowed mother of a family. And much less still to a widow who dies without children; the flames of the funeral pyre have scarcely consumed the mortal remains of such a one before she is forgotten. When a Brahmin woman dies, the married women, kinswomen, or friends of the family assist at the funeral ceremony, and it is they who receive the usual presents and distributions.

The obsequies of the Kshatriyas and Vaisyas are performed with nearly the same pomp as those of the Brahmins, the ceremonies which are observed lasting twelve days. It is always a Purohita who presides at the death-bed, and who directs the mourning ceremonies in both these castes. The chief mourner invites the Brahmins, to whom offerings and presents are made. These ceremonies are repeated every month during the first year; and after that it suffices if the anniversary is celebrated regularly.

## Among the Sudras

The last services which the Sudras render to their dead are accompanied by much less ceremony and formality. They have neither mantrams nor sacrifices. However, when a Sudra's last hour is come, it is Customary to call a Brahmin to go through the ceremony of Prayaschitta (expiation) for him. His family is also permitted to bestow on the Brahmins Godana and Dasha-dana, as well as the other customary gifts and presents. As soon as a Sudra dies, they wash his body and have him shaved by the barber. Then they pay attention to his toilet, which they strive to render as elegant as possible, and afterwards place him sitting cross-legged on a sort of bed of state. When all is ready for the obsequies, they remove him, still in the same position, to an open litter, or shrine, ornamented with flowers, green leaves, and valuable cloths, or else to an open palanquin splendidly decorated. The body is then carried to the funeral pyre by twelve bearers.

Musical instruments are employed in the funeral processions of the Sudras, but never in those of the higher castes. The two principal instruments are the long trumpet, called in Tamil Tami, and the Sankha, or Sangu, another no less lugubrious instrument made out of a large sea-shell (the conch). As soon as a Sudra has breathed his last, two of these are blown to announce the sad news to all the neighbours. Their harsh and piercing sounds are audible at a great distance, and cannot fail to inspire a pious horror wherever they are heard. One trumpet will sound a B flat, droning on this note for the space of half a minute; then another trumpet answers in G sharp; and thus they respond by turns. This continues without interruption from the moment of death until the end of the obsequies.

Mourning in the Sudra caste lasts for only three days. The third day is called the Day of Milk Offering. To perform this ceremony the chief mourner provides himself with three young coconuts, four coconut branches, a measure of raw rice, some boiled rice, herbs, fruits, etc. He fills an earthen pot with milk, places it in a new basket, and accompanied by the relatives and friends of the family, preceded by conch-players, goes to the place where the body of the deceased was burnt. On his arrival he draws some water in an earthen pot and sprinkles it over the ashes on the pyre. Above this he erects a small Pandal, covered with palm leaves and supported by four pillars, the interior of which he drapes with a piece of cloth. He collects the bones which have escaped the flames, puts the largest one on a flat cake made of dried cow-dung, and gathers up the rest in a heap. He calls the deceased by name and pours milk over the bones. During this libation the conch-players make the air resound with their lugubrious noise.

The chief mourner then piles up the ashes over the bones. At the side he places half a coconut, and on the top pieces of another coconut which he breaks, sprinkling the milk over this pyramid of ashes. He places a third coconut close by on a plantain leaf and invokes Harischandra.[1] Finally, he kneads the rice and other eatables which he has brought with him into a round mass and throws the whole to the crows, calling meanwhile upon the name of the deceased.

Then the relatives and friends come in turn to embrace the chief mourner, holding him in their arms and weeping with him. He takes the large bone which was placed in reserve; and all the mourners, to the doleful notes of the conches, go and throw this bone into the neighbouring tank. After bathing, all accompany the chief mourner to his house. There with much ceremony they put a new turban on his head, and each hastens to do justice to the repast prepared for the occasion. Thus ends the funeral ceremony.

Wealthy Sudras do not stop here. They proceed on the thirtieth day to a new ceremony, on which occasion they strive to rival the Brahmins in magnificence. And the Brahmins, since they enjoy all the honour and profit of the feast, take care not to show any jealousy.

The funeral ceremonies of the Sudras vary much in different districts. In some places Hindus of this caste bury their dead instead of burning them. In other places they throw the body into the river, deliberately feigning the river to be the Ganges. This kind of burial,

1. One of the kings of Ayodhya, who was famous for speaking the truth.

the most expeditious and least costly of any, is common enough among the sects of Siva and the poorer classes of Sudras.

The solemn occasion when man shuffles off his mortal coil naturally offers ample matter for speculation to the imaginative Hindus. They attribute to the moon a sort of Zodiac composed of twenty-seven constellations, each of which presides at one of the twenty-seven days of its periodical course. The last five are all more or less fatal. Woe to the relatives of him who dies in the period when the moon travels through them! The body of the deceased, in this case, cannot be removed from the house either by the door or the window. It is absolutely necessary to make an opening through the wall for this purpose. And this is not all. To escape the unfortunate accidents which would inevitably follow such an untimely death, the most prudent course is to abandon the house for six months, or at least three months, according to the degree of the malign influence of the constellation which was in the ascendant on the day of death.[1] At the erid of this time they remove the bushes with which they stuffed up the front door of the ill-fated house where the death occurred. The remotest corners of the building are carefully purified, a purification which can be completed only by the iritervention of a Purohita, who has to be called in, and of course paid for. Finally, a meal must be given to the Brahmins and presents must be made to them; after that the occupants will have nothing else to fear.

A death happening on Saturday entails almost equally serious inconveniences. It is a hundred to one in that case that another member of the same

1. Nowadays it is customary simply to shut up the room in which a man dies.

household will die before the year is our.[1] The only way to stave it off is to sacrifice a living animal, such as a ram, a he-goat, a fowl, etc., as a burnt offering.

Thus superstition follows the Hindu even to the last days of his existence. We have already seen what fancies assail him from his cradle. The child born under an unlucky star is not only himself destined, according to common belief, to all sorts of troubles and accidents during the course of his life, but he brings bad luck to those with whom he is united by the ties of blood; and it is not uncommon to see parents, convinced of the truth of these so-called malign influences, quietly abandoning on a high road innocent babes who happened to be born on a certain day which the prognostications of the professional astrologer have signified to be unlucky, or else handing them over to anyone who is bold enough to run the risk of assuming charge of such an ill-omened burden. There are even unnatural parents of this kind who go the length of cruelly strangling or drowning these tiny victims of most stupid and at the same time most atrocious superstition.

1. It is also believed that a death on a Thursday entails two other deaths in the same family.

## 7

# Women

The social condition of the Brahmanis, or wives of Brahmins, differs very little from that of the women of other castes, and I shall have little to say about it. This interesting half of the human race, which exercises such enormous power in other parts of the world, and often decides the fate of empires, occupies in India a position hardly better than that of slaves. Their only vocation in life being to minister to man's physical pleasures and wants, they are considered incapable of developing any of those higher mental qualities which would make them more worthy of consideration and also more capable of playing a useful part in life. Their intellect is thought to be of such a low order, that when a man has done anything particularly foolish or thoughtless, his friends say he has no more sense than a woman. And the women themselves, when they are reproved for any serious fault and find it difficult to make a good excuse, always end by saying, 'After all, I am only a woman!' This is always their last word, and one to which there is no possible retort.

One of the principal precepts taught in Hindu books, and on that is everywhere recognized as true, is that women should be kept in a state of dependence and subjection all their lives, and under no circumstances should they be allowed to become their own mistresses. A woman must obey her parents as long as she is unmarried and her husband and mother-in-law afterwards. Even when she becomes a widow she is not free, for her own sons become her masters and have the right to order her about!

As a natural consequence of these views, female education is altogether neglected. A young girl's mind remains totally uncultivated, though many of them have good abilities. In fact, of what use would learning or accomplishments be to women who are still in such a state of domestic degradation and servitude? All that a Hindu woman need to know is how to grind and boil rice and look after her household affairs, which are neither numerous nor difficult to manage.

Courtesans, whose business in life is to dance in the temples and at public ceremonies, and prostitutes are the only women who are allowed to learn to read, sing, or dance. It would be thought a disgrace to a respectable woman to learn to read, and even if she had learnt she would be ashamed to own it. As for dancing, it is left absolutely to courtesans; and even they never dance with men. Respectable women sometimes amuse themselves by singing when they are alone, looking after their household duties, and also on the occasions of weddings or other family festivities, but they would never dare to sing in public or before strangers.

Such feminine occupations as knitting or needlework are quire unknown to them; and moreover, any talents that they might develop in this direction would be wasted, as their clothing consists of one long piece of coloured calico, without any joint or seam in it, though most of them know how to card and spin cotton, and very few houses are without one or more spinning wheels.

When a young girl, who has been married in her early childhood, arrives at the age when she is fit to live with her husband, several ceremonies are performed. These festivities are called the consummation of the marriage. The young woman herself cannot appear, because she is, for the first time in her life, in a state of uncleanness, and for several days she is obliged to remain in a separate part of the house. But after she has gone through the usual rites of purification she returns to the family, and numberless other ceremonies are performed over her, amongst others several which are supposed to counteract the effects of witchcraft or the evil eye. She is then conducted with much pomp to her husband's house.

The Sudras, and even the Pariahs, have grand festivities when their daughters, though still unmarried, arrive at a marriageable age. The event is announced to the public with all the outward show that accompanies the most solemn ceremonies. A pandal is erected; toranams or strings of mango-leaves are hung in front of the entrance door of the house; feasts are given; much music resounds. In fact, it is a kind of advertisement or invitation to young men in want of a wife.

When a Brahmin's wife becomes pregnant, there are endless ceremonies to be performed, some indeed for each separate month. In any caste It would be considered a disgrace to the woman, and in a less degree to her parents, if her first child were born anywhere but under the paternal roof. Her mother accordingly comes and fetches her about the seventh month of her pregnancy, and she is not allowed to return to her own home till her health is entirely re-established.

When she departs, her mother is supposed to give her a new piece of cotton cloth and some more or less valuable ornaments according to her means and her caste. But in no case would the woman, to whatever caste she might belong, return from her parents to her husband's house unless her mother-in-law or some equally near relation came to fetch her. Her husband has to conform to this custom when his wife chooses to leave him and takes refuge under the paternal roof, sometimes for a mere whim, or for some very trifling cause. But in any case, even when the fault is all on her side, the husband must go and fetch her back.

## Domestic Life

These domestic quarrels and separations occur frequently, and are generally the fault of the mother-in-law, who looks upon her son's wife as a slave that has been bought and paid for. The elder woman, indeed, lives in constant dread of her daughter-in-law obtaining too much ascendancy over the husband, and by this means contriving her own emancipation; and accordingly, seizes every opportunity of breeding discord between them. This fear is, as a rule, perfectly uncalled for; for the men themselves show very little inclination to be ruled by their wives, and condescend to very little of what we call conjugal tenderness in their relations with them.

The women, on the other hand, are so thoroughly accustomed to harsh and domineering treatment from them; they would be quite annoyed if the husbands adopted a more familiar tone. I once knew a native lady who complained bitterly that her husband sometimes affected to be very devoted to her in public and allowed himself such little familiarities as are looked upon by us as marks of affection. 'Such behaviour,' said she, 'covers me with shame and confusion. I dare not show myself anywhere. Did any one ever see such bad manners amongst people of our caste? Has he become a Feringhi (European), and does he take me for one of their vile women.[1] As a rule a husband addresses his wife in terms which show how little he thinks of her. Servant, slave, etc., and other equally flattering appellations, fall quite naturally from his lips.

A woman, on the other hand, never addresses her husband except in terms of the greatest humility. She speaks to him as my master, my lord, and even sometimes my god. In her awe of him she does not venture to call him by his name; and should she forget herself in this way in a moment of anger, she would be thought a very low class of person, and would lay herself open to personal chastisement from her offended spouse. She must be just as particular in speaking of him to anyone else indeed, the Hindus are very careful never to put a woman under the necessity of mentioning her husband by name. If by chance a European, who is unacquainted with this point of etiquette, obliges her to do so, he will see her blush and hide her face behind her sari and turn away without answering, smiling .at the same time with contemptuous pity at such ignorance.

Politeness also forbids you to address a person of higher rank by his name. But if women enjoy very little consideration in private he, they are in some degree compensated by the respect which is paid to them in public. They do not, it is true, receive those insipid compliments which we have agreed to consider polite; but then, on the other hand, they are safe from the

1. It may be noted that at marriage feasts, etc., the males and females keep apart; and furthermore, the usual personal invitations to such feasts are invariably conveyed to men by men, and to women by women. —Ed.

risk of insult. **A Hindu woman can go anywhere alone, even in the most crowded places, and she need never fear the impertinent looks and jokes of idle loungers. This appears to me to be really remarkable in a country where the moral depravity of the inhabitants is carried to such lengths.** A house inhabited solely by women is a sanctuary which the most shameless libertine would not dream of violating. To touch a respectable woman even with the end of your finger would be considered highly indecorous, and a man who meets a female acquaintance in the street does not venture to stop and speak to her.

When travelling the men walk in front and the women follow some distance behind. You very rarely see the men address a word to their humble followers. If they come to a river which has to be forced the women tuck up their cloths above the hips, and in this naked state they approach near enough to their travelling companions to permit of the latter stretching out a helping hand behind them to help them to withstand the force of the current; but never would you see any one under these circumstances commit an indiscretion like that which caused Orpheus to lose his Eurydice.

I have often spent the night in one of the common resthouses, where the men and women lodging there were lying all huddled together anyhow and almost side by side; but I have never known or heard of any one disturbing the tranquillity of the night by indecent act or word. Should any person be so ill-advised as to attempt anything of the sort, the whole room would be up in arms against him in a moment, and prompt chastisement would follow the offence.

A woman's costume consists of a simple piece of cotton cloth, made all in one piece, and woven expressly for the purpose. It is from 30 to 40 feet long, and rather more than 4 feet wide. All sorts and kinds are made, in every shade and at every price, and they always have a border of a contrasting colour. The women wind part of this cloth two or three times round their waists, and it forms a sort of narrow petticoat which fall to the feet in front; it does not come so far down behind, as one of the ends of the cloth is tucked in at the waist after passing between the legs, which are thus left bare as far as, or even above, the calf. This arrangement is peculiar to Brahmin women, those of other castes arrange their draperies with more decency and modesty. The other end of the cloth covers the shoulders, head, and chest. Thus the clothing for both sexes is made without seams or sewing—an undeniable convenience, considering how often they have to bathe themselves and wash their garments; for Brahmin women have to observe the same rules of purification as the men, and are equally zealous in the performance of this duty. **The custom of women veiling their faces has never been practised in India, though it has been in use among many other Asiatic nations from time immemorial.** Here the women always go about with their faces uncovered, and in some parts of the country they also expose the upper half of their bodies.

Quiet and retired as is the life of a Hindu woman, it cannot be said to be one of complete and rigorous seclusion. Though all friendly intercourse with men is forbidden to them, still they may talk to those who come to the house as friends or acquaintances without fear of unpleasant consequences. **Eunuchs — those deplorable victims of oriental jealousy — are unknown in India, and the natives never dream of putting the virtue of their women under the care of these miserable beings.** They are not to be found even in the palace of a prince, where women are always guarded and waited on by women.

In several parts of India young girls and married

women wear a sort of little bodice under their cloth, which covers the breast, shoulders, and arms as far as the elbows; but this, I am told, is a modern innovation and borrowed from the Mahomedans. I have reason to believe that the custom of leaving all the upper part of the body uncovered as far as the waist was formerly common to both sexes in the southern parts of India. It still prevails on the Malabar coast, and in the neighboring provinces.

The custom of tattooing the arms of young girls with indelible designs of figures or flowers is very general. I have already described how this tattooing is done. When their skin is not very dark they generally ornament their faces in the same way, by putting three or four spots on the cheeks and chin. These marks produce very much the same effect as the black patches which were once the fashion with European ladies. I have already mentioned the habit which the beauties of India and Brahmin ladies observe of painting all the visible parts of their bodies with yellow saffron, and also of darkening their eyelids with antimony.

In order to make their hair more glossy and silky they frequently oil it. They part it exactly in the middle, and then roll it up behind into a sort of chignon, which is fastened behind the left ear. To make this chignon larger they often insert some tow, or else some cotton wool specially prepared for the purpose. Hindu women generally possess beautiful black hair, which is soft and straight. It is very rarely to be seen of any other colour. They are much given to wearing sweet-smelling flowers in their hair, and also ornaments of gold, none of any other metal being permissible, though they sometimes use a silver buckle to fasten the hair together at the back.

Silver ornaments may be worn on the arms, but are more frequently used to decorate the feet and ankles. It is remarkable that gold ornaments are never worn by Hindus on the feet, the reason being that it is a sacred metal, and would be thereby defiled. Some of their anklets are actual fetters, weighing as much as two or three pounds. There are special rings made for each toe, often entirely covering them.

Bracelets are sometimes made hollow, and are more than an inch in diameter. They are of different patterns, according to the country in which they are made and the caste of the person who wears them. They are worn either above the elbow or round the wrist, and are made of gold or silver, as the means of the wearer will allow. Quite poor women wear copper bracelets, and some have more than half their forearms covered with glass bangles.

Neck ornaments consist of gold or silver chains, or strings of large gold beads, pearls, or coral. In fact, beads of all kinds and of greater or less value are much in demand. Some women wear necklaces more than an inch wide, set with rubies, emeralds, and other precious stones. But to enumerate all the different kinds of ornaments worn by Hindu ladies would take a very long time. To give a single instance I could mention eighteen or twenty different kinds of ornaments that are used for the ears alone.

Even the nose is considered a suitable object for decoration. The right nostril and the division between the two nostrils are sometimes weighted with an ornament that hangs down as far as the under lip. When the wearers are at meals, they are obliged to hold up this pendant with one hand, while feeding themselves with the other. At first this strange ornament, which varies with different castes, has a hideous effect in the eyes of Europeans, but after a time, when one becomes accustomed to it, it gradually seems less unbecoming, and at last one ends by thinking it quite an ornament to the face.

It is no uncommon sight to see a woman decked out in all her jewels drawing water, grinding rice, cooking food, and attending to all the menial domestic occupations, from which even the wives of Brahmins not consider themselves exempt. It is, of course, needless to remark that all this extravagant display is very often obtained only at the sacrifice of other more useful and necessary requirements in their homes.

When a girl marries, everything that she receives from her future father-in-law, or that she takes away with her from her old home, is most clearly and distinctly set down, item by item, in a kind of legal document. All these things are her own personal property, which she takes care to claim when she becomes a widow.

## Rules of Conduct for Married Women

Nothing serves so well to illustrate the attitude and behaviour of Hindus towards their wives as the rules of conduct which are prescribed for the latter in the Padma, purana, one of their most valued books; rules which I will translate literally. They are reputed to be the work of the famous penitent Vasishta, who recommends their observance by every faithful wife. I cannot say that I altogether approve of them; some of them appear to me absurd; others there are which, from a social point of view, are harmful; all of them evidently have for their object the reduction of this interesting better half of the human race to the lowest state of subjection. It is not to be wondered at, therefore, if we find many foolish examples of Hindu superstition, which is a necessary element in every institution of the country. Order and continuity are not so conspicuous as one might desire in the ideas of the great penitent Vasishta' but I give a passage closely following the original, as a specimen of the style of writing that prevails among the Hindus:

'Give ear to me attentively, great King Dilipa! I will expound to thee how a wife attached to her husband and devoted to her duties ought to behave.

'There is no other god on earth for a woman than her husband. The most excellent of all the good works that she can do is to seek to please him by manifesting perfect obedience to him. Therein should lie her sole rule of life.

'Be her husband deformed, aged, infirm, offensive in his manners; let him also be choleric, debauched, immoral, a drunkard, a gambler; let him frequent places of ill repute, live in open sin with other women, have no affection whatever for his home; let him rave like a lunatic; let him live without honour; let him be blind, deaf, dumb, or crippled; in a word, let his defects be what they may, let his wickedness be what it may, a wife should always look upon him as her god, should lavish on him all her attention and care, paying no heed whatsoever to his character and giving him no cause whatsoever for displeasure.

'A woman is made to obey at every stage of her existence. As daughter it is to her father and mother she owes submission; as wife, to her husband, to her father-in-law, and to her mother-in-law; as widow to her sons. At no period of her life can she consider herself her own mistress.

'She must always be attentive and diligent in all her domestic duties; she should be ever watchful over her temper, never covetous of the goods of others, never quarrelsome with her neighbours, never neglectful of work without her husband's permission, and always calm in her conduct and deportment.

'Should she see anything which she is desirous of possessing, she must not seek to acquire it without the consent of her husband. If her husband receives the visit of a stranger she shall retire with bent head and shall continue her work without paying the least attention to him. She must concentrate her thoughts on her husband only, and must never look another than in the face. In acting thus she will win the praise of everybody.

'Should any man make proposals to her, and endeavour to seduce her by offering her rich clothes or jewels of great value, by the gods! let her take good care not to lend an ear to him, let her hasten to flee from him.

'If her husband laughs, she must laugh; if he be sad, she must be sad; if he weep, she must weep; if he ask questions, she must answer. Thus will she give proofs of her good disposition.

'She most take heed not to remark that another man is young, handsome, or well proportioned, and, above all, she must not speak to him. Such modest demeanour will secure for her the reputation of a faithful spouse.

'It shall even be the same with her who, seeing before her the most beautiful gods, shall regard them disdainfully and as though they were not worthy of comparison with her husband.

'A wife must eat only after her husband has had his fill. If the latter fast, she shall fast too; if he touch not food, she also shall not touch it; if he be in affliction, she shall be so too; if he be cheerful, she shall share his joy. A good wife would be less devoted to her sons or to her grandsons, or to her jewels than to her husband. **She must, on the death of her husband, allow herself to be burnt alive on the same funeral pyre; then everybody will praise her virtue.**

'She cannot lavish too much affection on her father-in-law, her mother-in-law, and her husband; and should she perceive that they are squandering all the family substance in extravagence, she would be wrong to complain and still more wrong to oppose them.

'She should always be ready to perform the various duties of her house, and to perform them diligently.

'Let her bathe every day, rubbing saffron on her body. Let her attire be clean, her eyelids tinged with antimony, and her forehead marked with red pigment. Let her hair be well combed and adorned. Thus shall she be like unto the goddess Lakshmi.

'Before her husband let her words fall softly and sweetly from her mouth; and let her devote herself to pleasing him every day more and more.

'She must be careful to sweep her house every day, to smooth the floor with a layer of cow-dung, and to decorate it with white tracery. She must keep the cooking vessels clean, and must be ready with the meals at the proper hours.

'If her husband be gone out to fetch supplies of wood, leaves, or flowers to perform the sandhya, or for any other purpose, she shall watch for the moment of his return and shall go to meet him. She shall go before him into the house, shall hand him a stool to sit down upon, and shall serve up the food prepared to his taste.

'She shall inform him in time of what is wanted in the house, and shall manage with care what he brings home.

'Prudent in her conversation, she must be careful

in conversing with gurus, sannyasis, strangers, servants, and other persons, to adopt a tone suitable to the position of each.

'In exercising in her house the authority given to her by her husband, she must do so gently and intelligently.

'She must, as in duty bound, use for the expenses of her household all the money with which her husband entrusts her, not taking any of it surreptitiously for herself or for her parents, or even, without her husband's permission, for works of charity.

'She must never meddle with the affairs of others, nor lend ear to stories of the good luck or misfortune which has befallen others.

'Never let her yield to anger or malice.

'Let her abstain from all food that is not to her husband's taste. Let her not oil her head when her husband does not oil his own.

'If her husband go away anywhere and ask her to accompany him, let her follow him; if he tell her to remain at home, let her not leave the house during his absence. Until his return she shall not bathe, or anoint her head with oil, or clean her teeth, or pare her nails; she shall eat but once a day, shall not lie down on a bed, or wear new clothes, or adorn her forehead with any of the ordinary marks.

'A woman during her menstrual period shall retire for three days to a place apart. During this time, she shall not look at anybotly, not even at her children, or at the light of the sun. On the fourth day she shall bathe, observing the proper notes for such occasions which were established before the Kali-yuga.

'A woman, when she is pregnant, must conform to all the rites prescribed for such occasions. She must then avoid the company of women of doubtful virtue and of those who have lost all their children; she must drive away from her mind all sad thoughts; she must be careful not to gaze at terrifying objects, or to listen to sad stories, or to eat anything indigestible. By observing these rules, she will have beautiful children; by neglecting them she will risk a miscarriage.

'A wife, during the absence of her husband, should strictly conform to his parting counsels. She should be heedless of her attire, and should not devote herself, under the plea of devotion to the gods, to any special acts of piety.

**'If a husband keeps two wives, the one should not amuse herself at the expense of the other, be it for good or for evil; neither should the one talk about the beauty or the ugliness of the children of the other. They must live on good terms, and must avoid addressing unpleasant and offensive remarks to each other.**

'In the presence of her husband, a wife must not look about her but must keep her eyes fixed on him, in readiness to receive his orders. When he speaks she must not interrupt him, nor speak to anybody else; when he calls her, she must leave everything and run to him.

'If he sing, she must be in ecstasy; if he dance, she must look at him with delight; if he speak of learned things, she must listen to him with admiration. In his presence indeed she ought always to be cheerful, and never show signs of sadness or discontent.

'Let her carefully avoid creating domestic squabbles on the subject of her parents, or on account of another woman whom her husband may wish to keep, or on account of any unpleasant remark which may have been addressed to her. To leave the house for reasons such as these would expose her to public ridicule, and would give cause for much evil speaking.

'If her husband flies into a passion, threatens her, abuses her grossly and even beats her unjustly, she shall answer him meekly, shall lay hold of his hands, kiss them, and beg his pardon, instead of uttering loud cries and running away from the house.

'She must not say to her husband: "Thou host hurt me, thou hast beaten me unjustly; I will no more speak to thee; hereafter the relations between ourselves will be no other than those between a father and his daughter, or a brother and his sister. I shall no more have anything to do with thy affairs; I will no longer have anything in common with thee." Such words ought never to fall from her lips.

'If any of her relatives or friends invite her to their house on the occasion of some feast or ceremony, she shall not go there without the permission of her husband, and unless accompanied by some elderly woman. She shall remain there for as short a time as possible, and on her return she shall render a faithful account to her husband of all that she has seen or heard; she shall then resume her domestic duties.

'While her husband is absent, she shall sleep with one of her female relatives, and not alone. She shall make constant inquiries after the health of her husband. She shall send constant messages to return as soon as possible, and shall offer up prayers to the gods for him.

'Let all her words and actions give public proof that she looks upon her husband as her god. Honoured by everybody, she shall thus enjoy the reputation of a faithful and virtuous spouse.

'If, in the event of her husband dying, she resolves to die with him, glorious and happy will she be in the world to which her husband will lead her after his death. But whether she dies before or with her husband, or whether she survives him, a virtuous wife may rest assured that all sorts of blessings will await her in the other world.

'A wife can enjoy no true happiness unless she attains it through her husband; it is he who gives her children; it is he who provides her with clothes and jewels; it is he who supplies her with flowers, sandalwood, saffron, and all good things.

'It is also through his wife that a husband enjoys the pleasures of this world; that is a maxim taught in all our learned books. It is through his wife that he does good works, that he acquires riches and honour, and that he succeeds in his enterprises. A man without a wife is an imperfect being.'

**These rules of conduct may seem extremely severe, yet they are faithfully observed, especially among the Brahmins.**

Among certain sects of the Vishnavite Brahmins a peculiar custom exists. A daughter-in-law is never allowed to speak to her mother-in-law. When she wishes to communicate anything to her, she does it by signs; and when the mother-in-law gives orders to the daughter-in-law, the latter answers by an inclination of the head, thereby indicating that she has understood the orders given her. She, however, at times manages to make up for this enforced silence by having recourse to spirited and expressive gestures; so much so, that her dumb repartees often cause her mother-in-law to boil with rage.

## Widowhood

The happiest death for a woman is that which overtakes her while she is still in a wedded state.

Such a death is looked upon as the reward of goodness extending back for many generations; on the other hand, the greatest misfortune that can befall a wife is to survive her husband.

Should the husband die first, as soon as he breathes his last, the widow attires herself in her best clothes and bedecks herself with all her jewels. Then, with all the signs of the deepest grief, she throws herself on his body, embracing it and uttering loud cries. She holds the corpse tightly clasped in her arms until her parents, generally silent spectators of this scene, are satisfied that this first demonstration of grief is sufficient, when they restrain her from these sad embraces. She yields to their efforts with great reluctance, and with repeated pretences of escaping out of their hands and rushing once again to the lifeless remains of her husband. Then, finding her attempts useless, she rolls on the ground like one possessed, strikes her breast violently, tears out her hair, and manifests many other signs of the deepest despair. Now, are these noisy professions of grief and affliction to be attributed to an excess of conjugal affection, to real sorrow? The answer will appear rather perplexing, when we remark that it is the general custom to act in this manner, and that all these demonstrations are previously arranged as a part of the ceremonies of mourning.

After the first outbursts of grief, she rises, and, assuming a more composed lock, approaches her husband's body. Then in one continuous strain, which would be hardly possible under real affliction, she apostrophizes her husband in a long series of questions, of which I give a summary as follows:

'Why hast thou forsaken me? What wrong have I done thee, that thou should thus leave me in the prime of my life? Had I not for thee all the fondness of a faithful wife? Have I not always been virtuous and pure? Have I not borne thee handsome children? Who will bring them up? Who will take care of them hereafter? Was I not diligent in all the duties of the household? Did I not sweep the house every day, and did I not make the floor smooth and clean? Did I not ornament the floor with white tracery? Did I not cook good food for thee? Didst thou find grit in the rice that I prepared for thee? Did I not serve up to thee food such as thou lovest, well seasoned with garlic, mustard, pepper, cinnamon, and other spices? Did I not forestall thee in all thy wants and wishes? What didst thou lack whilst I was with thee? Who will take care of me hereafter?'

And so on. At the end of each sentence uttered in a plaintive chanting tone, she pauses to give free vent to her sobs and shrieks, which are also uttered in a kind of rhythm. The women that stand around join her in her lamentations, chanting in chorus with her. Afterwards, she addresses the gods, hurling against them torrents of blasphemies and imprecations. She accuses them openly of injustice in thus depriving her of her protector. This scene lasts till her eloquence becomes exhausted, or till her lungs are wearied out and she is no longer capable of giving utterance to her lamentations. She then retires to take rest for a while, and to prepare some new phrases against the time when the body is being prepared for the funeral pyre.

The more vehement the expression of a woman's grief, the more eloquent and demonstrative her phrases, the more apparently genuine her contortions on such occasions, so much the more is she esteemed a woman of intelligence and education. The young women who are present pay the most minute attention to all that she says or does; and if they observe anything particularly striking in her flights of rhetoric, in her attitudes, or in any of her efforts to excite the attention of the spectators, they carefully treasure it in their memory, to be made use of should a similar misfortune ever happen to themselves. If a wife who was really afflicted by the loss of her husband confined herself to shedding real tears and uttering real sobs, she would only be thoroughly despised and considered an idiot.

The parents of a young widow once complained to me of her stupidity as follows: 'So foolish is she that, on the death of her husband, she did not utter a single word; she did nothing but cry, without saying anything.' The Hebrews also, on the death of friends and relatives, made a great parade of all the external signs of sorrow. They cried, rent their garments, beat their breasts, tore out their hair or beards, or else had them cut, and even inflicted cuts on their bodies.

In several parts of India, as formerly among the Greeks and Romans professional women mourners may be hired. When called in to attend the obsequies, these women arrive with dishevelled hair and only half clothed, wearing their scanty garments in a disordered fashion. Collecting in a group round the deceased, they commence by setting up in unison the most doleful cries, at the same time beating their breasts in measured time. They weep, sob, and shriek in turns. Then addressing themselves to the deceased, each, in succession, eulogizes his virtues and good qualities. Anon they apostrophize him, vehemently remonstrating with him for quitting life so soon. Finally, they point out to him, in the plainest possible terms, that he could not have committed a more foolish act. In discharging these duties, which are a curious mixture of tragedy and comedy, they take turn and turn about, and their affected sorrow lasts until the corpse is removed. As soon as the obsequies are over, they receive their wages and their faces, which were so lugubrious a few moments before, once more assume their wonted calmness.

Widows, who in the learned tongue are called Vidhava, a word akin to the Latin Vidua, are held in much less respect than other women; and when they happen to have no children, they are generally looked upon with the utmost scorn. The very fact of meeting a widow is calculated to bring ill-luck. They are called Moonda, a reproachful term which means 'shorn-head': because every widow is supposed to have her hair cut off. This rule, however, is not everywhere followed, especially among the Sudras. When women quarrel, this opprobrious term, Moonda, is generally the first abusive word that passes.

A widow has to be in mourning till her death. The signs of mourning are as follows:—

She is expected to have her head shorn once a month; she is not allowed to chew betel; she is no longer permitted to wear jewels, with the exception of one very plain ornament round her neck; she must wear coloured clothes no longer, only pure white ones; she must not put saffron her face or body, or mark her forehead.[1] Furthermore, she is forbidden to take part in any amusement or to attend family festivities, such as marriage feasts, the ceremony of Upanayana, and other; for her very presence would be considered an evil omen.

A few days after the death of her husband, a widow's house is invaded by female friends and relatives, who begin by eating a meal prepared for them. After this they surround the widow and exhort her to bear her miserable lot with fortitude. One after another they

---

1. She must, however, smear her forehead with sacred ashes if she is a widow of the Saiva sect, and mark her forehead with red powder if a Vaishnava. —Ed.

take her in their arms, shed tears with her, and end by pushing her violently to the ground. They next join together in lamenting her widowhood, and finally make her sit on a small stool. Then, one of her nearest female relatives, having previously muttered some religious formulae, cuts the thread of the Tali, the gold ornament which every married woman in India wears round Iter neck. The barber is called in, and her head is clean shaved. This double ceremony sinks her instantly into the despised and hated class of widows. During the whole time that these curious and mournful rites are being performed, the unfortunate victim is making the whole house resound with her cries of woe, cursing her sad lot a thousand times.

The thread of the Tali must be cut, not untied. This practice has given rise to a very common curse; two women when quarrelling never forgct to say to eacli other: 'May you have your Tali cut!' which means, 'May you become a widow!'

The signs of sorrow manifested by a Hindu lady who loses her husband are of so exaggerated a description that one cannot help doubting their perfect sincerity; yet it is impossible that any Hindu widow could face the sad future awaiting her with tearless eyes. Doomed to perpetual widowhood, cast out of society, stamped with the seal of contumely, she has no consolation whatever, except may be the recollection of hardships that she has had to endure during her married life.

I do not refer here to those unfortunate girls of five or six years of age, who, married to Brahmins of over sixty, very often become widows before they attain the age of puberty. Fortunately, their youth and inexpedience prevent their brooding over the sad condition in which they have been placed by such inhuman and iniquitous prejudices. But think of the numberless young widows in the prime of life and strength. How do they bear up against this cruel expulsion from the society of their fellow-creatures? The answer is better than one would be inclined to believe. The fact is they must perforce be resigned to their fate; and however despised a widow may be, there is this consolation, that one who remarries is a hundred times more so, for she is shunned absolutely by every honest and respectable person. Thus there are few widows who would not look upon proposals to remarry as a downright insult, though in this respect they are seldom put to the test. Even an old gouty Brahmin, as poor as Irus, would feel indignant at the very suggestion of marrying a widow, though she were rich and endowed with all the charms of youth and beauty.

One result of this prejudice, which is firmly and irrevocably established in India, is that **the country abounds with widows, especially among the Brahmins. Among this caste shorn-heads are to be seen everywhere.** Of course a certain corruption of morals is the inevitable result of such a state of things, but it is not pushed to such an extent as might be expected. The natural modesty of Hindu women, the way in which they are brought up, their ordinary chaste and circumspect demeanour , the calmness of their passions, all these go a great way towards providing as it were strong barriers against the attacks of the licentious, who, whatever may be said to the contrary by ill-informed writers, do not succeed in winning over women of the better class so easily as in many other countries where the lawful union of the two sexes is not beset with so many obstacles.

Besides, even if we refuse to believe that young widows possess in themselves sufficient strength of will to resist seduction, there are many other obstacles beyond their own control, which also serve as so many bulwarks to their modesty. Chief among such obstacles must be reckoned the diligent watchfulness exercised over them by their parents; the severity of the conventions which forbid any kind of familiar intercourse between men and women; the very heavy punishments which follow even the most trivial lapses; and, finally, the mere disgrace, which in India, above all the countries of the world, entails the most tremendous penalties on the person detected in an indiscretion.

## Suttee or Widow-burning

Although the ancient and barbarous custom of Suttee which imposes the duty on widows of sacrificing themselves voluntarily on the funeral pyre of their husbands has not been expressly abolished now, it is much more rare nowadays than formerly, especially in the southern parts of the Peninsula. In the North of India and in the provinces bordering on the Ganges, however, women are only too frequently seen offering themselves as victims of this horrid superstition, and, either through motives of vanity or through a spirit of blind enthusiasm, giving themselves up to a death which is as cruel as it is foolish.

The Mahomedan rulers never tolerated this horrible practice in the provinces subject to them; but, notwithstanding their prohibition, fanatics have more than once succeeded in bribing the subordinate representatives of authority to give permission to commit the deed in violation of the laws of humanity and common sense.

The European Power which nowadays exercises its sway all over the country has tried, by all possible means of persuasion, to put an end altogether to this barbarous custom; but its efforts have been only partially successful, and, generally speaking, it has been obliged to shut its eyes to this dreadful practice, since any attempt to remedy it by force would have exposed it to dangerous opposition.

Nobody is a greater admirer than myself of the wise spirit that animates this enlightened and liberal Government in manifesting to its Hindu subjects such a full and perfect tolerance in the practice of their civil and religious usages; and nobody is more fully alive than I am to the dangers and difficulties that an open defiance of these prejudices, which are looked upon as sacred and inviolable, would give rise to. But does the abominable custom in question form part of Hindu institutions? Are there any rules which prescribe its observance by certain castes? All the information which I have been able to gather on the subject tends to make me believe that there are no such rules. **The infamous practice, although encouraged by the impostors who regulate religious worship, is nowhere prescribed in an imperative manner in the Hindu books.**

It is left entirely to the free will and pleasure of the victims who thus sacrifice themselves. No blame and no discredit are attached nowadays to the wife whose own honest judgement suggests that she ought not to be in such a hurry to rejoin in the other world the husband who so often made her wretched in this. It would be quite possible, therefore, by the display of firmness, combined with prudence, to strike, without any considerable danger, at the very root of this shocking practice. Certainly it reflects discredit on the Government which tolerates it and manifests no great indignation with regard to it. During recent years, owing to the number of these abominable sacrifices being on the increase, especially in the Bengal

Presidency and in the districts bordering on the Ganges, the Government has thought fit to interfere to check this inconceivable mania by adopting at least persuasive measures. It has, therefore, directed the different magistrates scattered about the country to examine very minutely all the circumstances attending the custom of Suttee (this is the name by which these barbarous sacnfices are known), and never to sanction it except after exhausting all the means to oppose it which prudence may suggest to them.

No woman can, therefore, now devote herself to a death of this kind without the sanction of the magistracy. When such permission is sought, the magistrates call the victim to appear before them and question her carefully to assure themselves that her resolution is entirely voluntary, and that no outside influence has been brought to bear upon her. They then try by every possible exhortation and counsel to induce her to give up her horrible design. But should the widow remain firm in her resolution, they leave her mistress of her own fate.

The Protestant missionaries, when they first arrived in the country, expressed a just horror of these abominable sacrifices, and strove to diminish their number; but being ill acquainted with the character of the Hindus and with their devoted attachment to custom, they used brusque and violent measures which only resulted in augmenting the evil. I have seen the lists of widows who had sacrificed themselves on the funeral pyre of their husbands from 1810 (the period at which the missionaries commenced their labours) up to the year 1820; and I have remarked that the number of these victims progressively increased every year during that space of time. In 1817 there were 706 Suttees in the Bengal Presidency.

It is true that this insane practice is much more In

vogue on the banks of the Ganges than anywhere else. In the southern parts of the Peninsula of India Suttees are seldom seen. I am convinced that in the Madras Presidency, which numbers at least thirty millions of inhabitants, not thirty widows allow themselves to be thus burnt during a year.

It was principally in the noble caste of Rajahs that the Suttee originated. It was looked upon as a highly honourable proof of wifely attachment and love which enhanced the glory of the families of these wretched victims of blind zeal. Should a widow, by reason of a natural fondness for life or through lack of courage, endeavour to avoid the honour of being burnt alive, on the funeral pyre of her deceased husband, she was considered to be offering a gross insult to his memory.

I was once able to thoroughly convince myself of the influence which this false point of honour still exercises over the minds of fanatical Hindus, and at the same time to discern that this act of devotion to which these wretched victims sacrificed themselves is not always the result of their own free will and resolution. The poligar or prince of Cangoondy in the Carnatic having died, neither entreaties nor threats were spared to induce his widow to allow herself to be burnt alive with him. It was urged that this honourable custom had been observed for a long time past in the family, and that it would be a great pity, indeed, to allow it to fall into disuse. The funeral ceremonies were delayed from day to day in the hope that the widow would at last make up her mind to prefer a glorious death to a remnant of life spent in contempt and opprobrium. It was a fruitless attempt! The obstinate princess fumed a deaf ear to all the pressing entreaties of her relatives; and ultimately the deceased was obliged to depart alone to the other world.

It must, however, be confessed that some widows commit this folly readily enough, spurred on as they are by the thought of the wretchedness of widowhood, by vanity, by the hope of acquiring notoriety, perhaps also by a genuine feeling of enthusiasm. It should be remembered that they are awarded boundless honours, and are even deified after death. Vows are made and prayers addressed to them, and their intercession is sought in times of sickness and adversity. Such remnants of their bodies as have not been entirely consumed by the fire are most devoutly gathered together, and on the spot where they have sacrificed themselves small monumental pyramids are erected to transmit to posterity the memory of these brave victims of conjugal affection—a tribute all the more conspicuous, because the erection of tombs is almost unknown among the Hindus.[1] In a word, women who have had the courage to deliver themselves so heroically to the flames are numbered among the divinities, and crowds of devotees may be seen coming in from all sides to offer them sacrifices and to invoke their protection.

To these inducements of vain and empty glory—sufficient of themselves to make a deep impression on a feeble mind—must be added the entreaties of relatives, who, if they perceive the slightest indication on the part of the widow to offer up her life, spare no means in order to convince her and force her to a final determination. At times they go so far as to administer drugs, which so far deprive her of her senses that under their influence she yields to their wishes. This inhuman and abominable method of wheedling a

1. In some old Hindu houses, even to this day, may be seen, impressed with turmeric paste on the walls, the marks of the hands of women who underwent suttee. —Ed.

consent out of the unhappy woman is in their opinion justified, because her tragic end would bring great honour and glory to the whole of their family.

Some authors have maintained that this detestable practice originated primarily either from the jealousy of husbands, or rather, perhaps, from their fear that their discontented wives might seek to get rid of them by poison. As for myself, I have been unable, either in the writings of Hindu authors, or in my free and familiar intercourse with many persons well versed in the manners and customs of the country, to discover any justification for either of these two theories. And surely the lot of a wife, even when she is doomed to suffer wrong at the hands of a cruel and immoral husband, is far preferable to that of a widow, to whom all hope of a re-marriage under happier conditions is forbidden. It is hardly likely, indeed, that Hindu women would go to the length of committing a crime which must render their lot much worse than before! At the same time I am by no means inclined to attribute these voluntary sacrifices to an excess of conjugal affection. We should, for instance, be greatly mistaken were we to allow ourselves to be deceived by the noisy lamentations which wives are accustomed to raise on the death of their husbands, and which are no more than rank hypocrisy. During the long period of my stay in India, I do not recall two Hindu marriages characterized by a union of hearts and displaying true and mutual attachment.[1]

1. It is impossible to regard the conclusion here drawn as anything but greatly exaggerated. The influence of women, ignorant, and uneducated as they are, is in many Hindu households exceedingly strong, and it is an error to picture them as the mere slaves of the men, though the ascendency of the latter is still a marked feature of Hindu sociology. —Ed.

When a woman, after mature deliberation, has once declared that she desires to be burnt alive with her deceased husband, her decision is considered irrevocable. She cannot afterwards retract; and should she refuse to proceed of her own free will to the funeral pyre, she would be dragged to it by force. The Brahmins who regulate all the proceedings of the tragedy, and also her relatives, come by turns to congratulate her on her heroic decision and on the immortal glory which she is about to acquire by such a death-a death which will exalt her to the dignity of the gods. All possible means which fanaticism and superstition can suggest are brought to bear upon her in order to keep up her courage, to exalt her enthusiasm, and to excite her imagination. When, at last, the fatal hour draws nigh, the victim is adorned with rare elegance: she is clothed in her richest apparel, is bcdcckcd with all her jewels, and is thus led to the funeral pyre.

It is impossible for me to describe the finishing scenes of this dreadful ceremony without feelings of distress. But, in the meantime, I must solicit the indulgence of my readers for a short digression which is not wholly disconnected with my subject. When a husband has several lawful wives, as often happens in the caste of the Rajahs, the wives sometimes dispute as to who shall have the honour of accompanying their common husband to the funeral pyre, and the Brahmins who preside at the ceremony determine which shall have the preference. Here is an instance to the point extracted from the Mahabharata, one of their most esteemed books:

'King Pandu had retired into the jungles with his two wives, there to devote himself to acts of penance. At the same time a curse was imposed upon him, which doomed him to instant death should he dare to have intercourse with either of them. The passion which he felt for the younger of his wives, who was extremely beautiful, overcame all fear of death; and, in spite of the fact that for several days she continued to represent to him the dire results that must necessarily follow his incontinency, he yielded at last to the violence of his love; and immediately the curse fell upon him. After his death, it was necessary to decide which of his two wives should follow him to the funeral pyre, and there arose a sharp altercation between them as to who should enjoy this honour.

'The elder of the two spoke first, and addressing the assembly of Brahmins who had gathered together for the purpose, she urged that the fact of her being the first wife placed her above the second. She should; therefore, be given the preference. Besides, she urged, her companion had children who were still young, and who required their mother's personal care and attention for their bringing up. The custom of Suttee does not require widows who have young children to burn themselves with the body of their husbands; they are even forbidden to do so.

'The second wife admitted the seniority of the first but she maintained that she alone, having been the immediate cause of the sad death of their common husband in allowing him to defy the curse which doomed him to perish, was thereby entitled to the honour of being burnt with him. "As regards the bringing up of my children," she added, addressing the other wife, "are they not yours just as much as they are mine? Do not they too call you Mother? And by your age and experience are you not better fitted than I to attend to their bringing up?"

In spite of the eloquence of the younger wife, it was at last, unanimously agreed by the judges that the first wife should have the preference, a decision at which the latter lady was greatly delighted.

Most Sudras, as well as Hindus of the Siva sect, bury their dead instead of burning them, and there are several instances of wives having been buried alive with their deceased husbands. But the ceremonies in either case are nearly the same. I will relate here two incidents which took place at no great distance from the place where I was living, and which will give a good idea of what these deplorable scenes of mad fanaticism are like:

In 1794, in a village of the Tanjore district called Pudupettah, there died a man of some importance belonging to the Komatty (Vaisya) caste. His wife, aged about thirty years, announced her intention of accompanying her deceased husband to the funeral pyre. The news having rapidly spread abroad, a large concourse of people flocked together from all quarters to witness the spectacle. When everything was ready for the ceremony, and the widow had been richly clothed and adorned, the bearers stepped forward to remove the body of the deceased, which was placed in a sort of shrine, ornamented with costly stuffs, garlands of flowers, green foliage, etc., the corpse being seated in it with crossed legs, covered with jewels and clothed in the richest attire, and the mouth filled with betel. Immediately after the funeral car followed the widow, borne in a richly decorated palanvuin. On the way to the burning-ground she was escorted by an immense crowd of eager sightseers lifting their hands towards her in token of admiration, and rending the air with cries of joy. She was looked upon as already transferred to the paradise of Indra, and they seemed to envy her happy lot.

While the funeral procession moved slowly along, the spectators, especially the women, tried to draw near to her to congratulate her on her good fortune, at the same time expecting that, in virtue of the gift of prescience which such a meritorious attachment must confer upon her, she would be pleased to predict the happy things that might befall them here below. With gracious and amiable mien she declared to one that she would long enjoy the favours of fortune; to another, that she would be the mother of numerous children who would prosper in the world; to a third, that she would live long and happily with a husband who would love and cherish her; to a fourth, that her family was destined to attain much honour and dignity; and so forth. She then distributed among them leaves of betel; and the extraordinary eagerness with which these were received clearly proved that great value was attached to them as relics. Beaming with joy, these women then withdrew, each in the full hope that the promised blessings of wealth and happiness would be showered on her and hers.

During the whole procession, which was a very long one, the widow preserved a calm demeanour. Her looks were serene, even smiling;[1] but when she reached the fatal place where she was to yield up her life in so ghastly a manner, it was observed that her firmness suddenly gave way. Plunged, as it were, in gloomy thought, she seemed to pay no attention whatever to

1. Several travellers have said, and I am inclined to believe it, that they force upon these wretched victims of superstition a kind of drink, which confuses the mind and prevents them from forming a correct notion of the dreadful torture to which they are being led. This beverage, they say, consists of a decoction of saffron. It is known that dried saffron pistils (*Crocus sativus*), taken in large quantities, cause violent and convulsive laughter, sometimes terminating in death.

what was passing around her. Her looks became wildly fixed upon the pyre. Her face grew deadly pale. Her very limbs were in a convulsive tremor. Her drawn features and haggard face betrayed the fright that had seized her, while a sudden weakening of her senses betokened that she was ready to faint away.

The Brahmins who conducted the ceremony, and also her near relatives, ran quickly to her, endeavouring to keep up her courage and to revive her drooping spirits. All was of no effect. The unfortunate woman, bewildered and distracted, turned a deaf ear to all their exhortations and preserved a deep silence.

She was then made to leave the palanquin, and as she was scarcely able to walk, her people helped her to drag herself to a pond near the pyre. She plunged into the water with all her clothes and ornaments on, and was immediately afterwards led to the pyre, on which the body of her husband was already laid. The pyre was surrounded by Brahmins, each with a lighted torch in one hand and a bowl of ghee in the other. Her relatives and friends, several of whom were armed with muskets, swords, and other weapons, stood closely round in a double line, and seemed to await impatiently the end of this shocking tragedy. This armed force, they told me, was intended not only to intimidate the unhappy victim in case the terror of her approaching death might induce her to run away, but also to overawe any persons who might be moved by a natural feeling of compassion and sympathy, and so tempted to prevent the accomplishment of the homicidal sacrifice.

At length, the purohita Brahmin gave the fatal signal. The poor widow was instantly divested of all her jewels, and dragged, more dead than alive, to the pyre. There she was obliged, according to custom, to walk three times round the pyre, two of her nearest relatives supporting her by the arms. She accomplished the first round with tottering steps; during the second her strength wholly forsook her, and she fainted away in the arms of her conductors, who were obliged to complete the ceremony by dragging her through the third round. Then, at last, senseless and unconscious, she was cast upon the corpse of her husband. At that moment the air resounded with noisy acclamations. The Brahmins, emptying the contents of their vessels on the dry wood, applied their torches, and in the twinkling of an eye the whole pyre was ablaze. Three times was the unfortunate woman called by her name. But, alas! she made no answer.

The last king of Tanjore, who died in 1801, left behind him four lawful wives. The Brahmins decided that two of these should be burnt with the body of their husband, and selected the couple that should have the preference. It would have been an everlasting shame to them and the grossest insult to the memory of the deceased had they hesitated to accept this singular honour. Being fully convinced, moreover, that no means would be spared to induce them to sacrifice themselves either willingly or unwillingly, they made a virtue of necessity and seemed perfectly ready to yield to the terrible lot which awaited them.

The necessary preparations for the obsequies were completed in a single day. Three or four leagues from the royal residence a square pit of no great depth, and about 12 to 15 feet square, was excavated. Within it was erected a pyramid of sandalwood, resting on a kind of scaffolding of the same wood. The posts which supported it were so arranged that they could easily be removed, and would thereby cause the whole structure to collapse suddenly. At the four corners of the pit were placed huge brass jars filled with ghee, to be thrown on the wood in order to hasten combustion.

The following was the order of the procession as it wended its way to the pyre. It was headed by a large force of armed soldiers. Then followed a crowd of musicians, chiefly trumpeters, who made the air ring with the dismal sound of their instruments. Next came the king's body borne in a splendid open palanquin, accompanied by his guru, his principal officers, and his nearest relatives, who were all on foot and wore no turbans in token of mourning. Among them was also a large number of Brahmins. Then came the two victims, each borne on a richly decorated palanquin. They were loaded, rather than decked, with jewels. Several ranks of soldiers surrounded them to preserve order and to keep back the great crowds that flocked in from every side. The two queens were accompanied by some of their favourite women, with whom they occasionally conversed. Then followed relatives of both wives, to whom the victims had made valuable presents before leaving the palace. An innumerable multitude of Brahmins and persons of all castes followed in the rear.

On reaching the spot where their untimely fate awaited them, the victims were required to perform the ablutions and other ceremonies proper on such occasions; and they went through the whole of them without hesitation and without the least sign of fear. When, however, it came to walking round the pyre, it was observed that their features underwent a sudden change. Their strength seemed well-nigh to forsake them in spite of their obvious efforts to suppress their natural feelings.

During this interval the body of the king had been placed on the top of the pyramid of sandalwood. The two queens, still wearing their rich attire and ornaments, were next compelled to ascend the pyre. Lying down beside the body of the deceased prince, one on the right and the other on the left, they joined hands across the corpse. The officiating Brahmins then recited in a loud tone several mantrams, sprinkled the pyre with or holy water, and emptied the jars of ghee over the wood, setting fire to it at the same moment. This was done on one side by the nearest relative of the king, on another by his guru, on others by leading Brahmins. The flames quickly spread, and the props being removed, the whole structure collapsed, and in its fall must have crushed to death the two unfortunate victims. Thereupon all the spectators shouted aloud for joy. The unhappy women's relatives standing around the pyre then called to them several times by name, and it is said that, issuing from amidst the flames, the word *Yen*? (What?) was heard distinctly pronounced. A ridiculous illusion, no doubt, of minds blinded by fanaticism; for it could never be believed that the unfortunate victims were at that moment in a condition to hear and to speak.

Two days after, when the fire was completely extinguished, they removed from amidst the ashes the remnants of the bones that had not been entirely consumed, and put them into copper urns, which were carefully sealed with the signet of the new king. Some time afterwards, thirty Brahmim were selected to party these relics to Kahi (Benares) and to throw them into the sacred waters of the Ganges. It was arranged that, on their return from that holy city, they should receive valuable presents, upon producing authenticated certificates to the effect that they had really accomplished the journey, and had faithfully executed the task entrusted to them. A portion of the bones was, however, reserved for the following purpose:—they were reduced to powder, mixed with some boiled rice, and eaten by twelve Brahmins. This revolting and unnatural act had for its object the expiation of the sins of the deceased—sins which, according to the popular opinion, were transmitted to the bodies of the persons who ate the ashes, and were tempted by money to overcome their repugnance for such disgusting food. At the same time, it is believed that the filthy lucre thus earned can never be attended with much advantage to the recipients. Amidst the ashes, too, were picked up small pieces of melted gold, the remains of the ornaments worn by the princesses.

Presents were given to the Brahmins who presided at the obsequies, and to those who had honoured the ceremonies with their presence. To the king's guru was given an elephant. The three palanquins which had served to carry the corpse of the king and the two victims to the pyre were given away to the three leading Brahmins. The presents distributed among the other Brahmins consisted of cloths and of money amounting to nearly twenty-five thousand rupees. Several bags of small coin were also scattered among the crowds on the roadside as the funeral procession was on its way to the pyre. Finally, twelve houses were built and presented to the twelve Brahmins who had the courage to swallow the powdered bones of the deceased, and by that means to take upon themselves all their sins.

A few days after the funeral the new king made a pilgrimage to a temple a few leagues distant from his capital. He there took a bath in a sacred tank, and was thus purified of all the uncleanness that he had contracted during the various ceremonies of mourning. On this occasion also presents were given to the Brahmins and to the poor of other castes.

On the spot where the deceased king and his two unhappy companions had been consumed a circular mausoleum was erected, about 12 feet in diameter, surmounted by a dome. The reigning prince visits it from time to time, prostrates himself humbly before the tombs, and offers sacrifices to the manes of his predecessor and to those of his worthy and saintly spouses. Crowds of devotees also repair thither to offer up vows and sacrifices to the new divinities, and to implore their help and protection In the vanous troubles of life. In the year 1802 I heard accounts of a great number of so-called miracles performed through their intercession.

It is only after long and serious reflection on the many eccentricities and inconsistencies of the human mind that one can look without astonishment upon the deplorable scenes of which a few of the main features have just been described. It is indeed unaccountable how these Brahmins, who are so scrupulous and attach so much importance to the life of the most insignificant insect, and whose feelings are excited to pity and indignation at the very sight of a cow being slaughtered, can, with such savage cold-bloodedness and wicked satisfaction, look upon so many weak and innocent human beings, incited by hypocritical and barbarous inducements, being led with affected resignation to a punishment so cruel and undeserved. I leave to others the task of explaining these inconceivable contradictions, if, that is to say, it is possible to assign any reasons for such superstitious fanaticism, whose characteristic feature is to suppress all natural and rational sentiment.

# 8

# Property and Inheritance

When a Brahmin finds that he has no male issue, whether by reason of the barrenness of his wife or through the untimely death of all the sons he has had by her, he is permitted, nay, bound, by the rules of his caste to procure a son by means of adoption, in order that he, at least fictitiously, fulfil the great *debt to his ancestors*, namely, the propagation of a direct line of posterity. Although marriage constitutes the perfect state of man, this perfection is nevertheless deficient when a man does not leave a son behind him to perform his obsequies; and this defect alone, according to Hindu writers, is quite sufficient to deprive him of happiness in the next world.

This notion prevails so strongly among the Hindus that I have known barren women not only consenting to their husbands taking other wives, but even earnesly advising them to do so, and helping them in their quest. There is not one of them, however, who is not fully alive to the annoyances and discomforts to which she is exposing herself by thus introducing as her rival another woman, who must naturally, by her youthfulness and fecundity, soon become an object more beloved than herself by their common husband.

It has already been said that polygamy is tolerated among the ruling classes only; and when we find other women besides the lawful wife living in the families of private individuals of high caste, especially among the Brahmins, either they are living there, as already stated, with the consent of the lawful wife, or else they are merely hired concubines. However, a husband who has had no male issue by his wife, being fully alive to the unpleasant consequences arising from a second marriage, almost invariably prefers to have recourse to the system of adoption.

## Adoption

A Brahmin generally chooses from among his own relatives the child that he wishes to legally adopt as his son; and if perchance he finds nobody in his own family worthy of the honour, he applies to some poor fellow of his own caste who is burdened with many children. So long as the adoptive father is rich, he is sure not to meet with a refusal.[1]

The adopted son renounces wholly and for ever all his claims to the property and succession of his natural father, and acquires the sole right to the heritage of his father by adoption. The latter is bound to being him up, to feed him, and to treat him as his own son; to have the ceremony of Upanayana, or the triple cord, formed for him, and to see him married. The adopted son, in his turn, is obliged to take care of his adoptive father in his old age and in sickness, just as if he were his natural father, and to preside at his obsequies. On the death of his adoptive father he enters into full possession of his inheritance—assets as well as liabilities. Should there be any property left, he enjoys

1. The strict rule is that the natural mother of the adopted son must be a marriageable relative of the adoptive father. Nowadays however, a Hindu is allowed to adopt any boy provided he be of the same caste.

—Ed.

it; but if, on the other hand, there are debts, he is bound to pay them. He is, moreover, by his adoption admitted into the *gothram* or family stock of the adopter, and is considered to have left that in which he was born.

It is only natural that, in a country where everything is performed with so much solemnity, an event of such importance should be attended with great ceremonies. The following are a few of the most important:

The first thing to be done, as might be expected, is to select an auspicious day. They then adorn the portals of the house with toranams (garlands of leaves) and put up a temporary pandal. The festivities open with a sacrifice to Vigneshwara and the nine planets; and the other preparatory ceremonies already described are likewise gone through. The adoptive father and mother take their seats on the small dais raised in the middle of the pandal. The mother of the child is presented with a new garment and with a hundred or a hundred and fifty pieces of silver as her nursing wages. Then, with her son in her arms, she approaches the adoptive father, who asks her in a loud and distinct voice, in the presence of the whole assembly, whether she delivers over her child to be brought up. To this she answers in the same tone that she does deliver the child to be brought up. This utterance bears a comprehensive meaning. It is a formal intimation that she gives up her son not as a slave who is sold, but to be looked upon and treated as a child of the family into which he is about to enter. Generally a boy is adopted when he is fit for the Upanayana ceremony; and both ceremonies are performed simultaneously.

They next bring in a dish filled with water into which some powdered saffron has been thrown. The Purohita blesses this mixture by uttering mantrams and performing certain ceremonies. Then the mother of the child hands the dish to the adoptive father, and at the same time, invoking fire to bear witness to the deed, she thrice repeats the following words:—'I give up this child to you; I have no more right over him.' The adoptive father then takes the child, and seating him on his knees, addresses the relatives present as follows:—'This child has been given to me, after fire has been invoked as a witness of the gift: and I, by this saffron water which I will now drink, promise to bring him up as my own son. From this moment he is entitled to the enjoyment of all his rights over my property, sharing, at the same time, the burden of my debts.'

After these words, he and his wife pour out a small quantity of the saffron water in the hollow of their right hands and drink it up. They then pour a little into the hand of the adopted child and make him also drink it, adding: 'We have admitted this child into our gothram, and we incorporate him into it.'

It is the mother of the child who plays the most important part in this ceremony; the father being present there only as a mere formality. The reason is that in India all the children are supposed to belong by right to the mother. Should a married man, or a man living in concubinage, happen to separate himself, for some cause or other, from his wife or concubine, the latter would be entitled to take away all their children, without the possibility of the slightest opposition on the part of the father.

This is the last event in the ceremony of adoption. At the age of six months Hindu children are solemnly invested with the girdle or waist-string, to which, six or seven years later, is attached a small piece of cloth intended to cover the private parts. Should the adopted child be already wearing this string, they break it and supply him with a fresh one; but should he have none, they at once begin to invest him with it with all the usual ceremonies. It is by this act that his incorporation into the gothram or by the clan of his new father is sanctified.

The festivities, as usual, wind up with a repest and the distribution of betel and presents to the guests. The use of saffron water on this occasion accounts for the fact that an adopted child generally receives the appellation of the *'saffron-water child'* of such a one, a term which, it should be added, has nothing offensive about it.

The ceremony of adoption is almost identical among the Sudras and the Brahmins, with this one difference, that among the Sudras the adoptive father and his wife pour the saffron water on to the feet of the adopted child with one hand, and catch and drink it with the other. An adoptive father may choose not only a child of tender years, but even an adult, should that suit his taste and purpose better.

Persons whose means do not permit them to perform the ceremony of adoption with so much pomp and circumstance, have a simpler and more expeditious mode of performing it. It is deemed sufficient if the mother of the child and the adopted father invoke fire to witness their mutual bargain. Dwellers on the banks of the Ganges need simply call to witness, in such a case, the waters of that sacred river. In whatever fashion the ceremony of adoption be performed, the adopted child no longer retains any right either to the property or the heritage of his natural father, nor can he be held answerable for the debts which the latter may leave at his death.

The adoption of girls is rare, although instances of it are not wanting.

The work from which I have extracted these particulars relating to adoption also furnishes a solution of some of the difficulties that arise in certain cases with regard to the division of property. The little that it contains on the subject seems to me sufficiently interesting. We find there laid down the case of a man who, after adopting a son, has subsequently had contrary to his expectation, six children by his legitimate wife, four boys and two girls. The father and two of the boys die; one of the girls and the adopted son are married; there remain two boys and a girl who are unmarried; and provision must also be made for the subsistence of the widow. The question is, how in such a case, ought the property devolved by succession to be divided?

The answer given is to the following effect:—*First,* the amount necessary for the funeral expenses of the deceased father ought to be set apart, and the money required for the marriage of the three unmarried children ought to be placed in the hands of a trustworthy executor.

*Secondly,* the property that remains after these amounts have been set aside shall be divided into six shares. The adopted son shall take for himself a share and a half, and the remainder shall be equally divided among the brothers and the mother. Should the mother be dead, the property is divided only into five shares and a half, unless all the brothers, with common accord, relinquish on behalf of their unmarried sister, with the object of providing her with jewels, that part of the inheritance which would have fallen to the mother, who is perfectly at liberty, before her death, to dispose of this share in favour of her daughters, without the slightest objection being raised thereto by the sons. If she has not done so, the brothers alone, independently of the sisters, set apart a reasonable amount for a decent funeral, and divide equally among themselves whatever remains of her property.

This decision of the Brahmins, while in accordance with the general custom of the country, which entitles sons to equal shares of the paternal property, and excludes the daughters by merely granting them a dowry, departs from it in so far as mothers have no share whatever in the property of their husbands, their sons being conjointly bound to provide for their maintenance during their lives. Should a man, by reason of the barrenness of his first wife, marry a second, and the latter have a son, all the father's property belongs exclusively to this son; the first wife, after the death of the common husband, can claim nothing from the estate: but the son is bound to provide for her maintenance in a decent manner, and to meet all the expenses of her funeral. If the first wife does not choose to continue to live with the second, the relatives meet together and arrange for the allotment to her of a sufficient income according to her condition in life.

A certain man, finding that his first wife was barren, married a second, then a third; but it so happened that these two, like the first, were barren also, and the man, therefore, died without issue. The deceased had an elder and a younger brother, besides several cousins, sons of his paternal uncles. None of these, however, had been living with him. They had long before divided their family property, and each was living separately. The question arises, who ought to be regarded as the rightful heir of the deceased? The answer given is, that the rightful heir is the younger brother, because, being the youngest of the family, to him, according to the custom of the country, belongs the right of presiding at the obsequies—a right which carries with it the heirship. He thereby becomes the head of the family and the master of the house. It is he, therefore, who is obliged to provide for the maintenance of the three widows left by his brother. Should anyone of the three choose to return to her father's house, she would be at perfect liberty to do so, and even to take away with her all the jewels given to her by her deceased husband.

Furthermore, the family council would determine upon the allowance which her brother-in-law, as the heir to her husband's property, would be bound to make to her to enable her to subsist. If she elected to remain in her deceased husband's house and to have an establishment of her own there, she could not be refused permission; but in that case her brother-in-law would not be under the necessity of assigning her any considerable income; and she would be obliged, at her own risk, to supplement such income with alms. It is well known, however, that such a mode of living has nothing disgraceful about it, since begging is one of the six privileges of the Brahmins. Finally, the brother-in-law is bound to bear all the expenses of the funerals of the three widows should they happen to die before him.

If the deceased husband be the youngest of the brothers, the elder brother would then become the sole inheritor, and on him would devolve all the rights and obligations connected with the heritage. In the absence of brothers, the nearest relative on the father's side becomes sole heir.

In cases where doubts arise as to the transmission of the property, the relatives are called in to decide the matter according to the prevailing custom of the country, or as justice may dictate to them. But very often the partiality prevailing in these family councils turns the scale in favour of the one who is able to purchase the support of the others. The collusions, intrigues, and acts of injustice practised on such occasions are without number, and tend to throw discredit on an institution which owes its origin to truly patriarchal principles.

It may be observed from what has been already said that the right of inheritance and the duty of presiding at the obsequies are inseparable one from the other. When therefore, a wealthy man dies without direct descendants, a crowd of remote relatives appear to dispute with each other the honour of conducting the funeral rites. The contest is occasionally so tumultuous and prolonged that the body of the deceased is in a state of complete putrefaction before a definite settlement of these many pretensions is arrived at. On the other hand, on the death of a needy man burdened with debts, the survivors take every possible care to disprove near relationship.

## Succession

There is another rule regarding succession among the Hindus, which will, doubtless, appear to us highly incompatible with the true principles of justice.

A father dies, leaving several male children, who, from carelessness or some other cause, do not trouble themselves about the legal partition of the paternal inheritance. One of them, by his industry and diligence acquires wealth, while the others, leading a debauched and idle life, become seriously involved in debt. These, after a life of dissipation and wandering from place to place, learn at last that their brother, by his industry and good conduct, has amassed a brilliant fortune. They at once hasten to him and call upon him to share with them the property he has acquired by the sweat of his brow, and moreover render him jointly responsible for the debts resulting from their disorderly habits. The creditors themselves, too, have the right to recover from him by law what is due to them from his brothers. More than this, should brothers, who neglect to divide their family property, die before such partition has been actually effected, the same community of property and of debts holds good among their children, and it descends from generation to generation so long as the property remains undivided. It is by no means rare to see cousins of the third and fourth degree engaged in lawsuits concerning rights of succession dating back from time immemorial. Neither is it an uncommon thing to see the richer members of a family coerced by the poorer ones to admit the latter to a share of their hard-earned fortune while these burden them with their poverty and their debts.

In a country where nearly everything is regulated by custom, and where the usages are as many and as various as the different provinces, these lawsuits in connection with the partition of properties are an endless source of chicanery. There is one advantage however, from a social point of view, arising from this singular system, that it gives such relatives as are liable to be affected by the law of partition the right to watch over each other's conduct, and to restrain the debauchery and extravagance of those whose misconduct might involve them all in distress.

The appointment of a single heir among the male children of a family is a thing unknown in India. The brothers divide the paternal property equally, to the exclusion of the sisters, who have no share whatever in it. The father does not even possess the privilege of training one of his sons more generously than the rest.[1]

1. There is nothing, however, to prevent the father from allotting the whole or any portion of his self-acquired, as opposed to his ancestral property, to anyone of his sons, or disposing of it in any other way he pleases. —Ed.

The Hindus cannot conceive how a father could despoil several of his children in order to enrich one of them in particular; and they are simply astound when they are told that this custom prevails in many countries of Europe. But what makes us still more ridiculous in their eyes is that this favoured heir should very often be, not the son who distinguishes himself above the rest by his filial devotion, his virtues, and his talents, but one who by chance happens to be the first-horn, and who may perhaps be the most foolish and vicious of the whole family.

# 9

# Economic Condition

India has always been considered a most wealthy and opulent country, more favoured by nature than any other in the world, a land literally flowing with milk and honey, where the soil yields all that is necessary for the existence of its happy people almost without cultivation. The great wealth accumulated by a few of its native princes, the large fortunes so rapidly acquired by many Europeans, its valuable diamond mines, the quality and quantity of its pearls, the abundance of its spices and scented woods, the fertility of its soil, and at one time, the unrivalled superiority of its various manufactures: all these have caused admiration and wonder from time immemorial. One would naturally suppose that a nation which could supply so many luxuries would surpass all others in wealth.

This estimation of the wealth of India has been commonly accepted in Europe up to the present day; and those who, after visiting the country and obtaining exact and authentic information about the real condition of its inhabitants, have dared to affirm that India is the poorest and most wretched of all the civilized countries of the world, have simply not been believed. Many people in Europe, after reading what various authors have to say about India's manufactures and about the factories which turn out the delicate muslins, fine cloths, and beautiful coloured cottons, etc., which are so much admired all the world over, have supposed that the establishments producing such magnificent stuffs must have supplied models for those which are to be found at Manchester, Birmingham, Lyons, and other cities in Europe.

## Poverty Reigns

Well, the truth is (and most people are still unaware of the fact) all the beautiful fabrics are manufactured in wretched thatched huts built of mud, twenty to thirty feet long by seven or eight feet broad. In such a work-room the weaver stretches his frame, squats on the ground, and quietly plies his shuttle, surrounded by his family, his cow, and his fowls. The instruments he makes use of are, extremely primitive, and his whole stock in trade could easily be carried about by one man. Such is, in very truth, an exact picture of an Indian factory. As to the manufacturer himself his poverty corresponds to the simplicity of his workshop. There are in India two or three large classes whose only profession is that of weaving. The individuals comprising these classes are, for the most part, very poor, and are even desitute of the necessary means for working on their own account. Those who deal in the products of their industry have to go to them, money in hand, and after bargaining with them as to the price, quality, and quantity of the goods required, are obliged to pay them in advance. The weavers then go and buy the cotton and other necessaries with which to begin work. Their employers have to supervise their work and keep a sharp look-out lest they decamp with the money. Especially if the advances happen to be in any way considerable.

As regards the condition of the Hindus generally, I think that the following account may make things plain. It is based on a long acquaintance with the inhabitants of a large tract of country. Still, the casual observer may find fault with it if he judges it by what he has noticed in large towns, more especially on the coast. There, at least most of the natives possess houses of more or less value which they can dispose of if necessary, an advantage not shared by the rural classes. Besides, the towns are the rendezvous of the rich and industrious, and of those who intend to become so by fair means or foul, so it is not surprising to find a higher standard of comfort prevailing there. It is from experience of the masses of the population that I have been able to present this sketch of the different degrees of poverty or wealth amongst the people.

I should class the inhabitants of the Indian Peninsula in the following manner. The first and lowest class may be said to be composed of all those whose property is below the value of £5 sterling. This class appears to me to comprise nine-twentieths, or perhaps even a half, of the entire population. It includes most, of the Pariah class and nearly all the Chucklers or leather workers; and these together form at least a quarter of the population. To them must be added a considerable portion of the Sudras all the poorest members of the other castes, and the multitude of vagrants, beggars, and impostors who are to be met with everywhere.

Most of the natives of this class hire themselves out as agricultural labourers, and are required to do the hardest manual labour for the smallest possible wage. In the places where they are paid in coin, they receive only just enough to buy the coarsest of food. Their wage varies from twelve to twenty rupees a year, according to locality. They are better paid along the coast. With this amount they are obliged to feed and clothe themselves. In some places they are paid half in coin and half in grain, or else they get their keep and over and above that receive from four to eight rupees a year.

Some of the younger members of this class hire themselves out without wages, on condition that, after working faithfully for seven or eight years, their master will provide them with a wife of their own caste and defray all nuptial expenses. Married servants who are fed by their masters carry home their daily rations. This food is supposed to be sufficient for the wants of one person, or, to quote the native saying, 'to be enough to fill the belly'; but they have to share it with their wives and children, who also have to work and thus add to the provision. When they are in actual want, as often happens, they go and seek for food in the woods or on the banks of the rivers and tanks, where they find leaves, shrubs, roots, and herbs. These they boil, as often as not without even salt or any kind of condiment; and this primitive food forms, for the greater part of the year, the most substantial part of their meals. Clumps of bamboo abound in the woods, and its shoots form, for two or three months of the year, a great resource to the poor people who live near the places where It grows.

As soon as the children belonging to the class living in a state of servitude have reached the age of eight or nine, they join the same master who employs their father, the boys looking after the cattle and the girls sweeping, collecting the dung, grinding the grain, etc.

The well-to-do cultivators always employ men of this class; and, in order to keep them in perpetual bondage, they lend them money either on the occasion of a marriage or for other purposes. The poor wretches find themselves, on account of their small wages, quite unable to pay back the capital thus advanced, and in many cases even the interest, which soon exceeds the original loan, and are therefore reduced to the necessity of working, with their wives and children, until the end of their days. From the time this happens their masters look upon them as actual slaves, and refuse to grant them freedom until they have repaid both the principal and interest of the sum which they or their fathers borrowed perhaps twenty or thirty years before.

## Wage-earners

Those natives belonging to this class who are in a state of independence live by various industries. The greater number are carriers and coolies, or casual agricultural labourers in receipt of a small daily wage. The last-named are generally paid in grain, but when they receive money their wage varies from a penny to two pence a day, according to the district. However, they only work in proportion to their wage, and, whatever the task, a good European workman would, in most cases, do as much as four natives. But as the independent labourer is often out of work, and as the smallness of his wage or his improvidence does not allow of his putting by anything, his lot is no better, perhaps even worse, than that of his brother in slavery, and he is often in absolute want. Most of them have nothing of their own, or at the best only a wretched hut twelve or fifteen feet long by five or six broad, and from four to five feet high, which is full of insects and vermin and exhales an awful stench. Into this hovel they, with their wives and children, crowd higgledy-piggledy.

Their belongings consist of a few earthen vessels; one or two sickles, and the rags in which they stand. Those who are a little less poverty-stricken have a brass *lota* for drinking purposes, and another out of which they eat, a hoe, two or three sickles, a few silver bracelets, worth three or four rupees, belonging to the women, and two or three cows. Many Hindus own a few oxen and cattle, which are supposed to be the most valuable part of their property; in fact their degree of comfort is judged, more or less, by the number of these valuable animals which they possess. As soon as a Hindu has acquired a sufficient sum of money, he spends it as a rule on a pair of draught oxen and a cow. But the intrinsic value of these animals is small. The country oxen are, as a rule, stunted, weak, and incapable of enduring much fatigue. Four or five rupees is their outside value. These people are agriculturists and farm Government lands, on which they pay a tax varying from two to twenty-five shillings. Such, in truth, is the state of misery in which half the population of India passes its life.

## Upper Strata

I place in the second class all those whose property ranges from £5 to £25 sterling. This class, I should say, includes about six-twentieths of the entire population and is composed chiefly of Sudras. Those included in it are mostly agriculturists on their own account. Their poverty does not allow of their hiring others to work under them. They cultivate Government land, and pay a yearly tax from one to twenty pagodas, according to the value of the land. They sometimes require as many as three ploughs. Their entire property consists of a few cattle, a few small gold and silver trinkets, one or two copper vessels for drinking and a few more for eating purposes, and some iron farm implements. They live in thatched mud huts, rather more commodious and a little less filthy than those previously described. Weavers, barbers, washermen, and other workmen who cater for the wants of the public may also, for the most part, be included under this head.

The cultivators of this second class, although better off than those of the first, find it hard to make both ends meet even in the best seasons. They are obliged to sell at least half their crop beforehand at low prices, to enable them to pay their taxes, and the miserly usurers who profit by their poverty leave them hardly sufficient for the wants of their family during six or eight months of the year; if fact, many of them have only food enough to last four months. Some never even gather the harvest from the field they have sown, for as soon as the corn has formed in the ear they are day by day driven by hunger to cut off some of the green ears, with which they make a sort of soup. Consequently, by harvest time there is nothing but stubble left to gather, and to save themselves the trouble of cutting it they merely turn three or four cows into the field to graze. If by dint of self-denial they allow their crops to grow up intact, it is not they who benefit by them, for as soon as the grain has been threshed the money-lenders step in and take their due, and afterwards come those who lent them grain when they had nothing to eat, and demand payment of the original quantity plus twenty-five per cent interest; that is to say, a man borrowing twenty measures of corn has to repay twenty-five.

The grain takes about four months to ripen, and this-period is called the time of prosperity, or Sukha Kala. It is about the only season in the year when the poor have enough of even the coarsest kinds of food, consisting of various sorts of small pulse, much the same as that which is used in Europe to fatten pigs and fowls, and in India to feed horses. Hence the well-known proverb, 'Do not approach a Pariah during he Sukha Kala season, nor go within range of an ox during the Divuligai or Divali. Its celebration takes place in November, when the country is clothed in verdure. It is also called Deepavali. This is because both become unmanageaote then, from an unwonted state of prosperity.

In most provinces those who cultivate rice do not eat it, but sell it to pay their taxes. During the four months the Sukha Kala lasts, they live on the pulse and millet which they cultivate in their fields. During the rest of the year their only daily sustenance, in almost all cases, consists of a plateful of millet, seasoned with a little pounded salt and chillies. When after paying their taxes and debts they come to the end of their store of grain, supposing there has been any remnant, they are reduced to living from hand to mouth. Some of them borrow grain, which they promise to repay with interest after the next harvest; others explore the woods and the banks of rivers and tanks in search of leaves, bamboo shoots, wild fruits, roots, and other substances which help them to exist, or rather, prevent them from dying of hunger.

Thus for about three months of the year almost three-quarters of the inhabitants of the Peninsula are on the verge of starvation. In the south these three months are July, August, and September; and the saying is that those who have grain to eat then are as happy as princes. The scarcity begins to be less felt by October, for then several of the smaller species of grain are ready for harvesting, and the rains have brought out in the fields quantities of edible herbs, which suffice to allay the pangs of hunger.

Nor are men alone exposed to want during a great part of the year; domestic animals have to bear the same privations. Most families own cattle, and each hamlet possesses considerable herds which can only graze within the narrow limits assigned to them. The small amount of straw which the crops produce does not last long, and the animals are then reduced to nibbling at the few plants scattered here and there in the barren fields. During the three or four months when the sun is especially hot, all vegetable life is scorched up, and the wretched animals can scarcely find enough fodder for their daily sustenance. They may then be seen searching for clayey soil, impregnated with salt, which they proceed to lick with avidity, and that, together with the water they drink, comprises almost all their food. This is why, throughout the hot weather, they are mere skeletons and can hardly stand. I have often, at this time of the year, been in villages where there were more than a hundred cows, and yet sometimes I could not procure up much as half a measure of milk for my breakfast.[1]

Thirdly, I may reckon together those Hindus whose property varies in value from, £25 to £50 sterling. They comprise about one-tenth, of the population, and are principally agricultural. They farm lands large enough to require two, three, or even four ploughs, and their rental is from ten to thirty pagodas. This class lives in fairly comfortable circumstances, and most of the people are able to lay in sufficient grain for the whole year after meeting their taxes. Many of them have even more than they require for their own consumption, and are able to sell or lend the surplus to those in their village who have run short of food. We have seen on what outrageous terms these loans are effected. The well-to-do amongst them employ as servants one or more of those who come under the first class. They

1. The fact is, the slaughter of cattle being forbidden by the Hindu religion, large herds of old and useless animals are maintained which deprive the healthy and useful animals of their proper share of food.

—Ed.

have larger, more comfortable, and slightly cleaner thatched dwellings than the others, and they and their wives have at least a change of raiment, which is more than rare in the two preceding classes. But even their possessions are far from betokening wealth; they consist of a few gold and silver trinkets, some copper vessels and a great many earthenware pots piled up in a corner of the house; and besides these they own ploughs and other farming implements, some cotton-spinning wheels, and various primitive tools of small value. Cattle are their chief source of wealth. As to their comfort it is at best a relative term, for the contraction of debts is a custom common to all the Hindus we have hitherto spoken of. Most of them are debtors as well as creditors, but their assets seldom exceed their liabilities, and they are in no greater hurry to pay their creditors than their debtors are to pay them.

Besides tilling the land, many Hindus of this class keep goats and sheep, and their young, added to the one or two calves they are able to sell from time to time, bring in a small income. Two or three milch-kine and one or two buffaloes supply them with a certain quantity of butter for four or five months in the year, of which they make good use. The sale of pigs, fowls, eggs, etc., also contributes to their support, and even enables them to save for future needs, or to meet matrimonial expenses. Nevertheless, after a bad harvest numbers of these cultivators are reduced to the same state of want as those below them, and are obliged to have recourse to the same shifts.

In times of distress the Hindus have only their wonderful constitutions to fall back upon. Accustomed from their earliest infancy to privations of every kind, they are able to keep body and soul together on the smallest pittance of food. A pound a day of millet flour, boiled in water and reduced to a thin gruel, is enough to prevent a family of five or six persons from dying of hunger. With no food besides this gruel and water the majority of the natives manage to keep hale and hearty for months together. Furthermore, they possess the no less valuable faculty of sleeping at will. An idle Hindu invariably goes to sleep, and so does the man who has nothing to eat. If the homely proverb 'he who sleeps dines' can be taken literally, the Hindus certainly find consolation in it in times of scarcity.

The fourth class comprises those whose property varies in value from £50 to £100 sterling, and I should say it forms three-fortieths of the population. These people live in comfort, being chiefly Brahmins or well-to-do Sudras. They all keep servants belonging to the lowest class to aid them in cultivation. Besides this, some of them are rich enough to embark on commercial speculations in connexion with grain or other commodities, while others lend small sums of money at high interest. This class provides the villages with their Sudra headmen, and these men are at the same time the largest holders of Government lands. They also exercise in their villages the functions of collectors of revenue, petty magistrates, and public arbitrators. As they are usually held responsible by Government for the due payment of all taxes levied on their villages, they are obliged to conciliate the villagers, to prevent their secretly migrating elsewhere, which would mean the non-cultivation of the land, and consequent inability on their part to furnish the revenue due to the State. These men have quite a patriarchal authority in their villages, but those who attempt to abuse their power are soon confronted with deserted homesteads, waste lands, and ruin staring them in the face.

A striking example of this happened when a new and detested system was established by the creation of Muttadars, or hereditary farmers of revenue, which caused the ruin of most of the districts where it was enforced. No sooner were these Muttadars raised to what they considered an exalted position than they began to give themselves great airs and tried to carry things with a high hand. Men who had formerly been in a low position, or in obscurity, now indulged in horses, palanquins, trumpeters, and peons; in fact they gave themselves up, without any justification, to such pomp and splendour as the native delights in. As the crops produced by the lands whose revenue they had farmed could not possibly defray the cost of this expensive mode of life, they had recourse to a system of blackmailing to increase their incomes. The consequence of this arbitrary and unprecedented behaviour was the flight of their victims, who left the lands uncultivated. The final result was the ruin of the Muttadars.

The Sudra headmen of the villages are usually sensible, polite, and well-educated men. Most of them know how to read and write. Although they have the failings, common to all natives, of cunning and deceit, they are far from being proud, intolerant, and haughty like the Brahmins. By nature they are gentle, shy, and insinuating, and they behave with marked respect and submission towards their superiors. Towards their equals they are polite and complaisant, and towards their inferiors affable and condescending. In fact, they know well how to adapt themselves to their surroundings.

## The Most Respectable

The class occupying the fourth rung on the ladder which I have used to describe the various degrees of civilization in India is the one which, to my mind, is the most respectable and the most interesting. It is this class, chiefly, which influences public opinion amongst the Sudras, and maintains order throughout all ranks of society. One can tell at a glance that the natives of this class are all well-to-do and independent. As a rule, they are a more polite, better-educated, and better mannered race, and they look happier and more contented than the members of the other three classes. Most of the latter have thin, drawn faces, a heavy carriage, coarse minds, low manners, and a melancholy, and stupid appearance, all of which bespeak plainly enough the privations and sufferings of their lot. Just the reverse is noticeable amongst the natives of the fourth class.

In the fifth class I should include all those whose property varies in value from £100 to £200 sterling. It comprises about one-thirtieth of the whole population, and is composed chiefly of Brahmins or Vaisyas, and of the wealthiest among the Sudras. Agriculture, trading in grain or other commodities, money-lending on such usurious terms as twenty-five, thirty, and even fifty per cen such are the different forms of livelihood they thrive upon. Their clean appearance betokens comfort, and most of them live in tiled houses. They are also careful to conform to the rules of polite society. They perform daily ablutions, and their houses are kept ceremoniously clean by smearing the floors regularly with cow's dung. To appear more worthy in the eyes of the pubic the Sudras of this class usually abstain from all animal food, and, in imitation of the Brahmins, live entirely on milk and vegetables.

The natives belonging to this and the following classes constitute what may be called the gentle folk of Hindu society, and some of the faults which characterize the Brahmins, such as pride and intolerance, are noticeable in them. Those amongst them who are agriculturists do not till their own lands, unless very urgent works are necessary; they employ servants from the lowest class to do it for them.

The sixth class may be said to comprise individuals whose tangible property varies in value from £200 to £500 sterling, and it represents, I should say, about one-fiftieth of the population. Brahmins form quite half of this class, and the remainder is made up of the best representatives of the other castes. Their wealth consists partly of maniams, or hereditary lands exempt from taxation, partly of gardens planted with arecas, coconut and other fruit trees, and partly also of trinkets, money, and cattle. Besides this, they speculate in the same way as the natives of the preceding class. Some of them occupy the position of assistant collectors of public revenue, magistrates' clerks, and other posts in the public service. They are proud of the comfort they enjoy, and their arrogance is unrivalled.

Properties valued at more than £500 sterling are rarely to be met with in the villages. Natives who possess more than this live in Agraharams, or Brahmin villages, in towns, or in district boroughs, where they have more opportunity for commercial speculation and for furthering their ambitious schemes to procure posts under Government.

The seventh class may be said to be composed of those whose property varies in value from £500 to £1,000 sterling. I should say only one-hundredth part of the population belongs to this class, and at least half of them are Brahmins. The rest are the wealthiest among the Vaisyas and Sudras.

The eighth class includes those whose properties range in value from £1,000 to £2,000 sterling, and it comprises two-hundredths of the population. It is almost entirely composed of Brahmins, with a small percentage of Vaisyas and Sudras, who live in towns and capitals where they devote themselves almost entirely to commerce or are employed under Government. Properties valued at five to ten thousand pagodas are extremely rare, even in the towns, and are confined to the richest merchants and to those who have held for a long time the highest offices under Government. Still, there are some which exceed even ten thousand pagodas, but these are so few that they can easily be counted in each province.

Speaking generally, the following proportion may be established between properties in India and properties in Great Britain:

| **India** | **Great Britain** |
|---|---|
| Those of £500 to £ 1,000 | correspond to £5,000 to £10,000 |
| £1,000 to £2,000 | £ 10,000 to £20,000 |
| £2,000 to £5,000 | £20,000 to £50,000 |
| £5,000 to £10,000 | £50,000 to £100,000 |
| £10,000 and above | £100,000 and above. |

But a difference, more essential even than that between the characters of the two nations, is observable in connexion with properties. In Europe they are preserved intact, and are, with but few exceptions, transmitted from father to son generation after generation. In India, on the other hand, there is nothing permanent about them, especially among the Sudras. The latter make their money either by their industry, talents, or cunning, and once it is made they do not know how to spend it wisely. Realizing that, do what they may, they will necessarily be looked down upon as parvenus, they soon acquire all the characteristic vices of the rich. In time they become as proud and arrogant as any Brahmin, and their sole object seems to be to win a name for lordly extravagance. Money becomes no object to them, so long as it procures the gratification of their vanity. Immense fortunes seldom survive the second generation, owing to the manner in which the sons foolishly squander the wealth laboriously gained by their fathers. It is not uncommon to find sons who have inherited millions from their father end their days in beggary.

A native's house is besieged as soon as he is known to be a wealthy man, and this not only by his own relatives, but also by the indigent of his caste, and by a horde of parasites of every description, including poverty-stricken Brahmins, religious mendicants, ballad-mongers, and low flatterers, who feed his vanity by writing odes to his honour and glory, and by lavishing on him praise of the most fulsome nature. All these dependants stick to the wealthy native like leeches, fighting with each other as to who shall carry off the largest share of the prize, and never releasing their hold on their victim until they have stripped him of everything.

## Under the European Rule

As to the general condition of the natives now, as compared with what it was thirty years ago, the question arises, has it improved or has it deteriorated? I have occasionally heard this important question discussed amongst thoughtful and well-informed Europeans, but they could rarely agree with one another on the subject. Some maintained that the masses are enjoying greater prosperity than they ever did before; others that they have never been in a more wretched state; while a few hold that things are practically where they were before the change of government took place. But it is evidently absurd to suppose that a well-meaning, just, and equitable Government, which has succeeded one that was arbitrary, oppressive, and tyrannical, has produced no amelioration in the condition of the people, whatever peculiarities of character and disposition the latter may possess, and however great an obstacle their institutions may be to the philanthropic endeavours of the new regime to make their lives more bearable, if not actually happier.

This common-sense view of the case is borne out by my own observations. To me it seems undeniable that the condition of the people has improved in many important directions at least, and I have found that the most sensible natives themselves admit it. I do not mean to imply that the lowest classes in the land are better off, for in some provinces close observation will reveal an increase of misery; but where that is the case, I attribute it to causes beyond the power of any Government to prevent or put an end to; and further, I think that, given the same causes, the misery would have been more acute under the old regime.

Of these causes the chief one is the rapid increase of the population. Judging by my own personal knowledge of the poorer Christian populations in Mysore and in the districts of Baramahi and Coimbatore, I should say that they have increased by twenty-five percent in the last twenty-five years. During this period Southern India has been free from the wars and other decimating calamities which had been dealing havoc almost uninterruptedly for centuries before.

Some modern political economists have held that a progressive increase in the population is one of the most unequivocal signs of a country's prosperity and wealth. In Europe this argument may be logical enough, but I do not think that it can be applied to India; in fact, I am persuaded that as the population increases, so in proportion do want and misery. For this theory the economists to hold good in all respects the resources and industries of the inhabitants ought to develop equally rapidly; but in a country where the inhabitants are notoriously apathetic and indolent, where customs and institutions are so many insurountable barriers against a better order of things, and where it is more or less a sacred duty to let things remain as they are, I have every reason to feel convinced that a considerable increase in the population should be looked upon as a calamity rather than as a blessing.

It is in the nature of things that, in times of peace and tranquillity, when the protection of a just Government is afforded both to person and property, an increase in the population of India should take place at an alarming rate, since it is an indisputable fact that no women in the world are more fruitful than the women of India, and nowhere else is the propagation of the human race so much encouraged. In fact, a Hindu only marries to have children, and the more he has the richer and the happier he feels.

All over India it is enough for a woman to know how to cook, pound rice, and give birth to children. These three things are expected of her, especially the last, but nothing more. It would even appear displeasing if she aspired to anything else. No Hindu would ever dream of complaining that his family was too large, however poor he might be, or however numerous his children. A barren woman is made to feel that there can be no worse fate, and barrenness in a wife is the most terrible curse that can possibly fall on a family.

Another serious cause of the poverty of modern India is the decrease in the demand for hand labour, resulting from the introduction of machinery and the spread of manufactures with improved methods in Europe. Indeed, **Europe no longer depends on India for anything, having learnt to beat the Hindus on their own ground, even in their most characteristic industries and manufactures, for which from time immemorial we were dependent on them. In fact, the roles have been reversed, and this revolution threatens to ruin India completely.**

Just before returning to Europe I travelled through some of the manufacturing districts, and nothing could equal the state of desolation prevailing in them. All the work-rooms were closed, and hundreds of thousands of the inhabitants, comprising the weaver caste, were dying of hunger; for through the prejudices of the country they could not adopt another profession without dishonouring themselves. I found countless widows and other women out of work, and consequently destitute, who used formerly to maintain their families by cotton-spinning. Wherever I went the same melancholy picture confronted me.

**This collapse in the cotton industry has indirectly affected trade in all its branches by stopping the circulation of money**, and the cultivators can no longer reckon on the manufacturers who, in the days of their prosperity, were wont to buy up their surplus grain, and even to lend them money when they were in arrears with their taxes. This has led the cultivators to the hard necessity of relinquishing their grain to, and thus becoming the prey of, remorseless usurers.

Such is the deplorable condition into which the poor Hindus have sunk; and **it grows worse daily, thanks to the much-vaunted improvements in machinery which some nations glory in. Ah! if only the inventors of these industrial developments could hear the curses which this multitude of poor Hindus never tire of heaping upon them!** If only, like me, they had seen the frightful misery which has overtaken whole provinces, owing entirely to them and their inventive genius, they would no doubt, unless they were entirely wanting in human pity, bitterly repent having carried their pernicious innovations so far, and having thereby enriched a handful of men at the expense of millions of poor people, to whom the very name of their competitors has become odious as the sole cause of their utter destitution!

And let no one venture to assert that the unfortunate Hindus can, if they choose, find a recompense in the fertility of their soil. The sight of vast plains lying fallow and waste may induce the superficial observer to accuse the natives of indolence or the Government of mismanagement, but he is not aware that the greater part, if not the whole, of these vast plains are sterile, bare, and incapable of cultivation through want of water during most of the year. In Southern India, at the present time, there are few lands in the neighbourhood of wells, tanks, and rivers which are not under cultivation, even on the summits of the highest hills; and if by any chance a few fields still lie unreclaimed, it is due to the hopeless sterility of the soil, which, even in the best seasons, would never repay the labourer for his trouble, or else because, to yield any profit at all, they would require more capital and more courage than most of the people possess.

It is to my mind, a vain hope to suppose that we can really very much improve the condition of the Hindus, or raise their circumstances of life to the level prevailing in Europe. The efforts of a Government which is humane and generous, as well as just, may succeed up to a certain point in lessening some of their hardships; but as long as it is in the nature of the Hindus .to cling to their civil and religious institutions, to their old customs and habits, they must remain what they have always been, for there are so many insurmountable obstacles in the path of progress and to the attainment of a new order of things better calculated to bring them happiness. They will continue to grovel in poverty as long as their physical and intellectual faculties continue in the same groove.

Therefore, to make a new race of the Hindus, one would have to begin by undermining the very foundations of their civilization, religion, and polity, and by turning them into atheists and barbarians. Having accomplished this terrible upheaval, we might then perhaps offer ourselves to them as lawgivers and religious teachers. But even then our task would be only half accomplished. After dragging them out of the depths of barbarism, anarchy, and atheism into which we had plunged them, and after giving them new laws, a new polity, and a new religion, we should still have to give them new natures and different inclinations. Otherwise we should run the risk of seeing them soon relapse into their former state, which would be worse, if anything, than before.

Let our theoretical philanthropists, with their mistaken and superficial notions concerning the genius and character of the Hindus and the varied and multitudinous social links that bind them together, exclaim as much as they please in their unreflecting emhusiasm, that nothing has been done for the physical and spiritual improvement of the race. My reply is, 'Why do you expound your shallow theories in

Europe? Come and study the question on the spot; make personal inquiry into the manners and customs of the people; realize for yourselves whether all possible means have been tried with a view to gaining this desirable end. And then, but not till then, make up your minds on the question.'

Since our European ways, manners, and customs, so utterly different from theirs, do not allow of our winning their confidence, at least let us continue to earn their respect and admiration by humane examples of compassion, generosity, and well-doing. Let us leave them their cherished laws and prejudices, since no human effort will persuade them to give them up, even in their own interests, and **let us not risk making the gentlest and most submissive people in the world furious and indomitable by thwarting them.** Let us take care lest we bring about, by some hasty or imprudent course of action, catastrophes which would reduce the country to a state of anarchy, desolation, and ultimate ruin, for, in my humble opinion, the day when the Government attempts to interfere with any of the more important religious and civil usages of the Hindus will be the last of its existence as a political power.

# 10

# Language and Literature

The epistolary style of the Brahmins and of Hindus in general is in many respects so different from ours, that a few specimens may not be uninteresting to many of my readers.

## Letter to an Inferior

'They, the Brahmin Soobayah, to him the Brahmin Lakshmana, who possesses all kinds of good qualities, who is graced with all the virtues, who is true to his word, who, by the services he renders to his relations and friends, resembles the Chintamani;[1] Asirvadam (Blessings).

'The year Kilasa, the fourth day of the month of Phalguna, I am at Dharmapuri and in good health. I am very anxious to have news of thee.

'As soon as this letter reaches thee, thou must go to that most excellent and most virtuous Brahmin Anantayah, and, prostrating thyself at full length at his feet, thou must offer him my most humble respects.

'And then, without delay, thou must present thyself before the *chetty* (merchant) Rangappa, and declare to him frankly on my behalf that if he will now place in

1. This is a mythical stone which is supposed to procure every blessing for those who possess it.

thy hands the three thousand rupees which he owes me, with the interest due thereon at thirty per cent. I will forget all that has passed, and the matter shall be finally settled.' But if, on the contrary, he makes excuses and puts off the payment of the said amount, including interest, tell him that I am acquainted with certain efficacious means of teaching him that no person shall with impunity break his word with a Brahmin such as I am. This is all I have to say to thee. Asirvadam!'

## Letter to an Equal

'To them, the lords, the lords Ramayah,[1] who possess all those good qualities and virtues which render a man esteemed; who are worthy of all the favours which the gods can bestow; who are the particular favourites of the goddess Lakshmi; who arc great as Mount Meru; who possess a perfect knowledge of the Yajur-Veda; they, the Brahmin Soobayah. Namaskaram!

'The year Durmati, the fifteenth of the month Vaishaka, I and all the members of my family being in the enjoyment of good health. I shall learn with great pleasure that it is the same with you; and I trust you will let me know in detail all the matters which give you joy and contentment.

'The twenty-second of the above-mentioned month being a day on which all the good omens are combined we have selected it for the commencement of the marriage festivities of my daughter Vijaya-Lakshmi. I beg you will be good enough to be present here before that day, and to bring with you all the members of

1. A superior and even an equal is always addressed in the plural, both in speaking and writing. This is a rule invariably observed among the well-bred.

your household without excepting any. I beg that you will place yourself at the head of the ceremony, and that you will be pleased to conduct it.[1]

'Lastly, if there is anything in which I can be of service to you, I request you will be pleased to let me know. Namaskaram!'

## Letter to a Superior

'To them, the lords, the Brahmin lords, the great Brahmins Lakshmanayah, who are endowed with every virtue; who are great as Mount Meru; who possess a perfect knowledge of the four Vedas; who, by the splendour of their good works, shine forth like the sun; whose renown is known throughout the fourteen worlds, and who are highly praised therein; I, Krishnayah, their humble servant and slave, keeping myself at a respectful distance from them, with both hands joined, my mouth closed, my eyes cast down, my head bent—I wait in this humble posture, until they may vouchsafe to cast their eyes on one who is nothing in their presence. After obtaining their leave, approaching them with fear and respect, and prostrating myself on the ground at their feet, which are in reality *tamarasa* (lotus) flowers; after saluting those feet with profound respect and kissing them, I address to the following humble supplication.

'The year Vikary, the twentieth of the month Pushya. I your most humble slave, whom you have deigned to look upon as some chattel, having received with both hands the letter which your excellency humbled yourself by writing to me, having kissed it and put it on my head, I afterwards read it with all possible attention and care. Your excellency may rest

1. This is an expression used merely out of politeness in the case of everyone who is invited under similar circumstances.

assured that I will execute punctually the orders contained in it, without departing from them by the breadth of a grain of sesamum. The business mentioned in the letter has already been fairly begun, and I hope that by the efficacy of your excellency's benediction it will soon terminate to your excellency's honour and advantage. As soon as it is finished, I your most humble servant and slave, shall not fail to present myself at your excellency's feet to receive your orders.

'Lastly, I entreat your excellency to impart to me the commands and instructions necessary to enable me to act, in a manner agreeable to your excellency, and to point out to me in what way I may render myself most acceptable to your sacred feet, which are real *tamarasa* flowers. For this purpose it will not be necessary for your excellency to humble yourself still more by writing to me a second timc; but it will suffice that I receive from your excellency's bounty a leaf palm indented with your nail, through some confidential person who can verbally explain to me the orders of your excellency.[1]

'Such is my most humble prayer.'

The complimentary expressions used at the beginning of all these letters, and the humble and servile tone which pervades them, especially the third letter, present when translated sufficiently remarkable examples of epistolary style, yet I have by no means brought out the full force, or rather the extreme platitude, of all these expressions.

Our language has no equivalents for the expressions of base flattery and humility with which the Hindus are so lavish in their correspondence. These expres-

1. This device frequently serves for credentials in conveying verbal messages.

sions are, moreover, used with a certain amount of moderation in the letters just quoted. I have seen some the complimentary preface alone of which would have filled two pages of this book, The eloquence of a writer is inexhaustible under this head, especially when there is any question of obtaining some boon or favour. A petitioner can, indeed, without fear of seeing it thrown back in his face.

The thicker the smoke of the incense the more does it flatter him to whom it is offered.

In letters written by one Hindu to another, one never finds respectful assurances or compliments offered to a wife. The mere mention of her in a letter would be considered not simply as an indiscretion, but as a gross breach of politeness, at which the husband would have every reason to feel aggrieved.

When one Hindu has occasion to communicate to another the death of one of his relatives, the custom is to slightly burn the end of the palm-leaf on which the afflicting news is written; and this is similar to the black seal used by us in such cases. The same has been observed as a sign of displeasure, when one has occasion to administer a severe reprimand in writing.

When a superior writes to an inferior, he puts his own name before that of the person to whom he writes. The reverse is the case when an inferior writes to a superior. Any breach of this token of civility on the part of an inferior would be considered a dire insult by the person to whom he owed respect. Politeness also requires that, when writing to an equal, you shall place your own name last.

## Handwriting

Having said this much on the epistolary style of the Hindus, I will now offer some notes that I have collected in their handwriting.

Learned European scholars have made endless researches as to the origin of the art of writing, the manner in which it was transmitted by one people to another the different characters used, and the various kinds of tablets and other materials employed. Many conjectures have been offered concerning the systems invented by the Chinese and the Egyptians to transmit their ideas otherwise than verbally. The languages of India, however, seem to have escaped the learned investigations of philologists. Nevertheless, a careful study of these languages would, if I am not mistaken, throw a good deal of light on questions still shrouded in uncertainty.

I shall think myself fortunate enough if what I am about to say be considered worthy of the attention of the learned, and if it present some points of interest to those who are fond of discovering traces of primitive times in the usages that still exist.

The Hindu books attribute the credit of this invaluable invention to the great Brahma, the creator of men and the sovereign arbiter of their destinies. The serrated sutures to be seen on a skull are, they say, nothing less than the handwriting of Brahma himself; and these indelible characters, traced by his divine hand contain the irrevocable decrees regulating the destiny of each individual of the human race. It may be urged that this Hindu belief is a mere myth, and, as such, cannot be regarded as the basis of any reasonable conjectures. I am of the same opinion; but it must also be admitted that it is one of the oldest myths of India, and it proves at any rate that when it was invented the knowledge of writing already existed, Otherwise how could the Hindus of those remote times have discovered traces of writing in these marks on skulls?

Another fact, or another myth, if one prefers to call

it so, may be said to corroborate this. The four Vedas are considered to be the work of the god Brahma who wrote them with his own hand on leaves of gold. These books, which contain the ritual of the idolatrous ceremonies practised by these people, are held by them in great veneration, and their high antiquity is nowhere called into question. Other books, too many of which are undoubtedly very old, speak of the Vedas as of a far earlier date. Moreover, the language in which they are written had become unintelligible in many places. The Vedas, indeed, by whomsoever they may have been written, conclusively prove that the origin of Hindu writing dates from a period which is lost in remote antiquity.

One of the principal articles of the Hindu faith is that relating to the ten Avatars or incarnations, of Vishnu. The first and earliest is called the Matsya-avatar, that is the incarnation of the god in the form of a fish. And what was the cause of it? It was the loss of the four books of the Vedas. Brahma, under whose care they were left, fell asleep and a giant, his enemy, availed himself of the opportunity to steal the sacred volumes. Having escaped unperceived, the giant hid himself in the sea with his precious booty, which he swallowed, thinking it would be safer in his bowels. Vishnu, having been informed of what had happened, changed himself into a fish, and went in pursuit of this enemy of the gods. After a long search, he at length discovered the giant in the deepest abyss of the ocean. He attacked him, vanquised him, and tore him into pieces. He then plucked the hidden books from the giant's entrails, and restored them to the god who was their author and guardian.

Is there anything to be found in any books of ours whose unquestionable antiquity is recognized by European writers that might be said to compare with this fable, any indication of sources from which it could have been borrowed, thus proving its modern date? I think not.

Some of the Hindu authors ascribe the invention of writing to a famous Penitent called Agastya, who, it is said, was not taller than a hand's breadth. He is one of the most ancient persons recognized by the Hindus, in as much as they make him contemporary with the seven Penitents who were saved from the Flood in the ark, of which Vishnu himself was the pilot.

Again, the Gymnosophists, or naked penitents of India, have never been regarded as mythical personages. Even in the time of Lycurgus, that is to say, nearly nine hundred years before the Christian era, these philosophers enjoyed such a reputation for wisdom and learning that their fame had spread to countries far remote from their own. There is every reason to believe that their fame could only have been established gradually, and that their philosophy dated from a very remote period. True, some authors assert that their philosophy was handed down by oral tradition, and that they never committed anything to writing. It is, however, hard to believe that men who gave themselves up to the study of philosophy and astronomy could have done so without having recourse to written records.

Be this as it may, I will now briefly describe the present style of writing among the Hindus, mentioning (1) the written characters used, (2) the materials on which they are recorded, (3) the manner in which they are written, and (4) the shape of their books and of the communications which they address to each other.

It is generally stated that there are eighteen living languages in use in India, but as a matter of fact there are many more. All, or at any rate the majority of them, have their own distinct alphabetical characters. It is true that some of these characters, if carefully examined, bear a very close resemblance to each other; but in the majority of them one can distinguish no similarities. Yet, however diversified may be the characters employed in writing, there are many similarities to be observed in pronunciation and phraseology. In all these languages the arrangement of words admits of few changes or differences. In this particular they differ widely from the European languages, which, with a general resemblance in their alphabetical characters, admit of large variations in construction and phraseology.

What resemblance could, for instance, be found between the letters of the Telugu language? And the

| அ | ஆ | త |
|---|---|---|
| (a short) | (a long) | (tha) |

of the Tamil language and the letters

| అ | ఆ | ద |
|---|---|---|
| (a short) | (a long) | (tha) |

difference is not less striking in the other letters of the alphabet. Yet these two languages are spoken in countries bordering on each other, which in other respects present many points of resemblance. The same diversity with regard to alphabets is noticeable in other Indian languages.

Other facts worthy of note are that in all the languages of India (1) the letters are arranged in the same order; (2) the short and long vowels are always placed at the beginning of the alphabet and before the consonants; (3) these vowels are purely initial letters, which are never written except at the beginning of a word, special inflections being assigned to them when used in the middle of a word or after a consonant; (4) each consonant must have a vowel inflection: thus, *b, c*, can be pronounced *ba, ca*, and their form is changed when other vowel inflections are substituted. For instance, in Canarese the following letters change their form according to the vowel inflections to which they are subject, thus:

| ಬ | ಬೆ | ಬಿ | ಡ | ಡೆ | ಡಿ | ಧೊ | ಧು |
|---|---|---|---|---|---|---|---|
| ba | be | bi | too | they | thee | dho | dhu |

How is it that there is so much resemblance between the various idioms of these languages, and so much dissimilarity between the letters of their alphabets? Sanskrit appears to be the common type on which the other languages have modelled their phraseology; how comes it then that they have, in opposition to the mother-tongue, adopted letter formations so different from that of their common parent?

Similar variations are observable in the forms of their ciphers or symbols. Though they all use the decimal notation, they differ widely in the formation of their arithmetical figures. In the Tamil language, each decimal number is denoted by a different sign, thus:

| ௧ | ௰ | ௱ | ௲ |
|---|---|---|---|
| 1 | 10 | 100 | 1000 |

In Telugu, and in most of the other languages of the country, they follow exactly the system which we have adopted from the Arabs, the units being expressed by a single figure, the tens by two, the hundreds by three, the thousands by four, and so on.

This method, with the exception of a few slight differences in the shape of the figures, is the one most commonly used. The similarity which exists between this method and that of the Arabs can hardly have been the result of chance. If one nation did not borrow it from the other, it is at any rate probable that both borrowed it from the same source.

The Tamil arithmetical symbols seem, however, to bear a greater resemblance to the Roman than to the Arabic numerals. Like the Romans, the Tamils express the greater part of their arithmetical signs by letters of the alphabet, and use only a single letter to denote units, tens, hundreds, and thousands as stated above.

But, dissimilar as are the written characters of the various Hindu languages, they are still more dissimilar to the written characters known to us as used by other ancient nations, such as Syriac, Hebrew, Arabic, Greek etc. Unlike the majority of Oriental languages, which are written from right to left, Sanskrit and the various dialects of India are written, like the European languages, from left to right.

## Writing Practices

Paper is not unknown to the Hindus. They manufactured it, not from cotton rags, as is generally believed, but from the fibre of the aloe. I am, however, inclined to believe that the use of this coarse paper is of comparatively recent date in India, subsequent, that is, to the invasion of the Moghuls, who must have introduced it. At any rate, following the example of the Moghuls, the Hindus living in the interior of the country, where palm leaves are not procurable, use paper instead. But more generally they use black tablets named Kadatta, on which they write with a white pencil, called in Canerese Balapu, made of a calcareous quarried stone which is very common in the country. And it is with these materials that children learn writing in the schools.

Nevertheless the ordinary practice almost

everywhere is to write on palm leaves, of which there are two pieces, large and small. The latter are the commoner and are said to be the better; they are about three inches wide and two feet long. Seven or eight lines can be written on each leaf. They are thicker, stiffer, and stronger than double paper, so that one can easily write, or rather engrave, on both sides of them. The other kinds of leaves are broader, but not so strong. They are therefore used only in those places where the smaller kinds are not easily procurable. They are sometimes used specially as a mark of respect when writing to a person of rank. The island of Ceylon produces an enormous quantity of the smaller leaves, and they are so cheap that a half penny's worth of them would be sufficient for copying an entire folio volume.

Quintus Curtius relates that the Hindus, at the time of the invasion of Alexander the Great, wrote with an iron Stilus on the soft and smooth bark of trees. It is quite probable that palm leaves were mistaken for the bark of trees; for nowhere in India can any evidence be found to prove that the bark of trees has ever been used for the purpose of writing.

Aeneas, in Virgil's epic, implores the Cumaean Sibyl not to write her oracles on the leaves of trees, which the winds might speedily disperse. All the commentators are of opinion that the reference here is to palm leaves. It is therefore to be presumed that these leaves were quite different from those now used in India, which, on account of their weight and thickness, could not be blown about by the wind.

The Hindus write with an iron, Stilus, or pencil, which is from eight to nine inches long. The handle of the instrument generally ends in a knife, which is used to trim the sides of the leaves so as to make them all of one size. In writing with the *stilus* neither chair nor table is required. The leaf is supported on the middle finger of the left hand, and is kept steady by being held firmly between the thumb and the forefinger. The Stilus, in writing, does not glide along the leaf, as does our pen on paper; but the writer, after finishing a word or two, fixes the point of his instrument on the last letter, and pushes the leaf from right to left so the last line of writing is finished. This is executed with such ease that it is by no means a rare sight to see Hindus writing as they walk along.

As the characters thus traced are only a sort of faint engraving, of the same colour as the leaf itself, and therefore not easily decipherable, it is the common practice to besmear the whole with fresh cow-dung. The leaf is afterwards wiped clean, but the new material fills up the engraved letters and gives them a darker colour, thus rendering them more distinct and readable. This mode of writing is undoubtedly more convenient and more simple than ours, so far at least as writing on a small scale is concerned, for it does not require all the materials that we need on such occasions; but it will be readily understood that it is not equally convenient for writings of a somewhat voluminous nature.

As in our ancient manuscripts, the absence of every kind of punctuation, and the confusion arising from words and phrases not being sufficiently separated, render the perusal of the works of Hindu authors extremely difficult. The complicated rules of orthography pertaining to some of their languages, and especially to Tamil, tend to increase this difficulty still further. Very often the most experienced person is unable to read without difficulty, especially if the writer has adhered strictly to the rules of grammar, which are generally, however, either ignored or neglected.

When Hindus write on paper they do not use a quill pen. A Brahmin could not, without defilement, touch so impure an instrument. Consequently, a thin reed is used, called Kalam, a word evidently of modern origin borrowed from the Portuguese. The Kalam is somewhat thicker than our quill pen, and is mended in the same manner. Hindus employed under Europeans, however, lay aside these scruples, and use the same matenals as their masters.

When a Hindu wishes to make up a book of the palm leaves on which he has written, he has no need of a book-binder. He merely bores a small hole at each extremity of the leaves, and fastens them all together by means of two small pegs or sticks of wood or iron. Two thin boards, of the same length and breadth as the leaves, are then placed at the top and bottom of them, and thus form the binding or covers of the book. A long string fastened to one of the covers serves to hold the leaves together. If this plan is simple, it certainly is not convenient; for whenever one wishes to consult the book, the string must be loosened, the pegs by means of which the leaves are strung together must be removed, and the whole volume taken to pieces.

It will thus be seen that the Hindu system of writing and binding books closely resembles that of the ancient Romans, who wrote on extremely thin wooden boards, which they strung together and formed into a *codex*.

The following is the plan adopted by the Hindus in the transmission of letters:- They roll up the palm leaves on which they are written, and put them into an outer covering, upon which they write the address. At the junction of the two ends of the outer leaf, which are held together by means of a small incision in each, a kind of rough knot is made, serving as a seal. Due attention must be paid to the length and breadth of the leaves on which letters are written, which vary according to the rank and dignity of those to whom they are addressed.

To be the bearer of a letter denotes a kind of subordinate position. This duty cannot therefore be entrusted to superiors, or even to equals, unless they undertake it voluntarily. In the latter case, etiquette forbids the letter being given into the hands of the person who has offered to deliver it; the missive must be placed on the ground at his feet, and he picks it up and becomes responsible for its safe delivery.

The changes in the form of writing which time brings about in other countries do not offer a safe ground for conjecture in the case of Hindu manuscripts. I have seen a deed of gift written more than two hundred years ago on a plate of gold in Canarese characters, the letters of which were perfectly legible and exact like those at present in use, the form of writing having undergone no change whatever during that long interval of time. Nevertheless there are certain monuments in the country of very great antiquity, bearing inscriptions engraved in characters no longer in use. Some are also to be found in various places the characters of which are wholly unknown and evidently foreign.

The remarks I have made above concerning the dissimilarity of the written characters and the resemblance of the grammatical study in the various Indian languages are equally applicable to Siamese. At least, so it has been pointed out to me by persons who are familiar with that language, and who have discovered in its alphabet an arrangement exactly similar to that of the Hindu alphabets. In some languages of India the sign or inflection denoting the vowel that always accompanies a consonant is placed before it; the same practice is followed with regard to several letters in Siamese writing. Like the Hindus, the Siamese write from left to right. This coincidence can hardly be alleged to be the result of chance; it rather indicates some common origin. The investigations of modern authors with regard to this subject leave no doubt whatever that the *Pali* language, or the learned tongue of Siam, is a corrupt form of the Sanskrit. And this mother-tongue appears to have extended even still farther, since we find a large number of Sanskrit words in the Malay language. However, in shape the Siamese letters as written appeared to me to bear no resemblance whatever to the Hindu alphabets with which I was acquainted.

From the very earliest times poetry has been very much in vogue with the Hindus, and it is still held in by them. One is even inclined to believe they had no other written language. Not original ancient books is written in prose—not even the books on medicine, which are said to be very numerous in the Sanskrit language. We may naturally infer that the practice of writing in a style and idiom beyond the comprehension of the people was mainly due to the artful precaution of the Brahmins, who found in it a sure means of excluding all other castes from participating in a knowledge of which they wished to retain a monopoly.

It is quite certain that all the Hindu books in prose are of modern origin. It is in verse that the eighteen Puranas, and other similar works, have been translated from the Sanskrit into Tamil, Telugu, and Canarese, and, I think, into all the other vernaculars of India.

Tamil poetry seems to have been chiefly cultivated by the Sudras; and even Pariahs have been the authors of various poems In that language. The Tamil poets, however, while imitating the form and style of Sanskrit poetry, have added so many rules of their own that it is difficult to excel in the writing of it. Telugu and Canarese poetry is chiefly the work Brahmins.

## Literature

Having acquired some knowledge of the most important rules of Hindu prosody, which, I think, are the same in all the vernaculars of the country, Sanskrit not excepted, I will try to describe them briefly here. The subject seems to me likely to interest philologists. I will, therefore, describe: (1) the different kinds of poetry; (2) the long and short quantities; (3) the different feet; (4) the different meters; (5) the method of rhyme; (6) the composition of verses; (7) and the style of their poetry generally.

The Different Kinds of Poetry: There are five kinds of poetry, namely, *padam, padyam, dwipada, dandaka,* and *yakshakaram.* Some add to these another kind under the name of *padiya* but as this is, properly speaking, poetical prose, it is not generally considered as belonging to the province of poetry.

The *padam* includes not only the odes in honour of gods, princes, and other great personages, but also obscene and amorous ditties, sprightly dialogues between gods and goddesses, and other similar compositions, some of which are called *sringaram* (ornament), because they describe the beauty of women and their different methods of adornment.

The erotic songs are also called *sittinbam* (pleasures of the will). Of this sort there is an infinite varitey. They are sung, for the most part, by religious mendicants when they go from house to house asking for alms. The more coarse and indecent they are, the better they suit the tastes of the hearers, whose generosity is manifested in proportion to the enjoyment derived from them.

The hymns in honour of the gods are called *kirthanam* (praise), a term which these compositions well deserve on account of the high-flown eulogies with which they are replete.

The word *padam* corresponds likewise to our strophe, stanza, or couplet.

*Padyam* includes the great poems composed in honour of gods and heroes. They are divided into stanzas. There are at least thirty different forms of these stanzas, which may be introduced and interspersed in the course of the same poem. The *padyams* are also used in compositions dealing with moral and satirical subjects. The Telugu poet Vemana and the Tamil poet Tiruvalluvar excelled in these two kinds of composition.

The species of poetry called *dwipada* (two feet) is not subject to very strict rules. It might be described as free improvisation, and is used m the recital of short stories and adventures.

It is unnecessary to enter into details about the other kinds of poetry; it is easy to conjecture what they are like from what has been already said.

Long and Short Quantities: Hindu verses, like those in Greek and Latin, are formed of feet, composed of letters long or short in quantity. From these long and short feet are formed hemistichs, or lines which, combined in their turn, form stanzas.

The feet are composed of letters, because in the Indian languages there are no such thing as syllables. Every consonant carries its own vowel, which is incorporated with it. In several languages of India combinations such as bra, pla, etc. which we call syllables, are also written as one single letter.

The short letters are called *laghu-aksharam*, and the long ones *guru-aksharam*, in allusion, no doubt, to the slow and solemn gait of a Hindu guru. Even in ordinary writing they seldom fail to make a distinction between the long and short letters with their particular marks. This is scrupulously observed in pronunciation, and in verse it is quite indispensable.

In Hindu, as well as in Greek and Latin poetry, a long letter is equivalent to two short, and two long to four short. Thus the word *mata*, composed of two long letters, is equivalent to the word *iruvadu*, composed of four short ones. But there are letters which, though short in prose writing and in ordinary conversation, become long in verse by their position; thus the initial *a* in the word *aksharam*, though short generally, becomes long in versification, being placed before two consonants, *k* and *sha*. In the same manner the letter *ka*, though usually short, is long in such words as *Karm*, *karman*, etc., on account of the two consonants which follow it.

As I wished to know whether this rule admitted of that poetical licence of which we find some examples in the writings of the best Latin poets—that is, whether a final short letter could become long by position when the word which follows it begins with two consonants—I questioned a Brahmin whom I had asked to explain to me the structure of Hindu versification. He had already seemed somewhat surprised at the facility with which I understood his explanations, and I noticed that his professorial tone and arrogant self-conceit were gradually diminishing. But when I asked this question he stood dumbfounded, and for a while stared me in the face without uttering a word. At length he answered: 'I wonder how such a thought could have occurred to you, knowing as you do so little as yet even of the rudimentary elements of our poetry.' I told him that the different kinds of poetry which were studied in my own country bore many resemblances to the poetry of India, and that the knowledge I had previously derived from the former had led me to ask this particular question. But his astonishment, instead of decreasing, grew still greater. He found it very difficult to understand how such sublime things could ever have entered the minds of foreigners, and how poets could be found elsewhere than in India. This prejudice on his part easily impressed him with the idea that I was a person of wonderful mental penetration. One advantage which resulted from our conversation was that in future his conduct towards me become much more respectful.

As in Latin the last letter or vowel of a Hindu verse may be of any quantity at pleasure; but in such cases the distinction must always be marked in accentuation.

The poets of India, hold some letters to be of good and others of evil omen. The ambrosial letters *(amritam)* come under the head of the former, while the poisonous letters *(visham)* belong to the latter class. This distinction, however, is not observed in the poems in praise of the gods, who are supposed to be beyond such influences. But in verses which concern simple mortals the case is very different. Particular care must be taken never to begin any verse addressed to them with a *visham* or unlucky letter. In the Telugu and Canarese languages, the letters *he, ki, pe, pi, te, ti,* etc., are of this number, because these letters when written have the point turned downwards. On the other hand, the letters *ko, po, to,* etc., are considered to be lucky letters *(amritam)*, because they have the point turned upwards.

**The feet in verse:** The feet are called *ganams,* and there are two kinds, the simple *ganams* and the *upaganams.* The first are eight in number, and are expressed by the word *mahajasanarayala,* made up of the first letters of the following—(1) *maganam,* (2) *haganam* (3) *jaganam,* (4) *saganam,* (5) *naganam,* (6) *raganam,* (7) *yaganam,* and (8) *laganam.*

The first consists of three longs; the second, of a long and two shorts; the third, of a loog between two shorts; the fourth, of two shorts and a long; the fifth, of three shorts; the sixth, of a short between two longs; the seventh, of a short and two longs; and the eighth, of two longs and a short.

There are eight *upagartams* expressed by the word *gavahana-gamanala*, made up likewise by the combination of the first letters of the following words: (1) *gaganam*, composed of two longs; (2) *vaganam*, of a short and a long; (3) *haganam*, of a long and a short; (4) *nalam*, of four shorts; (5) *galam*, of two shorts; (6) *malagam*, of three longs and a short; (7) *nagan:* of three shorts and a long; and (8) *latam*, of two longs and two shorts.

The Hindu poets discern a certain relation between the *ganams* and the *upaganams*, according to the effects which they are severally supposed to possess the faculty of producing. They are all under the protection of different planets; and according to the good or evil dispositions of these latter, they bring good or ill luck. Those under the auspices of the moon, which in India is the symbol of comfort and coolness, are favourable; but the case is just the reverse with those governed by the sun. It therefore follows that a piece of poetry must never begin with a malign *ganam*. The Hindu prosodies are very diffuse and wearisome on this subject.

**The Different Metres:** The lines, properly speaking, of verses are formed of *ganams* and *upaganams*, and are called *padams* or *charanams*, words which signify literally *feet*. They may be compared to the hemistichs or lines of pentameter verse in Latin, or to the lines of ten and twelve syllables in French and English. The variety of *padams* depends on the number of *ganams* they contain; some having three, five, seven, or more.

In certam *padams* any of the *ganams* may be used, and these latter may be varied at pleasure provided the requisite number of shorts and longs is preserved. This variety, however, must be managed with a certain amount of taste and be free from all affectation; when it is done with discretion, it enhances the beauty and force of the verses which otherwise would become too monotonous. It is just the same with Latin hexameters, which would be wanting in grace if the poet were to put either all dactyls or all spondees in the first four feet.

The Hindu poets, however, cannot indulge in this interchange of *ganams* in all their compositions. There are cases in which it is absolutely necessary for them to use only such as the rules prescribe.

The various kinds of lines in Hindu verse have all special names. One is called the elephant, another the tiger, another the cobra, and so forth.

**Rhyme:** There are two kinds of rhymes in Hindu poetry. One occurs at the beginning of the line, and is called *yeti* or *vadi*. Thus where one line begins with the word *kirti* and the other with *kirtaoo, ki* is the *yeti*. The other kind of rhyme occurs in the second letter or syllable of the line and is called *prasam*. Thus, in two lines, one beginning with *gopagni* and the other with *dipantram, pa* is the *prasam*.

For the *yeti* rhyme the letters *ka, kaha, ksha, ga, gsha,* the simple *tsha,* and the aspirate *tshaha* etc. may be used.

For the *prasam* rhyme attention is, strictly speaking, paid only to the consonant, which ought to be absolutely the same; the vowel does not matter so much. Thus *da, de, di, do, du* all rhyme together. These kinds of rhymes, however, are not considered fine.

Generally speaking, the more words there are in a line having the *yeti* and the *prasam* alike, the more beautiful they appear to the Hindus. For our part we should look upon them as mere childish alliterations, recalling to our minds the line of Enuius so often in the mouths of schoolboys:

O Tate lute Tad tibi tanta, tyranne, tulisti!

There are also other kinds of poetry, which, like ours, have their ryhme at the end of the lines. In these cases they end as a rule with the same consonant and sometimes with the same word.

Generally speaking, the difficulties of rhyme are simply hopeless, and often puzzle Hindu versifiers themselves.

**Verses:** With the *padams*, or lines, arranged symmetrically with regard to quantity and rhyme, are formed the *padyams*, sometimes called *slokams*. They are, properly speaking, stanzas or couplets, sometimes regular, sometimes irregular.

These *padyams* are of several kinds, and each has its special name. In the sample *kanda-padyam* certain feet only can be introduced, in the same way as in Latin hexameters, in which dactyls and spondees only are used. But a single *ganam*, or foot, may sometimes comprise a whole line, such as the following; *Devaki-Deviki-Kamsudu.*

The limits of this work hardly permit me to enter into more minute details concerning the numerous rules to which the structure and arrangement of Hindu poetry are subject; but it will appear from what has been already said that Hindu versification is by no means easy. There are nevertheless a great many people of all castes who dabble in rhymes, and amuse themselves by reading out publicly and ostentatiously the pieces they have composed. In India, as in Europe, poetasters abound, while good poets are very scarce. The Indian languages, however, being very rich in synonyms, afford a great advantage to the Hindu poet.

There are five principal authors who have written on the subject of Hindu prosody; and these have laid down fixed and unalterable laws for making verses. Their collected works are called Chandas. The Brahmin who taught me was guided in his instructions by a book whose author had so arranged that every rule was comprised in a verse which served at once the double purpose of an example of the rule as well as the rule itself.

**Of Taste and Style in Hindu Poetry:** The predominating features of Hindu poetry are emphasis, affectation, and bombast. Every Hindu poet would seem to be a prototype of him who, in Horace,

*Proicit ampules et sesquipedalia verba,*

or of the Clitarchus compared by Longinus to a man who opens his mouth wide to blow through a tiny flute. The poetry of all nations has its peculiar turns of expression, its licences, its own vocabulary, etc., which render it difficult of understanding by foreigners; but in Hindu poetry the frequent use of elliptical phrases, of allegories, of metaphors, and of expressions not in vogue in ordinary language, renders the meaning so obscure that it is impossible to understand it properly unless one makes a special study of the subject. Even a thorough knowledge of Hindu prose works is of no avail.

Were Hindu literature better known to us, it is possible that we should find that we have borrowed from it the romantic style of our days, which some find so beautiful and others so silly. If the Hindu poet has occasion to describe any particular object, he seldom omits even the minutest details. He thinks it his duty to present it to the view in all its phases.

*S'il rencontre un palais, il m'en depeint la face;*
*Il me promene apres de terrasse en terrasse:*
*Ici s'offre un perron; la regne un corridor;*
*La ce balcon s'enfermeen un balustre d'or,*
*Il compte des plafonds les ronds et les ovales.*

If a Hindu poet has a beautiful woman for his theme, he will certainly never be content with merely stating, in a more or less flowery style, that she is endowed with all the charms of body and mind. Like the painter who reproduces on the canvas one feature after another of his model, so does our Hindu poet pass in review *a capite usque ad calcem* the various charms of the beauty he is describing. The colour of her skin, the expression of her face and eyes, in fine, everything connected with her, even her most secret charms, appear to him objects worthy of his praise. The finishing strokes of his brush are generally reserved for the touching up of all the moral and intellectual qualities which his imagination can impart to the fair subject of his verses. It may be easily imagined that these descriptive details, overloaded as they are with a vast display of epithets, become exceedingly diffuse, but we cannot deny to them at least the credit of exactitude.

Hindu poetry at first sounds harsh and inharmonious to a European ear, by reason of the frequent aspirations with which many of the letters at the beginning, in the middle, and at the end of the words are pronounced; but, on the other hand, this laboured pronunciation gives to the recital a stately and sonorous tone, which seldom fails to please one who has become used to it. At the same time it must be confessed that foreigners, and even natives who have not been well trained in it from infancy, find almost insurmountable difficulties in mastering this method of pronunciation.

The short pieces that I have seen have appeared to me generally weak. I know not whether the Hindus have any real dramatic works. I only know of a few productions of this nature, and these are mixed up with songs and dialogues. The *Dasa-avatara*, or the ten incarnations of Vishnu, is among the number. But I am not in a position to give any particulars as to their merit, or even of their contents, seeing that I have never taken the trouble to read any of them.

More fortunate than the French, who are never weary of repeating that no epic poem exists in their literature, the Hindus boast of a great number. The two most celebrated are the *Ramayana* and the *Bhagavata*. Both are of inordinate length. The former recounts the deeds and exploits of Vishnu under the incarnation of Rama, while the latter relates the adventures of Vishnu metamorphosed in the form of Krishna. Their authors have introduced into them the whole idolatrous system of the country—a system on which they are often at variance among themselves. It may be easily understood that the 'unities' prescribed by Aristotle have not been observed in these epics. The *Bhagavata* takes up its hero even before his birth, and does not quit him full after he is dead.

The fertile imagination of the ancient Greeks conceived nothing that can be compared with the incredible powers and wonderful achievements of the Hindu heroes, whose exploits are celebrated in these books. Even the colossal Enceladus and the giant Briareus, with his fifty heads and his hundred hands, were but pigmies compared with the wonderful giants who, according to the *Ramayana*, sometimes fought for Rama and sometimes against him.

# 11

## Military System

Here my self-imposed task should have been brought to a close, for it is hardly to be expected that I can treat the subject-matter of this chapter satisfactorily, seeing how foreign it is to my profession. However, as nearly all the public monuments of India, both civil and religious, commemorate some war, and as all the Hindu books are filled with descriptions of feats of arms and accounts of battles, I thought that a few details on this subject would not be entirely out of place in such a work as the present.

The Kshatriyas, or kings, and their descendants the Rajputs formerly held undisputed sway in India and they alone had a right to follow the military profession. All this, however, has nowadays undergone a complete change, ambition having found a way through this hard and fast rule. At the present time there are very few native rulers who belong to the old warrior caste. In this case, as in many others, the strongest have seized the reins of government. Indeed, in many provinces one may find princes of very low origin, who by their courage, their talents, or their intrigues have raised themselves to their high position. In the same way, the, profession of arms has now been thrown open to men of all castes, from the Brahmin to the Pariah.

On the one hand, one may see a Brahmin who has attained the rank of commander-in-chief of an army, while on the other hand, especially in the Mahratta armies, you may see them serving as common troopers.

## The Art of War

Though the habits of the Hindus appear more likely to impair their courage than to make them good soldiers, the art of war nevertheless seems to have been as well understood by them from very early times as any other, and those who followed the military profession have always been held in high esteem. In fact, military officers took rank in the social scale immediately after the priesthood. The Brahmins themselves, actuated by motives either of gratitude or of self-interest, allowed them to participate in some of their own high prerogatives, such as the valued privileges of being allowed to hear the Vedas read and of wearing the triple cord. But however much the Hindus may have honoured the profession of arms and however full their national wars, conquests, sieges, battles, victims; and shown at every epoch in its history so little skill in military science. When pitiless conquerors, at the head of savage and warlike hordes, forced their way over the northern mountains and spread themselves like a devastating torrent over the fertile provinces of India, the peaceable and docile inhabitants were unable to offer any effectual resistance. They saw their towns and villages ravaged by fire and sword, while rivers of blood, ingloriously and fruitlessly spilt, deluged their fields. The readiness with which they bent their necks beneath their oppressors' yoke, and the feebleness of the efforts which they put forth to recover their independence, proved how inferior they were in courage and discipline to the proud Tartars who invaded and conquered them.

The wars of India may be classified under three heads: those of the mythical ages, those of the ancient kings, and those of modern times. By the last I mean only the intermission wars between native princes before the time when these princes, convinced of the superiority of European military science, determined to introduce foreigners amongst their troops, and to this end enlisted in their service those European adventurers who offered to help them in their undertakings. It was an imprudent policy, and the native princes did not see until too late the danger of surrounding themselves with such intriguing and ambitious auxiliaries.

I will say nothing about the wars of the gods and the giants, which the majority of Hindu books describe with equal bombast and prolixity. Such exaggerated flights of imagination can hardly be considered worthy of a place in serious history. It is always the same story of armies of giants whose heads touched the stars, and who were mounted on elephants of proportionate size. One of these giants, for example, is depicted as upheaving the very firmament with his shoulders, giving it such a violent shock as to overthrow all the gods who dwelt therein, and thereby warning them of what they might expect from an adversary of such prowess.

On the other hand, a god who is about to engage these formidable enemies takes the earth for his chariot a rainbow for his bow, and Vishnu for an arrow. He shoots this extraordinary missile, and with one shot overthrows an immense city, in which all the villains that he is pursuing are entrenched, burying them all in the fallen ruins of the city.

*Ab uno disce omnes.* I do not think that the history of the wars of the ancient kings of India is one whit less absurd. It is only the poets who have undertaken the task of transmitting details to posterity, and as Hindu poets are not wont to do things by halves, they have freely availed themselves of the privilege of exaggeration and embelishment. Facts are so interwoven with senseless efforts of the imagination that it is impossible to disentangle the truth. Why should on feel astonished at Xerxes being able to gather together and maintain a million soldiers when he set forth to conquer Greece? Such an army would have formed only a small detachment of one of the armies of the kings of India. These latter never took the field at the head of less than several hundreds of millions fighting men! If the reader will recollect what he remarked several times, namely, that only that which is extraordinary and extravagant has the power of pleasing the Hindu, he will hardly be astonished at the strange mania which has induced Hindu authors to carry exaggeration even to puerility. In every country writers adapt their work to the taste of the public being anxious to gain from them the greatest possible approbation.

## The Game of Chess

The one fact that I have been able to glean for certain is that the armies of the ancient Hindu kings were divided into four arms or sections, of which the whole formed a Chaturangam. These four corps were the elephants, the chariots, the cavalry and the infantry; such indeed were the component parts of the army of Porus, who was vanquished and taken prisoner on the banks of the Hydaspes by Alexander.

No one at the present day denies the fact that the Hindus invented the military game of chess. The following is the story, according to Oriental writers, of how this game was invented. At the beginning of the fifth century of the Christian era a very powerful young monarch was reigning in India, who was of excellent character, but who allowed himself to be corrupted by flatterers. This prince soon forgot that the love of the people is the only sure support of a throne. The Brahmins and Rajahs uttered many remonstrances, but in vain. Intoxicated by his greatness, which he fancied was unassailable, he despised their counsels. Accordingly, a Brahmin named Sissa undertook to open the young monarch's eyes by strategy. To this end he invented the game of chess, in which the king, though the most important of all the pieces, can nevertheless neither attack nor defend himself without the assistance of his subjects. The game speedily became famous, and the king expressed his anxiety to learn it. Sissa, while teaching him the rules, made him a right man.

It is very evident that it was the composition and tactics of the ancient Hindu armies that originally suggested the game. The Hindus, in fact, called it Chaturangam. Though with some few small variations we have adopted their method of playing, it must be admitted that the innovations which we have introduced in the shapes and names of the pieces are certainly not happy. What can be more ridiculous than the castles which move about from place to place, the queen who rushes about fighting with the king's people, or the bishops who occupy such an exalted position?

As with us, the most important piece on the Hindu chessboard is the king. The second piece, which we call the queen, they term the Mantri, a title which signifies a minister of state, who is also commander-in-chief of the army. Chariots occupy the place of out bishops. Like us, the Hindus have knights, but instead of our battlement castles they have elephants. The pawns or foot-soldiers are, as with us, the simple rank and file of which the army is composed. The chessboard is called by the Hindu Porsthalam, or field of battle.

But to return to the ancient Hindu armies. In the first line came the elephants. It is certain that these animals carried castles or *howdahs* on their backs, containing several men armed with javelins, But I think it would be wrong to suppose that these castles or *howdahs* were of any great size, as might be imagined from certain illustrations. Like those which may still be found in the present day amongst the armies of some Eastern princes, these towers or *howdahs* resembled large boxes without lids, as long and as broad as a large bed, placed crosswise on the back of the elephant, and capable of holding six or seven archers when sitting in Oriental fashion. Though an elephant is very strong, so as to be able to carry two small cannons and their carriages, there is nevertheless a limit to its powers; and naturally a much larger erection, with a still larger number of men in It, would be a burden, under which even an elephant would succumb. And there is yet another point, namely, the difficulty of fixing a lofty structure with any degree of security on an elephant's back, a difficulty which would be rendered practically insurmountable by the brusque movements and rolling gait of the animal.

Be this as it may, elephants in days gone by were formidable adversaries amongst these half-disciplined nations. They broke the ranks, frightened the horses, trampled the soldiers underfoot; and at the same time it was very difficult to wound them, on account of their hard and horny epidermis. These powerful creatures are still employed in the armies of native princes, but rather from ostentation than from any warlike purpose that they serve. A native general or senior officer considers an elephant to be the only mount befitting his dignity; the animal being usually covered with magnificent trappings. It is only with great difficulty that elephants can be made to stand fire, though every method is employed to familiarize them with it. Without these precautions the rattle of firearms and the squibs that are hurled at them would excite them to frenzy, and would consequently cause the death of their riders.

They were also used for battering the gates of besieged towns; and it was with a view to counteracting this that most of the gates were thickly studded on the outside with long and stout iron spikes. In the Mogul armies, before the introduction of European tactics, an elephant always marched in the van, bearing on its head a long pole, from which floated a large flag. Sometimes this was followed by another elephant carrying a rich *howdah*, on which was placed a box containing a priceless relic, which usually was, if one may believe it, an actual hair from Mahomet's beard.

The chief service which these animals render nowadays is in the transport of artillery and equipage. When a swamp, a ditch, a canal, or any other obstacle arrests the progress of the bullocks that drags the cannon, one or more elephants are brought up to push the gun-carriage with their heads and trunks and thus help them over the difficulty. When rivers which are not fordable have to be crossed, elephants are often used to carry men and heavy baggage over on their backs. But the services of these animals are dearly bought, considering the vast expense which their food and keep entail. Thus they are falling more and more into disuse. Every day the camel is growing in favour as being more patient and tractable.

Chariots formed the second division of the ancient Hindu armies. If one may believe what early Hindu writers say, these chariots were used in considerable numbers and were of considerable size. That of the king was the most magnificent. The rest belonged to his subordinate chiefs. When two hostile armies met, the leaders on each side were in the habit of interchanging compliments with each other before joining battle. One, for instance, would drop an arrow just short of his adversary's chariot, and the other would return the salute. Splendid horses were harnessed to these war-chariots. One reads in the *Bhagavata* that one of the old kings of India, when setting out on a campaign, harnessed a troop of demons to his chariot, to ensure the pace being good. The chariots were usually ornamented all round with large bells, which made a great noise, and this custom is still occasionally observed at the present time in the case of private carriages. The latter, however, in no way resemble the ancient war-chariots, about which I have not been able to collect any trustworthy information.

The cavalry formed the third division. Indian generals in ancient times, however, did not rely much on this arm. The infantry played the principal part in their wars, which is contrary to the practice of more modern times, for until quite recently no use whatever was made of infantry, only a few undisciplined regiments of followers being maintained to pillage, ravage, and destroy all the villages in their way, and to devastate the enemy country. This idea they had evidently borrowed from the Tartars, who had invaded their country and whose superiority in arms they had been forced to acknowledge to their cost.

The Moguls and Mahrattas, the two rival powers who for a long while disputed the supremacy of India, placed on some occasions as many as 100,000 horses in the field. The Mahratta princes combined could have commanded as many as 300,000 horses. But they never knew how to utilize this unwieldy multitude to its full advantage, because they did not understand how to manoeuvre it in a scientific manner. The lessons which the European invaders gave them time after time, for more than 300 years, seem hardly to have taught them to appreciate their mistakes. Even at the end of this long period, and when it was too late to mend matters, there was a vast inferiority in their tactics compared with those of their dreaded opponents. They never could be brought to understand the value of strict discipline, good tactical handling, orderly arrangements in marching and camping, and, in 'short, all the skilled dispositions by which it is possible to manoeuvre large bodies of troops without confusion. They thought their work was done when they had collected a miscellaneous horde of men, who marched to battle in a disorderly mass and fell upon the enemy without any method or concerted plan.

## The Armies

Indian armies always contain a large number of chiefs who command as many troopers as they are able to raise at their own expense. Each recruit brings his own horse, which remains his private property. He receives a fixed sum for himself and for the keep of his horse. If he happens to lose his horse, he is dismissed as useless. This plan certainly puts the State to little expense but it renders the cavalry as a body less effective, for at close quarters the rider's first care is for his horse, which belongs to himself; nay, often, when he sees that there is much danger, he will take; to flight at the first order to charge. Desertion indeed is very common in the armies of Indian princes. As a rule, little trouble is taken to catch the deserters and they and severely punished when caught. In order to honour fidelity amongst their troops the chiefs are in the habit of keeping their pay in arrears, and this prevents a large number of mercenaries from deserting as they fear to lose what is due to them. Nevertheless, whole armies have been known to throw down their arms in the face of the enemy and refuse to take them up again until they had received their pay. It is by no means a rare occurrence for large bodies of troops to refuse to set out on a march for a similar reason. Mutinous soldiers, too, frequently put their generals under arrest, send them to prison, menace them sword in hand or try to intimidate them by loud threats and insults. The generals, strange to say, will calmly and patiently put up with these mutinous outbursts. Usually they will pay the mutineers a part of their arrears and promise the rest in a short time. Quiet is then restored, and the men return to duty until another such occasion presents itself.

Although these undisciplined mercenaries make very inferior troops, still there are instances on record of honourable and brave conduct among their chiefs, especially among Mahomedan chiefs of high rank. The latter never cry for quarter; and, even when the day is going against them, they will not retreat a step as long as they have the support of a few of their followers. Flight or retreat under such circumstances is considered by them even more ignominious than it is by their European opponents.

The ordinary cavalry troopers, be they Mahomedan or Mahratta, are usually very badly mounted, and their equipments are still worse. Nevertheless, their weedy looking chargers are so inured to fatigue and so accustomed to privation that they will make, with only a little coarse hay for food, a succession of forced marches which would be quite beyond the capabilities of our best European cavalry, covering as they sometimes do as much as sixty miles a day. Mounted on these wretched animals, detachments of troops are able to cover great distances, and to sweep down suddenly on districts from which they were supposed to be far away. It must not be supposed that there are not very good horses to be found, especially in the Southern provinces of India; but they are only to be bought for very high prices that are quite beyond the means of ordinary persons. Only the chiefs possess really fine horses. They take remarkably good care of them. They usually decorate them in various ways, and often paint their bodies in different colors. They train them in an extremely clever manner, and ride them most gracefully. Many indeed would be able to carry off prizes in our European riding schools. The Mahrattas, for instance, accustom their horses to stop at a given signal. The rider dismounts and goes away, leaving his steed loose. Sometimes for hours together the animal will remain as still as a milestone until his master returns.

A horse-stealer who one day came across a solitary steed, which had thus been left without anyone to look after it, mounted it and galloped off. The owner of the horse, seeing from a distance what had happened, thereupon gave the call by which he always stopped the animal. At the sound of its master's voice the horse perceived its mistake and stood stock still. In spite of every effort on the part of the thief it refused to budge; whereupon the latter thought it more prudent to take to flight on his own two legs.

The troopers, Mahomedan and Mahratta, are armed with lances, javelins, and *katharis,* or daggers. Some, few have blunderbusses in addition, while others have indifferent sabres. A few may be seen armed with nothing but the whip or switch which they use in urging on their horses. Each man, in short, is expected to arm himself at his own expense, and consequently a remarkable variety may be noticed in the equipments of a troop of native cavalry.

They march in the most irregular fashion, and have no idea of regular military movements. Indeed, any such knowledge would be of little or no use to them for they very rarely take part in a pitched battle; their campaigns are reduced to mere skirmishes and constant surprises on one side or the other in which very little blood is shed. The chief operations of native armies are confined to ravaging the country that they happen to be passing through, without distinction of friend or foe, and pillaging without mercy all the defenceless inhabitants, who are put to inconceivable tortures in the attempt to force them to disgorge imaginary treasure that they never possess.

The infantry is, if possible, in even a worse plight; or at any rate it was up to the time when native princes were induced to admit European adventurers into their service, to reorganize and drill their armies.

The ancient kings of India placed most reliance on their infantry. It formed the fourth division of their armies, and was numerically larger than the other three. It formed, in fact, the main strength of the combined forces. At the present day, too, it constitutes the principal, and indeed almost the only, force of the smaller native princes who are known by the name of Poligars. These Poligars rarely have any cavalry, the smallness of their revenues and the character of the country they inhabit rendering it almost impossible to maintain them.

The Poligars in many respects resemble the European barons of the Middle Ages, who from their strongholds ventured boldly to defy the royal authority. They are fairly numerous in the various districts of the Peninsula, and they were much more numerous before the great European Power extended its dominion over the territories in which they were established and subdued the greater number of them. These petty despots waged almost incessant war against each other. Safely ensconced in deep jungles or on inaccessible mountain-tops, they were able to defy the princes whose territories surrounded them; and the latter unable to surprise these turbulent vassals for fear that they would pillage and devastate their own states, tried to live amicably with them.

These Poligars or self-styled princes made war according to methods of their own. The use of cannon was unknown to them; their only arms being arrows, pikes, and flintlocks. They never risked a pitched battle. When attacked by a superior force they took refuge in their jungles and on their mountains. Their object would be to surprise the advancing enemy. Lying in ambush behind trees or thick brushwood, they would pour well-directed volleys upon their opponents, forcing them to retire in disorder with considerable loss. It was in the midst of their jungles or on the tops of their mountains that the English, after much labour and the loss of many men, managed to lay hands upon these brigand chiefs and their lawless followers. Only by these means were the newcomers able to restore peace and tranquillity in provinces which had previously been the scene of perpetual outrages.

The art of laying out camps is as little known to Indian generals as that of marching an army. The greatest confusion always reigns both in their encampments and on the march. When an army makes a halt, the most important point, offcourse, is to see that there is food and supply of water close at hand. This is not always to be found where it is wanted, especially at certain times of the year, and while armies have been reduced to the direst straits by being temporarily deprived of this indispensable element, the want of which is much more keenly felt in a tropical climate than elsewhere.

An officer usually goes on ahead, selects a suitable site for the camp, and there sets up a large flag, which is visible from a long distance. Each division then encamps in any sort of order beyond this landmark. Each chief pitches his tent in the midst of his own followers, and hoists his distinctive banner. Confusion and disorder prevail everywhere. Things are, however a little more orderly around the commander-in-chief's tent. Fairly good discipline is also maintained in the spot set apart as a market-place. Here provisions and commodities of various kinds, pillaged from the country through which the army has passed, are exposed for sale; for the progress of an Indian army is always attended by fire, sword, and robbery. In fact, it is considered unnecessary and troublesome to establish regular depots for provisions, or in fact to make commissariat arrangements of any kind. It was only when an army was obliged to pass through a country which had already been devastated that these precautions were considered necessary. Strings of bullocks were then employed with the army to carry its provisions. And all other chiefs relied for their commissariat on a crowd of purveyors attracted by the hope of gain, and especially on the Lambadis, or Sukalers, professional pillagers, and who kept the camp market well supplied by their continual raids on the unfortunate inhabitants of the surrounding country.

The most abominable debauchery is openly authorised among the soldiery, especially in Mahomedan armies. A special quarter in the camp is set apart for the vile and depraved wretches who give themselves up to this hideous form of prostitution.

Charlatans of all kinds swarm in these disorderly camps. There are conjurers, soothsayers, astrologers, tight-rope dancers, acrobats, quacks, pickpockets, fakirs, religious mendicants, blind men; and furthermore, each soldier is generally followed by his whole family. Thus you may often see an army of from twenty-five to thirty thousand soldiers with three hundred thousand followers of all sorts and conditions in its train, who, profiting by the confusion which reigns in the camp devote their whole time to robbery with impunity. The Mahratta armies are less troubled with these encumbrances, for they often make forced marches, and it would be impossible for the follower to keep up with them.

The generals' tents, especially in the case of Mahomedans, are very large and commodious. Oriental taste and luxury are conspicuous in them. They are richly adorned and provided with every kind of comfort. They are divided into several compartments, some of which are destined for the wives or concubines of these pleasure-loving commanders, who are almost invariably accompanied by their women. Even in the midst of a tumultuous camp, Indian princes and generals never neglect anything that can pander to their sensuality.

One may well believe that it is easy to surprise a camp composed of such a rabble. There are rarely any outposts. The spies who are maintained in the hostile camp partly supply this deficiency; for, as soon as they perceive anything unusual going on, they hurry off to warn their employers, who are thus prepared to receive the enemy. The latter usually retire as soon as they perceive that their opponents are on the alert. Moreover, surprises and night marches are not at all to the taste of Indian warriors, who do not like to be deprived of their sleep. Thus it has sometimes happened that a mere handful of Europeas has thrown into disorder and routed a whole army by unexpected attacks of this nature.

Nevertheless, however inferior the people of India may be in discipline and courage, they have one great advantage over Europeans, which, had they only known how to make use of it, would certainly have rendered the struggle between them and their formidable adversaries much less unequal. I mean their soldier could live on three or four pounds of rice per week with a little salt, and on that, with the addition of a little water, he will keep himself in good health, be active, cheerful, and in condition to undertake forced marches fer several days consecutively, without suffering inconvenience. What a fund of latent force the Indian armies possessed in this useful faculty for the purpose of harassing and annoying an enemy whom they were afraid to meet in pitched battles, but who, infinitely less abstemious, would soon have become disheartened without a plentiful supply of substantial food!

## Areas of Neglect

The art of fortifying, besieging, and defeat strongholds was equally neglected in India. The method generally followed was to surround a town and trust to famine to force the besieged to capitulate. To take a place by assault appeared far too dangerous a proceeding to Indian tacticians; consequently it frequently happened that a wretched little fortified town surrounded by nothing but mud walls and defended by a few hundred peasants armed with a few war matchlocks, was able to hold out for months the attacks of a host of assailants, who, tired out at last by the perseverance of their adversaries, were obliged to ignominiously raise the siege. Even in recent times, though they might have learnt by sad experience to what horrors a town taken by assault is exposed, several Indian generals have been known to shut themselves up behind walls of mere mud or earth and obstinately refuse to listen to any suggestion of capitulation, treating the European besiegers with insolent bravado, and fearlessly awaiting the force of an assault.

It is true, however, that the honour of commandant of any fortress is at stake on occasions. However advantageous the conditions to him might be, he would never willingly capitulate; for should he be weak enough to do so, he would find it difficult to escape the suspicion, on the part of his king and of the people, that he had acted with treachery or cowardice, and consequently, his dignity would be for ever tarnished.

Neverthless, the art of approaching a fortified position by mines and entrenchments has long been known to Indian generals. When such works have been carried as close to the main fortress as possible, the besieged and the besiegers delight in insulting and challenging each other by word of mouth. For instance, the Hindus will say to the Mahomedans: 'If you do not now take the place, it will be as great a slur on your good name as if you had eaten pork.' And the besiegers will answer: 'If we take the place, it will be as great a disgrace to you as if you had eaten cow's flesh.' Another proof that bluster is no indication of courage.

A device upon which Indians place great reliance under such circumstances is enhancement. The magicians of either party are called upon to exercise all the resources of their black art. But unfortunately, the sorcerers of the besiegers are nearly always as clever as the sorcerers of the besieged. One charm is consequently nullified by a counter-charm, and it comes to the same thing in the end, namely, which side is able to display the greater amount of courage and skill. Whatever the result may be, however, the magicians always enjoy a large share of the glory of success or bear the greater part of the shame of defeat. These absurd illusions were still in vogue when I left India.

The fortifications of the most important strongholds, even up to recent times, consisted of one or two very thick walls with round or triangular towers at the angles, on which were placed a few guns very badly served. The fort was surrounded by a broad and deep moat, but as the natives of India did not understand the use of the drawbridge, the ditch was hidden by a curtain wall to prevent its being visible from a distance.

In several places in the Peninsula strongholds may be seen which owe little of their strength to the skill of the engineer being situated on the top of steep and almost inaccessible hills. These fortresses are called Durgams. Alexander besieged a fortress of this kind on the banks of the Indus and found great difficulty in capturing it. But there is a great drawback to these Durgams. The air is always cold and damp, even when extreme heat prevails in the plains below and this renders them most unhealthy to live in and the men who garrison them being subject to long spells of fever which are difficult to cure.

The people of India have lately learnt from Europeans the warlike art of exterminating the human species in a more scientific and practical manner. They have introduced great changes in their methods of attack and defence and, in fact, in the whole of their military system. A sad and fatal gift, which they may perhaps one day use against those who brought it to them!

Before finishing this subject I will add a few words on the different kinds of weapons that have been used in India at different times. There are thirty-two different kinds of old fashioned weapons each of which has a name and shape peculiar to itself. Models of these are to be found in the hands of the principal idols. Each deity is provided with the one that he most affected. As my readers would find no counterpart to them in a European armory, it would be difficult to describe them without illustrations. All that I can say about them is that besides many instruments for cutting, there were others for hacking stabbing and felling.

Among Indian arms of more modern times the most important defensive ones are the helmet and the shield. The latter is made of leather and ornamented in the centre with large bosses. Most Indian soldiers can use it very skilfully. Some wear a thick-quilted corselet as a cuirass or breast-plate, which, it is said, is impervious both to sword and arrow. The Greeks and Romans, and many other nations of old used this sort of cuirass, but they also wore metal ones of different shapes. But as this breast-plate affords no protection against a bullet and is undeniably most uncomfortable to wear in a hot climate, its use has been almost entirely abandoned. Among the offensive weapons of India are bows and arrows. The bow measures only about two feet and a half when strung, and each arrow is nearly two feet long. These are but poor specimens of the weapons which history credits the Hindu gods with using. The bow used by Rama, for instance, was so enormous that the fifty thousand men who were employed to bring it to him succumbed beneath the burden. Vishnu's favourite weapon was the Chakram, and many of his devotees have it branded on their shoulders with a red-hot iron. It is still used in some parts, and consists of a metal disk about nine or ten inches in diameter, with well-sharpened edges.

There is a hole in the centre, and through this is passed a stick by means of which a rapid rotatory motion is given to this disk, which flies off and inflicts a severe cut on anyone that it strikes.

Large grenades or squibs are also frequently used, eight or ten inches long, and armed at one end with a keen-edged crescent-shaped blade. These are fired off horizontally, and are used to produce confusion amongst bodies of cavalry. They are less effective than our hand-grenades, but carry very much further. According to Hindu authors, these grenades, called Vanams, were used in very early times. The *Ramayana* speaks of Rama's Vanam as one of his most important weapons. It is therefore to be inferred that gunpowder was known in India in very early times. It is quite certain that the Hindus possessed the secret of compounding explosive substances long before the invasions of Tartars or Europeans. Still they can hardly have been aware of the terrible effect which inflammable materials can produce when enclosed in a metal tube: it was reserved for those who conquered this peaceable nation to teach them the power of this agent of destruction.

The Hindus still use the pike, the dagger, and the sword. The last is at present their favourite weapon, and they have fencing-masters who can teach them to use it with great skill.

The gun is also much used by them, although in their hands it is not a very deadly weapon. Until quite recently they only used matchlocks, and their gunpowder was extremely bad, as indeed it is even at the present time. Amongst Hindu soldiers musketry practice is unknown, as their princes consider that it is useless expense to employ powder for this purpose.

Europeans have recently introduced bronze and cast-iron cannon. In former times Indian cannon were made of iron, and were of enormous calibre. From these wretched guns they fired stone balls more than a foot in diameter. They took no trouble whatever to learn how to aim. I have read in a manuscript written nearly eighty years ago that the Rajah of Tanjore, having declared war against the Dutch, sent an army to a besiege their fortress at Negapatam. When it drew near, the Dutch fired an ill-directed salvo from the top of the ramparts. The Rajah's troops, observing that the balls passed well over their heads, thought that they had nothing more to fear the enemy's artillery, and labouring under this delusion, they boldly approached the glacis. Just at that moment the garrison fired a few well-aimed volleys of grape-shot which annihilated the rash assailants, who learnt to their cost that a cannon can be aimed both above and below its true level. The author adds that the palanquin of a Brahmin who held a high command in the Rajah's army, and who had approached a little too close to the fortress, was struck by a cannon ball and shattered to pieces. The Brahmin got off scot-free with only a fright; but his alarm was so great that he ran off as fast as he could, and, when he found himself in a place of safety, swore by his three hundred and thirty million gods that never again would he venture within ten miles of any place inhabited by those dogs of Feringhis.

# 12

## Justice

Governed from time immemorial by despotic princes, who recognized no law but their own free will and pleasure, India has been acustomed to a form of judicial administration peculiar to herself. There has been no legal code, neither has there been any record of legal usage. There are, it is true, a few works containing general legal principles, and a few wise legal maxims which have helped to guide the judges in their decisions; yet nowhere have there been properly organized courts of justice. Ordinary cases have generally been settled, without any right of appeal, by the collectors of public revenue, assisted by assessors selected from the principal inhabitants and by the military officer commanding the district.

The Hindus have neither barristers nor solicitors neither are they compelled to submit to those long proceedings and interminable delays, the cost of which often equals the value of the matter under dispute. When it is a question of dividing property or of other business of any importance, it is generally submitted to the arbitration of relatives or of the headmen of the caste, and if the nature of the suit or the high rank of the litigants render it advisable, all the principal inhabitants of the district assemble to decide the point at issue.

When a case is brought before the revenue officer of the district and his assessors, no difficulty is experienced in getting them to settle the dispute if they think that they are likely to make any money out of it. Otherwise they will easily invent some pretext for putting off the matter till some future time when they may have more leisure to attend to it. In any important case they try their best to bring the parties to an amicable understanding; and if that is impossible, they leave the decision to a Panchayat, or 'tribunal of five arbitrators,' which may be composed of a larger, but never of a smaller number than five. If caste customs are the subject of dispute, the settlement devolves upon the heads of the castes.

## Common Sense Justice

The procedure generally followed is that dictated by common sense, by ordinary intelligence, and by such principles of equity as one always expects to find established, in theory at any rate, in all civilized countries. Besides, almost every member of a caste is well acquainted with its different customs, which are handed down by tradition from father to son, and thus are never lost. In short, the form of judicial procedure in India is less complicated than that of Europe, and would leave little to be desired if the scales of Themis were not much more easily put off their balance there than in other countries. Impartiality and disinterestedness are virtues with which Hindu judges have but a very slight acquaintance. Too weak to be able to resist the bribes that are offered them, to be independent of the prejudices and predilections of their own circle, or to be above all considerations of personal interest, their judgements are rarely conspicuous for unswerving uprightness and integrity. Almost invariably it is the richer suitor who gains the day; and even the most guilty generally find some means of blunting the sword of justice.

If the parties to a suit have an equally good case or an equally bad one, the party which makes the most noise and is loudest in its abuse of its adversary usually gains the day, for eloquence at the Indian Bar consists in shouting with all the strength of one's lungs, and in pouring such a flood of invective on one's adversary that he has not all answer left.

There are two or three Hindu works which contain rules and directions concerning the administration of Justice, both civil and criminal. The best known is the *Dharma-Sastra*, which contains, amongst other things a treatise on Hindu polytheism. There are also the *Niti-Sastras*, and the *Manu-Sastra*, which have been part translated into English. Many legal precepts and decisions, which would be most useful helps to a judge, might be gathered from these works; but, as usual, they are a farrago of nonsense, religious and otherwise. For instance, one may find there numbers of decisions in hypothetical cases that are either perfectly ridiculous or morally impossible and also numbers of idiotic theses propounded. Futhermore, whatever valuable information may be found here and there in these books is quite beyond the comprehension of the majority of Hindus, who do not in the least understand the learned terms in which they abound.

The Hindus, it may be remarked, recognize no prescriptive rights. A person in actual possession of any property, who happens to have no legal and authentic document stating 'that it belongs to him, is liable to be proceeded against judicially and evicted by the representatives of a soi-disant legitimate proprietor, even though the actual possessor could prove that he and his ancestors had enjoyed the property without question and in good faith for a century or more. The same principle holds in the case of debts. It is not at all an uncommon thing for creditors to sue the great-grandson of the original debtor for a debt contracted more than a hundred years before, and to force him to pay it even though he himself might be totally unaware of its existence.

## Usury

Usury is a recognized institution everywhere; and there is no limit to the rate of interest. In the parts of the country where I lived the lowest rate was twelve per cent and that they call the *dharma-vaddi* or fair interest, a rate that would not shock the most sensitive conscience.

Indeed to lend money at that interest is considered a meritorious action. Eighteen to twenty-five per cent is the usual rate, and moneylenders have been known *to* exact the extortionate rate of fifty and even a hundred per cent. Happily the cupidity of these moneylenders often ends in their over-reaching themselves, for only people who are ruined and absolutely penniless will consent to pay such interest, and consequently the greedy creditor runs the risk of losing both interest and capital. Borrowers of this class do not, as a rule, offer any security which the credited can .pounce upon in case of default of payment. A Hindu's whole property generally consists of a few head of cattle; but such property is inviolable. If a creditor tried to seize a debtor's cattle, the magistrates would interfere to prevent it; not altogether in the interests of the agriculturist, but because by thus taking away the means of cultivating his fields, the creditors would, at the same time, prevent his being able to pay the taxes which belong to the State. Even the hut which the

Hindu inhabits does not belong to him, but is the property of the State. When he leaves his village to settle elsewhere, he has no right to dispose of his hovel. It remains unoccupied either until some other inhabitant comes, and with the consent of the headmem of the village takes possession of it, or until it falls to pieces;

Thus it may readily be understood that usurious money-lending does not always tend to enrich the usurer. It very often happens that the borrower and lender are both completely ruined together. Nevertheless, the lenders need relinquish all hope. The legal system of bankruptcy, which the dishonest man will so gladly avail himself of and by which he can grow rich at the expense of his creditors is unknown in India. If a debtor dies insolvent, his descendants to the sixth generation continue to be responsible for his debts.

## Criminal Cases

Criminal jurisprudence in India varies greatly. In some cases, for instance, the woman who commits adultery renders herself liable to capital punishment, but neither her parents nor the headmen of her cast have to carry out or assist at her execution. Her husband alone has the right to put her to death. These severe measures, however, have never been put in practice except in countries governed by native princes. The Mahomedans always opposed them wherever their rule extended. They thought it would be less cruel and more advantageous to the State to inflict very heavy fines for offences of this nature. Thus, a woman or girl not a prostitute by profession, who is proved to have committed adultery, particularly if she afterwards became pregnant and thereby convicted herself, would be sentenced to a very heavy fine, quite beyond her power to pay; and her seducer would also be fined to the same amount. If the guilty pair were unable to find the money, the fine would fall on their nearest relatives, who would he obliged to pay it for them. The same form of punishment was meted out in any cases of a glaring nature where caste customs had been broken. These fines were collected by the revenue officer of the district in which the offences had been committed. It was further the custom for the offenders to give a feast to the headmen of their caste after their fines had been paid, in consideration of which their fault was considered to be wiped out.

There used to be, and still are in some districts, contractors who collected the revenue derivable from such fines. These men agree to pay a fixed sum to the public treasury, and in exchange they are allowed to keep all the fines they collect for minor offences against caste customs, or other peccadilloes. One can well imagine that all their energies are directed to preventing any persons from going unpunished.

As to more serious crimes, such as theft, homicide, etc., either the ruling prince, his minister, or the governor of a province usually passed sentence on them. The governors, however, had not the right to condemn a man to capital punishment without the ruler's sanction. Thieves, as a rule, got off by giving up what they had stolen, and a good deal more besides, if they had it. The unfortunate man whose goods were stolen only received a very small portion of what he had lost, by far the larger portion remaining in the hands of the judge who had kindly consented to look into the matter. Highway robbery was punished by mutilation - the right hand, nose, and ears of the robber being cut off.

Murder itself was rarely punished by death. If the person accused was rich and knew what to give to the governor who tried the case, means could always be found to divert well merited punishment from the culprit. If the offender was a poor man, they took away the little that he possessed and banished him and his family from the province. Thus the most abominable outrages on society were encouraged or only lightly punished in India, whilst imaginary crimes invariably entailed punishment on any who might be accused of them. A poor Pariah was put to death in Tanjore for having hurled a stone at and killed a bull dedicated to Siva, which was devastating all the rice-fields in the neighbourhood. I knew another man of the same caste whose hand was cut off for having killed, also with a stone, a calf which was trespassing on his field. He too would have certainly lost his life had he not been able to prove that the offence was unintentional, and had not several persons of note interceded in his behalf.

A person condemned !o capital punishment is either shot, hanged, or beheaded. There are many forms of punishment and torture prevalent in India. For instance, the offender may be banished from the country, severely flogged, or rolled naked on burning hot stones; or he may be-condemned to carry a heavy weight on his head or shoulders until he faints from exhaustion; or he may be tied to a stake and exposed to the burning rays of the sun with bare head and naked body; or, his hands and feet may be put into fetters tightened till they almost dislocate the joints; needles may be inserted under his nails; the pungent and acrid juice of the pepper plant may be injected into his eyes and nostrils; or large bodkins may be plunged into the most sensitive and fleshy parts of his body, and on their withdrawal the parts be rubbed with salt and vinegar or burning acids. These are only a few of the horrors invented as punishments by the Hindus. It is not on murderers, thieves, and offenders of that class that these terrible punishments fall. They are much more likely to be inflicted on Government officials guilty of malpractices or malversation of public moneys, or on anybody who is known to be well off, but who declines to allow himself to be fleeced.

In those provinces which are still under native government, and especially in those where the rulers are Mahomedans, no man's fortune is safe, however honestly it may have been acquired. Government agents, aided by a highly organized system of espionage, contrive to obtain most accurate information respecting the amount of every person's fortune; and whenever an unhappy individual is ascertained to have saved enough to attract the prince's cupidity, he is denounced, arrested, and imprisoned. If these high-handed proceedings are not sufficient to induce him to transfer the contents of his strong book into the prince's treasury, harsher measures, such as torture, are resorted to.

Mahomedans treat even the Brahmins in their service with the same severity. But, it must be admitted, the latter only experience the kind of treatment that they have so often inflicted on their fellows. No one can be harder, more cruel, or more pitiless towards the poor agriculturists than a Brahmin invested with authority, when he sees a chance of money from them. Nevertheless there are many Hindus, and Brahmins particularly, who endure with unshaken firmness and courage the most horrible tortures inflicted on them, even when their lives are in danger, rather than give up their treasures. I have known Brahmins who have been thus persecuted for year after year and without success. They may be seen with their bodies so covered with bruises and wounds, that they appear to be but one large festering sore, a prey to all kinds of vermin; and in this sad plight all relief is denied them, even to the extent of refusing dressing for their wounds.

If the poor prisoner survives these cruel tortures, his tormentors, astonished at his fortitude, will set him at liberty, ashamed at last of their unsuccessful efforts at coercion. This faculty of bearing the most excruciating pain with calm endurance is very common among the Hindus. There are some, however, who are not thus gifted by nature, and who, after resisting as long as possible, at length submit and come to terms with their oppressors. These weaker members receive a present, perhaps, of a new turban or a piece of cloth. Their persecutors express much regret at having been obliged to resort to such harsh measures, remarking at the same time that their victims might have spared themselves much pain and torment by acceding to their requests in the first instance. The victims are then restored to their former honours and employments.

Filled with the desire to recoup themselves for their losses, they seize every opportunity for extortion, until they become rich once more and forced to disgorge their plunder. But whatever crimes they may commit or whatever tortures they may endure, no disgrace is attached to either. The penalty of death itself leaves no stain on the memory of the man who has undergone this supreme punishment; and, as a natural consequence, no sort of disgrace is reflected on the family of the victim. A Brahmin would be degraded and vanished from his caste for having eaten food which had been prepared, or drunk water that had been drawn, by a person of lower caste; but were he convicted of stealing, of uttering vile calumnies, of attempting to take another man's life, or of betraying his prince or country, none of these offences would prevent his appearing without fear or shame in public, or would hinder his being well received everywhere.

In civil as well as in criminal cases, **when the evidence does not completely establish a fact, the**

**Hindus often have recourse to ordeals to decide the point at issue. There are four ordeals generally recognized among Hindus, namely, by the scales, by fire, by water, and by poison.**

It is not the magistrates only who order these trials by ordeal. Anyone has the right to insist on such a trial. Thus, if a theft has been committed, the head of a household compels each member to undergo an ordeal. In the same way, the head of a village may force it upon all the inhabitants on whom criminal suspicion may rest; and a jealous husband may order the same in the case of his wife whose fidelity he doubts. These ordeals sometimes produce such an effect on the real culprits that they are convinced that discovery is inevitable, and think it more prudent to confess their guilt at once than to aggravate the matter by keeping silence. On the other hand, such ordeals often occasion deplorable miscarriages of justice, and result in the conviction of innocent persons, who, strong in the knowledge of their innocence, fondly believe that the natural course of things will be reversed in their favour.[1]

---

1. This method of deciding a case, degrading example as it is of the foolish beliefs of which the human mind is capable, was common enough amongst all ancient heathen nations. Indeed it was still in existence in most Christian countries till the thirteenth century. In the belief that it was impossible, even in the most barbarous ages, for the obvious abuses of this system to have escaped the eyes of the judges who were bound to uphold it, some people have suggested that, while the long ceremonious prayers and exorcisms which preceded the ordeals were going on, the judges were able to determine the guilt or innocence of the accused by their demeanour, and that in the former case they left them to the ordeal, while in the latter they found means, either by the application of medicines or

*Contd.*

A certain young woman who lived close to my house became the victim of her husband's jealous suspicions. To prove her innocence, he forced her to plunge her arm up to the elbow into a bath of boiling oil. The unhappy woman, sure of her inviolable virtue, did not hesitate to obey, and the result was that she was most frightfully scalded. The wound became inflamed and blistered, finally mortified, and caused the unhappy woman's death.

No doubt the disregard of the sanctity of an oath prevailing among the Hindus has, to a certain extent, necessitated the adoption of this system of trial by ordeal. Certain it is that there is no nation in the world who think so lightly of an oath or of perjury. The Hindu will fearlessly call upon all his gods - celestial, terrestial and infernal - to witness his good faith in the least of his undertakings; but should fresh circumstances demand it, he would not have the smallest scruple in breaking the word that he had so solemnly pledged. Woe to the imprudent person who

*Contd. from last page*

drugs or by some other trickery, to ensure their passing through the ordeal safe and sound. It appears moreover that Hindu judges used to protect by other means the accused who were to undergo any dangetous ordeal. Thus, for instance, in some provinces, if a stolen object was of small value, such as a gold ornament, the judges would order a vessel full of water to be brought, and each suspected person received a smaller vessel of soft clay, which he had to place in the larger vessel. These soft earthen vessels were easily dissolved in the water, and the lost property was generally found at the bottom. Thus the culprit escaped undiscovered, and there was no need for the ordeal to take place. —Dubois.

The detection of crime by ordeal is not entirely dead even now. But it is not, of course, recognized in the regular court, and in fact is illegal. —Ed.

confides to Hindus any private matter that affects his fortune, his honour, or his life! If it served their purpose, they would divulge it without any hesitation.

The unscrupulous manner in which Hindus will perjure themselves is so notorious that they are never called upon to make a statement on oath in their own courts of justice, unless they are persons who bear an exceptionally high character.[1]

**But the jurisprudence of the Hindus, like the rest of their political institutions, has undergone a complete change since a great European Power has dominated the country. Regular courts of justice have been established at great expense in every district to protect the rights and settle the differences of persons of all classes, irrespective of rank, position, and caste.** And this is, undoubtedly, one of the greatest benefits that a just and enlightened Government can bestow on any country. However much opinions may differ as to the usages of these courts, it seems to me that no one can deny that they have already been productive of immense benefit. Nowadays every member of society can rest assured that, sooner or later, the wrongs under which he suffers, either in his person or his property will be redressed, and he can also rely unreservedly upon the impartiality of his judges, an advantage he was far from enjoying under the iron rule of his former despotic masters. At the

1. In *India: What can* it *teach us?* Professor Max Muller defends with no little skill the general credibility of the Hindus. He quotes, *inter alios,* Sir John Malcolm, who asserted: 'I have hardly ever known, where a person did understand the language, or where a calm communication was made to a native of India through a well-informed and trustworthy medium, that the result did not prove that what had at first been stated as falsehood had either proceeded from fear or from misapprehension.'

—Ed.

same time, it must be admitted that the present judicial system has by no means realized all the objects for which it was established. Indeed, how could anyone reasonably expect that such a huge measure of reform would be sealed with perfection from its very commencement?

Every creation of the human brain can always be improved upon when the light of experience has shown up its defects and revealed the mistakes that have been committed. For example, the fact cannot be disguised that the slow and cautious method of procedure which is customary in a European court of law is by no means adapted to the majority of Hindus, who from their straitened circumstances and the nature of their occupations cannot afford such long and expensive modes of litigation. Is it likely that they would find it convenient to wait about at the place where justice is dispensed, it may be for many days, till their turn to be heard comes, leaving, as they must, in the meantime their families without any means of subsistence? From this point of view the new system is all to the advantage of the rich and influential and to the detriment of the poor against whom the former can bring vexatious suits with impunity.

So great is the dread amongst the poorer Hindus of these lengthy processes, and of the prolonged absences from their homes which they entail, that when they are cited to appear as witnesses before these new tribunals, they will often spend large sums in bribing the official who brings the summons, if, any means whatever can be found by which they can elude the hateful business. If brawls or quarrels arise in a village, the neighbours, far from interposing and trying to restore peace, retire promptly to their own houses, terribly afraid lest they may be called as witnesses in court, and thus waste much precious time which otherwise might be profitably employed in the fields or in the house.

The conclusion to be drawn from this seems to be that under the new system of judicial administration sufficient attention has not been paid to the peculiar character, disposition, and prejudices of the people for whose benefit it was devised. It was not sufficiently borne In mind that nowhere In the whole world is where another race of men so obstinate, so deceitful and so litigious as the Hindus, partly from faults of training and partly from their deep-seated attachment to caste customs. What we should think trifles appear to them of the utmost importance, and are often the cause of lawsuits. Three-fourths at least of the legal proceedings have to do with the most petty concerns, though they are far from being regarded as such by the complainants. They are usually about small debts, quarrels, slanders, tiffing assaults without bloodshed, petty larcency etc.

The settlement of these small matters might very well be removed from the jurisdiction of the higher courts and placed in the hands of village panchayats or petty courts of arbitration, composed of the best materials available or they might in part at any rate, be left to the village headmen, whose judgements in either case would be expeditious and without appeal. It could certainly not be expected that these subordinate courts would fulfil their duties with very scrupulous integrity or strict impartiality; but the parties concerned would always have as compensation for the small injustices of which they might now and then be the victims the immense advantage of not losing their time or being put to an expense which more often than not is out of all proportion to the value of the matter in dispute.

## Debt Matters

Of the penalties sanctioned by the European courts of justice, imprisonment for debt, amongst others, strikes the Hindus as a ridiculous expedient, and it is one at which they often laugh. To be deprived of liberty without any additional coercion or torture appears to them no punishment at all. Any Hindu who has sufficient private means would be quite contented never to leave his house night or day; he would be in a state of indolent repose, chewing betel, smoking his pipe, eating, drinking, and sleeping without taking the least interest in what was going on in the world outside.

There are two classes of persons who are imprisoned for debt: firstly, those who are fraudulent debtors, who can pay but refuse to do so, and whom torture alone would bring to their senses; and, secondly, those who are absolutely insolvent. The first of these two classes will go to prison with the utmost indifference, while the second are positively delighted to be sent there, because the aggrieved party is obliged to feed them while they are in prison. And what can be more pleasing to Hindus than to be maintained in idleness? It must be borne in mind that most Hindus, when they borrow money, do so with the lurking hope that circumstances will arise, or that they will think of some expedient, by which they will be able to elude repayment.

Thus strong measures have to be resorted to as the only means by which payment can be exacted from such very unscrupulous debtors. When the time for payment comes and the creditor demands his money, the debtor declares he has none and begs for further grace, swearing by all his gods that he will pay everything, capital and interest, at the time stipulated. More time is granted, once and even twice, and each time the debtor's fine promises end in smoke. At last the creditor becomes tired of these interminable delays, grows angry, and arrests the debtor in the name either of the ruler of the country or of the governor of the province.

The creditor forbids his debtor to eat or drink without his permission, and at the same time he himself is bound to fast. If this method does not succeed, the creditor places a huge stone on the debtor's head and a similar one on his own, and thus burdened they remain motionless opposite each other, exposed to the heat of the sun; or they walk till one of them faints from exhaustion; or they both stand on one foot like cranes; or sometimes the creditor seizes the debtor's cattle and shuts them up, forbidding anyone to feed them until payment has been made in full. At last the debtor is so worried that he is unable to bear it any longer; he comes to terms, pays a large sum on account, and gives good security for the remainder. Creditor and debtor then part on the best of terms. Very often the creditor is so hard pushed himself that he is obliged to relinquish a part of what is due to him in order to get back some of his money.

Is it likely, I may ask, that men who carry obstinacy and tenacity to such lengths would be alarmed at the prospect of enjoying a few idle weeks in prison?

The only object of a prison, according to the Hindus, is to prevent the accused or the criminal running away. No disgrace is attached to imprisonment, and consequently, it is no punishment at all. In fact mere imprisonment is not looked upon as a punishment even by magistrates in native provinces. Everyone condemned to prison has to undergo more or less severe torture according to the gravity of his offence. If it is but a trifling misdemeanour, the delinquent is beaten and then set at liberty.

All intelligent Hindus are agreed that the penal laws introduced by Europeans into their country err considerably on the side of leniency. They consider them quite inadequate to protect society against evildoers. To keep peace and order amongst a nation constituted like the Hindus, they say, much harsher measures must be resorted to.

Even capital punishment appears to produce no impression whatever on these apathetic people. The sight of an execution, far from moving the spectators to feelings of pity or compassion, is only looked upon as an amusement; and they are even much diverted by the convulsive contortions of the poor wretch who is hanging on the gallows. Perhaps the utter want of feeling shown by the crowd under these circumstances was one of the reasons why native princes resorted to capital punishment. Probably they reflected that punishments were inflicted quite as much for the sake of their determent effect on others as for the chastisement of the guilty. Mutilation appeared to them to be a much more efficacious way of repressing vice. Criminals deprived of nose, ears, or right hand, dragging out their miserable existence before the eyes of all men, were living and lasting witnesses of the severity of the law, and their woeful appearance served as a daily example to others; they seemed to say to every passer-by, what a sad fate awaits those who break the laws!

The death penalty, on the other hand, barely excites a passing terror, and I very much doubt whether the fear of it ever restrained any Hindu who was bent on comminuting a crime.

## Trial by Ordeal

When the evidence against a man accused of either a civil or criminal offence is not sufficiently strong to convict him, the Hindus as already have recourse to trial by ordeal, noted, The principal ordeals are those by scales and weights, by fire, by water and by poison.[1]. The following are the rules to be observed. The months of *Chaitra, Vaisakha,* and *Margasira* (April, May, and December) are the most favourable for ordeals, though that of the scales can take place at any time when there is not too much wind. The ordeal by fire should be practised during the rainy season, that by water in the hot weather and in autumn, that by poison in winter and in foggy weather. If careful attention is not paid to these points grave errors are liable to occur. An ordeal which took place at an unfavourable moment would be of no assistance in ascertaining the truth. The accused who is to be tried by ordeal prepares himself by fasting and ablutions. He then goes to a Brahmin Purohita, explains the circumstances of the case, and receives his advice and instruction. After this he offers a sacrifice to all the Brahmins present, asks for their *Asirvadam* (blessing), and then speaks as follows:

'Say that this day shall be a fortunate one for me, a day of virtue, a day on which it will be recognized that I am innocent of the crime of which I am accused, a day on which 1 shall receive many blessings.'

To this the Brahmins reply three times:

---

1. There are ten forms of trial by ordeal:- *Tula,* 'the balance'; *Agni,* 'fire'; Jala, 'water'; *Visha,* 'poison'; *Kosa,* 'drinking water in which an idol has been washed'; *Tandula,* 'ejecting chewed rice grains'; *Tapta masha,* 'taking a *masha* weight of gold out of heated oil'; *Phala,* 'holding a hot ploughshare'; *Dharmadharma,* 'drawing concealed images of Virtue and Vice out of a vessel filled with earth'; *Tulasi,* 'holding the leaves of holy basil.' This holy basil is sacred to Vishnu.

—Ed.

'May this day be a fortunate one for thee, a day of virtue, a day on which thy innocence will be proved, a day on which thou shalt receive many blessings.'

This preliminary ceremony, which is called the Sastivassa, being ended, they offer homam in honour of the nine planets. The scales are then brought in. Over them is a little white flag, and a stake is driven into the ground to support them. The Purohita presiding 'over the ceremony takes a vessel containing water, rice, and flowers, and turning towards the east says:

'Glory to the three worlds!

'Goddess of Yirtue, approach this place, come near, accompanied by the eight divine guardians of the eight corners of the world, and by the gods of wealth and of winds.'

He offers puja to the goddess of Virtue; then turning successively to the eight principal points of the globe, he says:

To the east, 'Glory to Indra!' (the king of the gods).

To the south, 'Glory to Yama!' (the Hindu Pluto).

To the west, 'Glory to Varuna!' (the Hindu Neptune).

To the north, 'Glory to Kubera!' (the Hindu Plutus).

To the south-east, 'Glory to Agni!' (fire).

To the south-west, 'Glory to Nairuta!' (the Chief of the Devils).

To the north-west, 'Glory to Vayu!' (the wind).

To the north-east, 'Glory to Isana!' (the Destroyer).

He then offers puja to these eight deities. He also offers it to the eight gods of wealth, to the twelve suns, to the twelve Rudras, to the sixteen mothers, to Ganesha, and finally to the eight winds. He offers to Virtue the lesser puja, that is to say, sandalwood, flowers, incense, a lamp, and neiveddya.

Then follows the homam. The fire having been consecrated and purified by the Purohita according to Vedic rites, and the Gayatri mantram having been recited, they throw into the fire a hundred and eight, or twenty-eight, or at least eight pieces of the *villi* tree, dipped in a mixture of butter and rice. At this juncture presents must be given to the Brahmins.

Then the accused, who must be fasting and be wearing very damp clothes, is placed on that side of the scale which is towards the west. They then put bricks and darbha grass on the other side until a perfectly just balance has been obtained. The accused then leaves his scale and is sent to perform his ablutions without taking off his garments. During this interval the Purohita writes in two lines of equal length, and each containing an equal number of letters, the mantram of which the following is a translation:

'Sun, moon, wind, fire, Swarga, earth, water, virtue, Yama, day, night, dusk, and dawn, you know this man's deeds, and whether the accusation is true or false.'

He then specifies below the offence which the accused is supposed to have committed. This writing must not be in black ink; ink of some different colour must be used.

The Purohita places the writing on the head of the accused, and addresses the scales in these words:

'Scales, you know everything that is in the hearts of men; you know their vices and their virtues. What escapes man's perspicacity is not hidden from you. Behold a person who is accused of a crime of which he declares himself to be innocent, and who desires to prove his innocence to the public. If he is not guilty, justice demands that you should pronounce in his favour.'

The duty of watching the movements of the scales must be left neither to a religious recluse, nor yet to a person of doubtful honesty. The former would be too likely to be influenced by compassion; the latter would not scruple to trifle with his conscience. A Brahmin of tried wisdom and virtue is therefore chosen to fill the office, and he in his turn makes this speech to the scales:

'Scales, the gods have appointed you to dispense justice to mankind and to reveal the truth. Show it, therefore, on this occasion; and if the man you are about to try is really guilty, do not allow him to preserve his equilibrium, but make the weight of his sin turn the scale against him.'

The Purohita then puts the accused again in the scales. He chants five times a stanza suitable to the occasion. If the scale on which the accused is standing forthwith drops, he is declared innocent. Ii the scales remain equal, he is considered to be partially guilty; and if the tope breaks, he is reckoned altogether guilty. The ceremony, as usual, terminates with a distribution of presents to the assembled Brahmins.

In the ordeal by fire they first of all draw eight circles on the ground, each sixteen fingers in diameter, leaving the same amount of space between each. Fire is the presiding genius of the first circle. Varuna, the wind, Yama, Indra, Kubera, the moon, and Savitra preside over the seven others. These eight circles are arranged in two parallel lines. A ninth, placed by itself, is dedicated to all the gods. All the circles are purified by being smearedover with cow-dung, on the top of which they scatter darbha grass. They then offer puja in turn to the deity presiding over each circle.

Meanwhile, the person about to undergo the ordeal bathes without removing his clothing, and while still quite wet, places himself in the first circle of the line on the west side, his face towards the east. They then dip his hands into wheat flour mixed with curdled milk, and cover them over with seven leaves of the Aswattha tree, seven leaves of Choni, and seven stalks of darbha grass.

A blacksmith then heats a small iron rod in the fire to a red heat. The rod should be about eight inches long, and the weight of fifty rupees. Then the Purohita places some fire purified according to the rites of his Veda to the south of the ninth circle and performs the homam. He invokes the goddess of Virtue in the same words as those used in the ordeal by scales. He throws the red-hot iron into water; and after it has been re-heated to the same degree, he speaks as follows:

'Fire, you are the Four Vedas, and as such I offer you homam. You are the countenance of all the gods, and you are also the countenance of all learned men. You take away all our sins, and that is why you are called pure and purifying. I am the greatest of sinners, but I have the happiness to see you. Purify me from all my sins, and if this man who is about to undergo this ordeal is really innocent, refrain for his sake from making use of your natural power of burning, and do him no harm.'

He finishes his discourse by doing homage to the power which this element possesses of penetrating into the inmost recesses of the human heart and discovering the truth. Then he says —'Glory to the three worlds!' and finally pronounces this evocation: '0 fire, come near! come near and stay here! stay here!' and he offers puja. The accused places himself in the first circle, and the Purohita, taking up the bar of hot iron with some tongs, says again: '0 fire, you know the secrets of men! Reveal the truth to us on this occasion!' At the same moment he puts the red-hot iron on the hands of the accused, who then, still keeping hold of the iron, runs over all the circles, in such a manner as to place his feet alternately on all. Arrived at the eighth circle he throws the iron into the ninth on to some straw, which should be set on fire by the contact.

In the case of the accused dropping the iron before he has covered the whole distance, the trial would have to begin over again. If, on an inspection of his hands, it is seen that the iron has not injured the skin, he is considered innocent. An accidental burn on any other part of his body would not count. To make quite sure that contact with the red-hot iron has produced no sensible effect on the skin, the accused is given some unhusked rice, which he has to rub vigorously between his hands to separate the grains from the husk.

The preparatory formalities for the ordeal by water are much the same as the preceding ones. For this they draw a single circle in which they place flowers and incense. A stake is also driven into a tank or a river where the current is not too strong. Near this stake the accused must place himself, the water being up to his waist. The Purohita, with his face to the east, then speaks his words.

Someone is then told to go a certain distance and to return. During this time the accused must immerse himself completely, holding on to the bottom of the stake. If he raises his head above the water before the person returns, he is accounted guilty; if he comes up afterwards, he is declared innocent. If both accuser and accused are condemned to undergo the ordeal, they must both go under the water at the same time, and he who first comes to the surface is considered guilty.

The ordeal by poison is preceded by all the usual ceremonies. A little powdered arsenic is mixed in some melted butter. The Purohita then says:

'Poison, you are a harmful substance, created to destroy the guilty and impure. You were vomited by the great snake Vasuki to cause the death of guilty giants. Behold a person who is accused of a crime of which he declares himself to be innocent. If in reality he is not guilty, divest yourself of your injurious qualities and become to him as Amrita (nectar).'

The accused then swallows the poison; and if, though he may feel unwell, he survives for three days, he is proclaimed innocent.

There are also several other kinds of trial by ordeal. Amongst the number is that of boiling oil, which is mixed with cow-dung, and into which the accused must plunge his arm up to the elbow; that of the snake, which consists in shutting up some very poisonous snake in a basket, in which has been placed a ring or a piece of money which the accused must find and bring out with his eyes bandaged; if, in the former case, he is not scalded, and in the latter is not bitten, his innocence is completely proved.

• • •